THE
ART
OF
LOSING
IT

THE
ART
OF
LOSING
IT

A MEMOIR OF
GRIEF AND ADDICTION

ROSEMARY KEEVIL

SHE WRITES PRESS

Published 2020
Printed in the United States of America
Print ISBN: 978-1-63152-777-7
E-ISBN: 978-1-63152-778-4
Library of Congress Control Number: 2020908450

For information, address:
She Writes Press
1569 Solano Ave #546
Berkeley, CA 94707

She Writes Press is a division of SparkPoint Studio, LLC.

All company and/or product names may be trade names, logos, trademarks, and/or registered trademarks and are the property of their respective owners.

This is a work of non-fiction and, as such, reflects the author's memory of the experiences. Many of the names and identifying characteristics of the individuals, places and institutions featured in this book have been changed. Certain individuals are composites. Dialogue and events have been recreated to convey their substance rather than written exactly as they occurred.

For my late husband and my two beautiful and resilient daughters.

PART ONE

Prologue
"Just Like a Pill"
Pink
Friday, April 12, 2002

I n my bed on a Friday afternoon. I can't seem to sleep off this cocaine. Why did I do that? I gulp some more Bâtard-Montrachet from the lovely, large goblet on my nightstand and study the familiar green bottle. Still half full—that'll do.

I sneak out to the porch off the bedroom and scan for anybody who might notice me and my wired state. No neighbors? No gardeners?

The Camel Light I smoke offers no relief. I drink more fine wine. A shower will work—will help me sober up and wash off the stink of the smoke at the same time. A check in the mirror reflects paranoia. My God, I'm shaking; my stomach and heart are knotted together, pounding, pounding . . . maybe I'm having a heart attack.

I need sleep. It's only one thirty. I have a couple of hours. One of those little blue pills will do the trick.

Two thirty: passed out.

Three o'clock: still passed out.

Three thirty: I raise my weighted eyelids and try to focus on the clock radio. I am suddenly wrenched out of my anesthetized state, as if stabbed with a shot of adrenaline. Oh my God! Fuck! I'm a half hour late!

Jump up. Check the mirror. Brush teeth. Grab purse, then the four daily newspapers by my door—never know when you might have idle time. Jump into Mazda RX7. Convertible hood is down. Shit! I'll be so obvious with my wild hair flying everywhere. Oh well—no time to close it now. Ram car into reverse. Get out of the garage. Hope for no rain. Check mirror. Paranoia. First gear. Move forward fast. Concentrate—very, very hard. Second gear. Third. Fourth. Highway. Concentrate. Concentrate.

Pull up to the curb by the grassy area in front of school. Still a number of kids in blue plaid uniforms—running, screaming, chattering, doing what young teen girls do. My thirteen-year-old, Dixie, spots me. Separates from her pals. Rushes over, face scrunched in confusion.

She opens the door. "Where were you?"

Newspapers spill out onto the ground. "Ah-ha-ha-ha-ha . . ." Even to me it sounds like a crazed laugh.

"Mom! Did you take an Ativan?"

"Of course not, dear."

Dixie hazards a glance at her friends. "Let's just go, Mom."

Earlier this week, she asked me to take her to Surrey on Friday after school for a sleepover at her cousin's. The dreaded drive to Surrey can be an hour and a half long in rush-hour traffic.

"Mom! Get going," Dixie pleads. "Let's just go."

But by the time we're on the Upper Levels Highway, there is something wrong with her.

"Mom, take me home. Pleeeease, just take me home."

I look at her. At the cars in front of us. At the cars behind us. Cars beside us. At her again. Are people honking? Her eyes are tearing; she is yelling something at me.

"Turn around!" she cries. "Don't take the highway."

I pull over to the side of the highway. Dixie is screaming. Maybe I should go home. I start driving, most gingerly, to the next exit and turn around.

We make it home, and I go immediately to my room and collapse on my bed. Dixie's fifteen-year-old sister, Willow, arrives home from a friend's and charges into my room.

"Mom, aren't you taking me to youth group *now*?"

She shakes me out of my unconsciousness. I desperately try to register.

"Mom! I'm gonna be late. Are you taking me?"

"Where?"

"Mom. My youth group in Coquitlam. You promised!"

"Of course, dear. I'll meet you in the car." Oh, yes, fucking Coquitlam—as difficult to drive to as Surrey.

I drag myself into the bathroom, check the mirror . . . and see a terrified, maybe even insane person staring back at me. I hear Willow yelling to me and manage to maneuver my ravaged body down the stairs and out to the garage. Willow is just getting in the car when I get there. She is putting the family dog, fluffy little Angel, onto her lap.

I choose the Lions Gate Bridge and Barnet Highway route—far less intimidating than the Upper Levels. Somehow I make it to the Coquitlam rec center, where the youth group meets.

"Which driveway?"

"This one, Mom. Don't you remember?"

Her friends come out to meet her. I paint a smile on my face as they look at us in the RX7 with the top down and Angel panting away, excited to see everyone.

"Nice car," her buddy says.

"Yeah, it was my dad's."

"It's awesome."

"Nice dog."

"When shall I pick you up?" I ask, anxious to get home and back to bed.

"I'll call you later," she says. "I can't take Angel into the rec center. But remember to bring her back when you pick me up."

As I am driving home, I notice that Burrard Inlet and the mountains are on my left.

If the mountains are on my left, I must be going east. But we live west of Coquitlam, so I must be going the wrong way. Street signs? Crossroad? Where the fuck am I? I need to check the map.

I pull into a gas station parking lot, and Angel immediately jumps out of the car. She maybe little, about twenty-five pounds, but she sure can move. Holy shit! I left her window down. She's bolting behind the building. Oh my fucking God. I'm going to lose Angel.

"Angel. Angel. *Angel!*" I scramble out of the car and chase after her. As she runs behind the back of the station, some twenty yards away, I am terrified I will never see her again. As I round the corner, I see her about to go around the next corner. But there's a person coming my way. A middle-aged woman with flowing clothes.

"Grab that dog, *please!*" I yell to her. "She's the family dog. If I lose her, my kids'll die!"

As Angel is about to run by her, the woman puts her cloth bag down, as if in slow motion, reaches out with both hands, grabs Angel, and picks her up. I cannot see the woman's face, as the entire scene is silhouetted by the late-afternoon sun behind them.

"Oh my God. Thank you. Thank you. Thank you." I run up to the woman, squinting, and take Angel.

"You're most welcome. He's a cute little thing, isn't he? What kind is it?"

"She's a Shih Tzu Chin," I say, short of breath. "She likes to take off. I almost had a heart attack. Thank you sooooooo much." The sun shines directly in my eyes, like one of those brilliant lightbulbs used in dramatic interrogations and torture scenes in the movies. I am able to position myself so my face is in her shadow. Still, she can see me better than I can see her. I pray she does not detect how out of it I must be. She could report me to the police.

Back in the car, I leash Angel to the seat belt, then ensure the window is up all the way and the child lock is on. I am able to get my bearings from my map and go in the correct direction with one thing in mind: bed.

When I walk into the house, Melba is there. Thank God for Melba, our intelligent, grounded, patient, and invaluable Filipino nanny. Oh, and loyal, too. She is willing to work anytime. My last job entailed screwy hours. I worked for a radio station hosting *The Rosemary Keevil Show* (original, I know). When I started, the show aired live at five in the morning. Then it shifted to nine at night, going until midnight. Somehow I managed not to drink or use before going on air, but that meant I had a lot of drinking catch-up to do when I got home after midnight. Then the radio station changed its format, and my show was canceled.

"What's happening, Rosemary?" Melba asks in her strong Filipino accent. "I thought you were taking Dixie to Surrey. *I* took her. Is everything all right?"

"Melba, I don't feel well. I'm going to lie down. When Willow calls, will you please pick her up? Oh, and take Angel with you, please. Don't forget." The least I can do is remember to tell Melba to take the dog for Willow. "Thank you," I say, before fleeing to my bedroom. "What would I do without you, Melba?"

1

"It's a Wonderful Life"
Louis Armstrong
Monday, December 24, 1990

"You do this one, Dixie."

"How, Daddy?"

"Well, you take the spatula and get gobs of whipped cream on the chocolate wafer; then you put it on the other chocolate wafer so they stick together. The whipped cream is the glue. . . . Very good, just like that."

My husband, Barry, and two-year-old Dixie are at the table by the small kitchen in our Whistler condo. We drove up from our home in West Vancouver for Christmas after an early dinner and arrived an hour ago. I busied the little ones as Barry hauled the stuff—Christmas presents, the turkey and makings for dinner, the suitcases—in from the car. He dumped most of it in the narrow hallway by the front door for me to dismantle and put away. Now he's moved on to kids' play.

"Yes, that's right, Dixie. Now another one," Barry continues to coach her in the intricacies of making a *bûche de Noël*, our traditional Christmas dessert. "Nooooooo . . . not like that, Dixie," Barry warns her, as she gobs some whipped cream onto his balding head. He dabs a bit of the cream on her nose. She squeals and grabs the spoon in a motion that looks distinctly like she's got it in for Daddy.

"Oh, man, you guys. *No.* Don't do it! This could get really messy," I say with a grin as I stop abruptly en route into the kitchen, wanting to witness, but not encourage, the shenanigans.

"That's enough, Dixie," Barry says gently, pressing down on her miniature forearm with his strong male hand to stop the spoon midair.

"I wanna help." Four-year-old Willow marches over to the table.

"Okay, Willow, sit here. Dixie's losing interest anyway."

"No, I wanna do boosh," Dixie says.

"Now, now, Dixie, here." I guide her down from the table to the array of plastic animals decorating the floor by the fire.

Thank goodness for the short attention span of two-year-olds. She plunks herself down and grabs the donkeys. "Hee-haw, hee-haw."

Barry and Willow finish the *bûche de Noël,* and I put it in the fridge so the wafers will soften overnight.

I take the girls upstairs for their nightly bath and then call on Barry to help tuck them in. He has an easier time than I do settling Dixie. She loves her bedtime routine with Daddy, who seems to magically make her teddies—Joey and Bloomy and Fluffy and Bongo—come alive and mesmerize her into submission.

Because it's Christmas Eve, it takes longer than normal to calm the girls; they require at least one extra bedtime story each. We savor the lull after the kerfuffle of the last few hours.

As we go downstairs, Barry says he has a present for *us* to go with our turkey dinner, and suggests I take a seat and close my eyes.

Some thirty seconds later, he says, "Okay. Open sesame." When I open my eyes, he has a bottle of wine resting on the inside of his forearm, just like a waiter in a fine dining restaurant.

"Wow," I say, "that looks really special."

He gingerly takes off the thin layer of brown tissue covering the label to reveal . . .

"A Château Mouton Rothschild!" I exclaim.

"It's been in the cellar for a while. It's a 1961, one of the best years ever. I've been saving it for a special occasion like Christmas."

"I can't wait. You think of everything." I smile, put my hand on his cheek, look up at him, and kiss him on the lips. "Thank you, hawney."

"Speaking of everything," says Barry, "you'd better set it someplace safe, away from those rowdy kids. And I'd better stuff the stockings. Now, make yourself scarce while I play Santa."

On Christmas morning, our two precious daughters clamor down the stairs in their footed pink pajamas. At the sight of the tree overflowing with gifts, they react with the heartwarming exuberance we were hoping for, just like the rosy-cheeked, gleaming kids in the Christmas storybooks.

Willow is enamored with her new Teddy Ruxpin, the talking bear. She moves the dial on his neck, which triggers his talking. "Hello, my name's Teddy Ruxpin. Can you and I be friends?"

"Hello, my name's Teddy Ruxpin," mimics Willow, giggling with glee. "Can you and I be friends?" She passes it to her daddy. "You talk to Teddy Ruxpin!" she says in her little-girl garble.

Barry takes Teddy. "Hi, Teddy Ruxbear. Will you play with me?"

"Teddy *Ruxpin*!" repeats Willow.

Daddy: "Teddy Ruxbear."

Willow: "Teddy Ruxpin."

Daddy: "Teddy Ruxbear."

Willow: "Ruxpin!"

Daddy: "What are you saying, Willow?"

Willow: "Teddy Rux*pin*."

"Get with the program there, Daddy. Rux*pin*," I butt in. "It's Dixie's turn for a present."

As Dixie rips the wrapping off a box containing a pair of skates, she jumps up and down. "Jus' whad I wanned. I wanna go to the lake and skate, go to lake 'n skate, lake 'n skate," she sings, amusing herself and the rest of us, too.

"Hold your horses there, Whistlin' Dixie—those things are sharp," Barry says, as he puts his hand on Dixie's shoulder to calm her. "It's Mommy's turn now."

"Don't worry about the blades, Barry," I reassure him. "Those skate guards are on tight."

Then I open my present and find a dazzling necklace from Barry: two strands of large pearls holding a two-inch, brushed-gold lion with diamond eyes. I lean into him and plant a big smooch on his cheek.

"Thank you so much, hawney. And thank you, too, for showing me how joyful Christmas can be."

I never liked Christmas until I spent my first one with Barry. He had prepared a treasure hunt for me. One clue led to another, which led to yet another—and at the end of the hunt was a silver-tipped fox-fur coat. Despite its opulence, this was a practical gift for a news reporter. I was a TV reporter in Toronto when Barry and I were first together. I was often outside, braving frigid weather.

I have only sad memories of Christmases growing up. There was no money for lavish gifts. One year I was given a Raggedy Ann doll that a seamstress neighbor had made. I cherished that little Annie but was told it was just on loan and that I had to return it. And my dad was always so cranky. He resented these milestones in the calendar year; the relentless passage of time reminded him that he was growing older. One Christmas, he threw a pair of new gloves my brother had given him into the fire. He resented both my brothers. I think he felt threatened by them.

In hindsight, Dad was probably hungover on Christmas mornings. He used to come home plastered in the evening and create pandemonium in the kitchen, throwing around pots and pans or anything else he could get his hands on. Then he would go hunting for Mom, who was hiding in my bed, "for protection." I could hear him stomping down the long hallway toward the bedroom I shared with my sister, yelling, "Audrey, Audrey, *Audrey*," each call getting progressively louder as he approached and eventually punched the door open. He never came much closer than the threshold of the door, though. Maybe Mom's ill-conceived plan worked.

Now it's Barry's turn to open my special gift to him.

"Let me guess. It's a pizza," he jokes, as he unwraps the thirty-by-twenty-four-inch original oil painting. He holds it in front of him with both hands and studies it with a knowing smile on his face. "This is Whistler golf course from the south, right? This is perfect for the new place at Blueberry Hill."

"Yes," I say with a nod, admiring the art and my husband at the same time.

We are building a three-story home in a new development at Blueberry Hill, beside the Whistler Golf Club. Barry and I donned snowshoes to inspect the property before we bought it. There isn't even a road into it yet. We will be selling the condo we are in now and moving there in the new year. It seems surreal that I will have such a lovely home in Whistler, British Columbia. I remind myself how lucky we are to be able to afford it. Barry works as a corporate lawyer and inherited enough money to build the new home.

"Mommy, Daddy, lake 'n skate," squeals Willow. Dixie echoes the demand.

"I think the natives are getting restless," I say to Barry.

"Lake 'n skate, lake 'n skate," both girls say in unison.

"Now, *there's* an idea. I just need a few minutes to finish the turkey and get it into the oven before we go. Why don't you get them dressed and organized?"

The scene at Alta Lake—families skating together on Christmas Day—exudes the warmth of a Norman Rockwell painting. I have to capture the feeling on film.

"Hey, Barry and Willow and Dixie," I call, "stay still a bit. I'm going to take a pic."

"Easy for you to say. These two are a little unsteady," Barry replies, as he helps Dixie up onto her feet. He manages to get the girls on either side of him and hold their hands, which is about all that's keeping them up. I just notice, now, that Willow has left the house with about three scarves wrapped around her neck. Dixie's pink toque has slipped over her eyes, and she can't see a thing. As I center the three of them in my viewfinder, I breathe a deep sigh of appreciation.

2

"Late in the Evening"
Paul Simon

Wednesday, January 9, 1991

"How much do you want?"

"Two fifty a ticket."

Barry looks from the scalper to me with questioning eyes, his face a blur through the heavy snowflakes. The chilly wind gusts around us, and the biting winter air defines every breath we take.

I return a look of uncertainty, as I am flabbergasted at the price but really want to see Paul Simon. "Well, I love Paul Simon almost as much as I love you, hawney."

Barry rubs his bare hands together. He turns his head to look at the scalper from the corner of his eye.

"You certain they're good seats? Not rippin' me off, are ya?"

"You won't be disappointed."

Barry buys the tickets.

It is six thirty, and the show begins at eight.

"Well, I guess we should grab a bite to eat," I suggest.

"Where?" Barry asks. "It's so cold, I'm shaking, and so are you."

"Doesn't make much sense to drive and have to park again. I think there're restaurants a short walk away—down Hastings and around the corner over there," I say, pointing toward a large intersection.

Barry shrugs. "Yeah, there's gotta be something."

We start walking. It's a treacherous journey over bumpy, icy footprints.

"Gosh, this is tough sloggin'," I say. "There's obviously been no snow clearing since yesterday's storm."

I am thinking that this will be a good time to bring up the topic of my working. Shortly after Willow was born, four years ago, we moved to Vancouver from Toronto, where I was reporting for a national TV station. I had to quit my job when we relocated and have not had a chance to really pursue my career again. I did have one contract, with the Vancouver International Film Festival, last fall for two months—I was a media liaison officer—but it required me to work over Thanksgiving weekend. While I didn't really mind, Barry did.

I have realized, and am having a hard time accepting the fact, that Barry probably really does not want me to work—and certainly not at any job that necessitates odd or excessive hours. So I am a little nervous to tell him about the interview I had yesterday. It is for a job with Burson-Marsteller, an international PR company. I could start by telling Barry I feel I am on the verge of a job, because I think I am—but I could also start with something lighter, like perhaps that acting gig I auditioned for. And maybe—considering the kids and my warm family life—acting is a better fit. Perhaps a big job is not the answer. But I really, really think I have to try for it.

What do I say to Barry? He gets up in the morning, puts on a nice suit, and comes to say goodbye to me as I rinse poo out of a cloth diaper in the toilet. Then he is off to an interesting job as the legal VP for a forestry company that his dad founded. I am sensitive to the fact that I may look less than desirable in my housecoat, with poo in my hands, compared with the freshly showered and perfumed career women floating about Barry's office. I don't doubt his devotion to me, but I believe it is important to continue to make the effort to look attractive for my husband. I have noticed that some wives let themselves go, get left by their husbands, and *then* lose fifteen pounds and dye the gray out of their hair. What's wrong with that picture?

"Yeah, it's pretty tough going. My knee's bothering me a lot," Barry says, interrupting my thoughts.

"Really?" I ask, snapping back to the present. "Which one?"

"The right one, same one that bothered me during hockey." He stops and pulls the collar of his leather bomber jacket over his ears, and I button up the neck of my red winter jacket.

"We need those scarves Willow was wearing at Christmas," I say. "Too bad you don't have a hat."

"I'm used to having an exposed head. You could lend me some of your hair. You've got enough to spare." He looks down at his legs. "You know, this is really aggravating my knee."

"Oh dear. Shall I hail a cab?"

"Nah, we're almost there. We'll take one back."

Hmm, I think, *tonight is not the night to talk about my career.*

We find a sushi diner, and as we wait for the food to come out, we discuss the new house. I have carpet and wallpaper samples at home for Barry to see. He says he picked up three full bags of light switches and, being his meticulous self, has studied every single one of them and found that two of them are the wrong style.

When we return to the Coliseum, everyone is pushing and shoving to get to their seats. We discover that ours are in the second row, center stage. The scalper was not lying.

The buzz of anticipation is intoxicating. When Paul Simon strides onto the stage, the audience erupts with adoration. An orchestra of musicians and singers from Africa surrounds him, playing one hit after another: "Boy in the Bubble," "Me and Julio," "I Know What I Know," and "Bridge over Troubled Water."

This last one reminds me of the summer I turned fifteen. My sister and I were waitressing at Elgin House, a resort in Muskoka, Ontario. I got drunk for the first time that summer, on gin and tonic. I puked on the resort golf course at five thirty in the morning as we made our way back to the staff dorms.

When Simon plays "Graceland," I almost start doing jumping jacks. I exercise to this in the family room of our home on the mountainside in West Vancouver. I sing along with Paul on the chorus.

At the first few bars of "Late in the Evening," Barry looks down at me knowingly, and when Simon gets to the words about getting that girl no matter what, Barry squeezes me and we sing along.

I freeze this moment in my mind, willing it to be one of those moving scenes that stay vibrant in one's inner life forever.

I cup my right hand to Barry's left ear and try to yell above the noise, "Thank you."

We live off the high of that concert for days.

The following day, Barry discovers a small lump on his right thigh that looks somewhat like a varicose vein. When he shows it to me, he says he feels generally crappy all over. I secretly wonder whether, and hope that, the malaise can be attributed to Barry's tendency for hypochondria.

On the weekend, Barry is feeling a bit better, and we all go out to the snowy front yard. The kids are bundled up in snowsuits, scarves (of course), hats, and mittens. We start building a snowman as Barry shovels the walk. Dixie quickly loses interest and lies on her back to make snow angels, grunting as she flaps her arms and legs.

"Dixie, snow angels don't grunt like that," Willow declares.

"Daddy's grunting," Dixie protests.

I look over at Barry and realize he does seem to be almost wincing as he shovels.

"Mommy, Mommy," Willow yells out, "help me with the snowman."

"Yes, sweetie," I say. "I'll just go to the kitchen and get his nose."

"You mean his carrot?" she asks.

"Yeah," I answer, distracted, as I walk toward Barry. "Barry, what is it? Your knee?"

"Yes. It's really painful," Barry says, as he stops shoveling and leans one elbow on the handle of the shovel.

"Really? Again?" I frown. "Hmm. Yeah, don't shovel anymore. I can finish up. This is the third time it's really bothered you," I say, as if he needs to be reminded of the icy walk by the Coliseum and his hockey game. "When are you seeing the doctor?"

"I made an appointment for tomorrow."

That is when I have an interview at the Waterfront Center Hotel. I want to tell Barry about both my interviews and the acting classes I have lined up, but it seems like it would be insensitive to talk of my plans for the future now. This reminds me I have to ensure that Dianne, the part-time nanny we've had since Willow was two, is coming tomorrow.

The next evening, I am anxious to hear details of Barry's trip to the doctor. I also hope to maybe get an opportunity to talk about my job interview.

The calm that follows the kids' tuck-in is the sweet spot of time that Barry and I have for each other. I want to feel attractive for my sexy husband, so I change into a fresh, crisp white shirt and my favorite tight jeans and touch up my makeup.

I am in the kitchen, organizing our dinner, when Barry walks in. He's changed from his business suit into a sweatshirt and jeans, and when he looks at me with those gentle green eyes of his, I think of the moment I first saw those eyes.

I met him on a warm Saturday evening in rural southern Ontario. Barry and my sister's boyfriend, Hal, were in a band that was booked to play at a barn party, and my mom wanted to set me up with Barry.

Mom had gotten to know Barry a bit because the band practiced in the garage of our house in Toronto, where we all grew up. It was a large stone-and-stucco house with copper awnings. That house had presence. It was perched on the large ravine that cut through Rosedale—a neighborhood that, in Toronto, is synonymous with money. But we lived in incongruity. There was little money around, but Mom went to herculean efforts make it appear as if there were. She even managed to forage enough to send her four kids to private schools. But we all went about the world shouldered with the huge secret that, in reality, we could ill afford this extravagance. Mom was the president of the Toronto Symphony Orchestra Women's Committee simply so our family could attend the type of functions that symphony-goers do. For her, it was all about having us meet the "right" people—including appropriate suitors for me and my sister, Sal. Barry, who was from a well-to-do, interesting family, made the cut.

Hal invited me to the party and went ahead of me to the barn to practice with the band. I had curled my hair and put on my favorite summer frock. I entered the barn, tingling all over inside, and scanned the band members on the makeshift stage . . . and when I saw the guy who I realized must be *him*, I froze. His bright green eyes beamed right into mine. He was deeply tanned and wearing a baseball cap and a loose, sleeveless sweatshirt. He must have known that Mom was playing Cupid—and, as it turned out, she was very qualified.

I shake myself out of the memory and focus on the Barry standing in front of me today. "Tell me about your visit with Dr. Bradley. Does he have an idea what the pain might be?"

"He says it could be a sports injury from hockey, or maybe arthritis or a bone infection. He's ordered an X-ray."

"When does that happen?"

"He's going to get it done tomorrow at the hospital."

"What about the lump?"

"He says it's really small. He didn't sound too concerned. Said to keep an eye on it to see if it changes."

"You're really worried, aren't you?" I set my hand on his, which is resting on the counter.

"My knee and now my calf are really, really painful."

"Oh, hawney, if it's an infection, it will be quite treatable. And it sounds like the bump on your thigh is nothing to worry about. You're gonna be great. Look at you." I playfully beat his chest with my fists. I believe my own words without reservation. "You're a strapping forty-one-year-old man glowing with health. What's that you have there?" I look at the bottle of white wine sitting by the sink, beaded with condensation, that he took out of the fridge as he walked into the kitchen.

"Pouilly-Fuissé."

"We better have some before it warms up," I say, and give him the corkscrew.

He opens the bottle and pours two generous glasses. We both take a sip.

"Lovely." I smile. "What do you think?"

"Hmm, yes, nice and light." He studies his glass.

"I have to say," I comment, "I've grown quite fond of that Bâtard-Montrachet. I like that really buttery Chardonnay."

"Well, you have good taste," says Barry.

"Yes, that's why I'm with you," I say grinning. "Let's have a bite to eat. I made chicken drumsticks and veggies with cheese sauce—the kids' favorite."

"And I like it, too," he chirps, imitating the woman in the Irish Spring soap commercial. I am relieved to hear his lightheartedness.

—

"Hi, Mom. How are you?" I say to my mom on the phone when she calls the next morning.

"Hello, Rose, *dahh-link*. How are you and those adorable little girls and your handsome husband?" Mom, as always, is her effusive self, and always available for me.

"Well, good. It's busy. Willow's loving preschool, but we thought she had a hearing problem. Her—"

"Oh, no," Mom interrupts, sincere alarm in her voice.

"Hear me out," I say, chuckling. "The teacher was so concerned, she suggested we have her tested. We went through the entire rigmarole, and at the end the doctor explained that her hearing is perfect. I turn to Willow, who's sitting on a chair, looking at the open book in her lap, and say, 'Hear that?' and she doesn't even look up 'cause she's too absorbed in her darn book. She's a daydreamer!"

"Oh, the precious," Mom says. "She's reading, isn't she?"

"Yes, and get this: We get home, and Dixie asks us, 'How was the hearing contest?'"

Mom laughs. "That Dixie. What a card. She reminds me of Gav when he was growing up. Always crackin' up the joint."

Gavin is one of my two older brothers, though people often thought we were twins when we were little since we were barely a year apart in age. Gavin and I were really close emotionally, too, until he got diagnosed with schizophrenia in his twenties and ended up living on the street. He used to come by Hal and Sal's house, which was in Lawrence Park, another tony area of Toronto, in his street-bum clothes, bushy hair, and full beard, asking for money for cigarettes. Once, when Gavin was living in subsidized housing, he called the police because of what he called "the stench of a decaying dead body" in the unit next to him. The police came and arrested him for public mischief, and Hal, who is a lawyer, had to go down to the courts and bail him out.

"Anyway, the girls are good," I continue. "But Barry's had some worrisome pain in his knee. We thought maybe it was a sports injury—you know, he plays hockey, and it bugged him when he was shoveling snow and stuff. Mom, there is so much snow here. We're having a blast with Willow and Dixie."

"Yeah, and the outside play tires them out but good! Has Barry seen a doctor?"

"Yeah, he's ordered an X-ray, and—"

"What did it say?" Mom asks, not letting me finish.

"Well, we don't have the results yet. But he's feeling crappy all over—not enough to miss work, but his knee hurts more and more all the time. He's got a bit of a fever at night—well, like, you know, when he's sleeping. Last night, he sweated like a pig. Pardon the expression, but he really did soak the bed."

"Oh, sweetheart, that may be just a passing thing," Mom says. "He's a strong, robust young man."

I hear Dixie screaming in the background and have to set the phone down for a second to assist Dianne, who is remarkably patient with the kids. By the time I get there, Dixie is starting to reduce the decibel level of her tantrum. Dianne distracted her with a compelling rhyme: "Beans, beans, the musical fruit, the more you eat, the more you toot, down your leg and in your boot." Dianne is a little rough-around-the-edges sixty-year-old.

I rush back to the phone. "Hi, sorry 'bout that. Dixie was acting up, but Dianne seems to have it under control." I take a breath. "But, Mom, Barry also has a little lump on his leg. Mind you, the doc is not too concerned about that. It's so small. He says to wait and see if it changes."

"But you say he's going in to work. As I said, it sounds like it could be a passing thing."

"Yeah, I know . . . I don't know. I really, really hope so, but I don't know."

"Have you seen Rob lately?" Mom asks.

Rob is my eldest brother, who also lives in Vancouver. He's the same age as Barry, forty-one.

"I haven't seen him in a while, but I'll be seeing him tomorrow."

"Tell him I love him and I'll talk to him soon."

"'Kay. Thanks, Mom. I better go."

"Hang in there, sweetie. Remember, babe, no one ever said it was going to be easy," Mom says in her sassy-but-fun tone.

"Yeah, yeah."

We both giggle and say goodbye.

3

"Raise a Glass"
Rob Parr

Wednesday, January 16, 1991

I t has been almost a week since the Paul Simon concert, and Barry's knee is getting more and more painful. Despite feeling so poor, he continues to go to work every day as if everything were normal. We attend his doctor's appointment together. Dr. Bradley says the X-ray of his leg does not show anything, but he is concerned about all the other symptoms: the pain in the knee, the headaches, the lumps (now there are two), and the fact that Barry is achy all over and increasingly uncomfortable trying to sleep at night.

"I've booked a gallium scan, which should tell us more, for tomorrow," Dr. Bradley says. "You have to swallow a radioactive liquid and be tested hours later. In fact, you'll be admitted for the night. Come to Lions Gate Hospital at nine in the morning, for blood tests, too. I'm also ordering a chest X-ray and a CAT scan of the brain."

Dr. Bradley looks right at Barry with professional compassion.

—

Later, after I tuck the kids in, Barry and I try to settle down as well. But a shroud of nagging foreboding engulfs us.

I start to give him a massage in bed to help him relax. As I'm kneading his shoulders, the phone rings.

Goddamn, who the hell? I think. *It's ten thirty at night, for fuck's sake.* I move off Barry's back, lie on the edge of the bed, and reach for the phone. I have barely said hello, when I hear Mom's voice.

"Rose, darling?"

"Mom, what's wrong? It's one thirty in the morning for you."

"It's Rob, dear. He's in the hospital."

I sit upright on the side of the bed and grip the receiver. "What? What are you talking about? Is he okay?"

"He collapsed in his apartment, I think. I don't have much information." She is trying to sound composed, but I sense a distinct weakness in her voice. "Oh, dear, can you go see what's going on? I hate to ask you now, with all that's going on with Barry. Have they found out anything yet?"

"No, Mom. He's going to be admitted for more tests, but that doesn't matter right now. Of course, I'll go see Rob. Right away! Where is he?"

"In Vancouver General Hospital, in Emergency. Is that near you?"

"It's not that far. I'll go now. I'll be in touch as soon as I know something. I love you."

I feel disloyal leaving Barry and promise I will be back as soon as possible. I hope the kids stay asleep so they're not demanding of their daddy.

I head across town to VGH, some eight miles and two bridges away. I park as close to the emergency entrance as possible—only to find out Rob is not there but in Acute Care. The hospital is frustratingly difficult to navigate. There are numerous different wings—A Wing, B Wing, C Wing—and all the hallways blend in with one another, exuding a predictable but depressing odor of laundry bleach mixed with illness and medicine. The elevators are painfully slow. I negotiate my way past faceless health care workers in hospital garb and weak patients on gurneys in revealing robes. Finally, I see a sign above another long, unwelcoming hallway: ACUTE CARE.

I walk up to the nurses' station, which is positioned like the Great Wall of China in front of the patients' rooms. One cannot enter the ward without being screened.

"Is Rob Parr here?" I ask the nearest person in the nurses' pit.

"Who are you? Are you a relative?" she says.

"I'm Rosemary Keevil, his sister."

She seems disappointed that I am actually related, a fact that forces her to be helpful.

"Oh, we need his birthday."

"April 2, 1949."

She writes on her chart, looks up at me, and points across the hall. "Rod is in room 603, right there."

"It's Rob. And thank you."

I peek in the doorway of room 603 and quietly step in. I shudder when I see the man propped up in the bed. Is this really Rob? His head is swaddled in bandages, his face so swollen that his eyes are tiny slits. He does not notice me. He's attached to an IV tube, the dispenser standing beside him like a guard, and the bandage that is keeping the needle in place is bloody. I do not recognize this person and have to trust it is my brother. I stare long enough to register the gravity of his condition and am drained of momentum to carry on. I force myself to return to the desk and the sour nurse.

"What, what happened? What happened to my brother? Is he going to be okay? How did this happen?" I put both my hands on the counter and then turn them both over, palms up, looking right into her eyes, anticipating an answer.

"Rob has a brain tumor. He's in stable condition," she says perfunctorily.

"But what happened? How would he get a brain tumor?"

She checks her chart. "I cannot provide you with that information."

"What do you mean? What happened to his head? How'd he get here?"

"You'll have to talk to the neurologist. I cannot give you any information." She moves her head back and forth to reinforce her message.

"Where is the neurologist? Who is the neurologist? Is he here at this time of night?"

"His name is Dr. Henry Flanagan. You'll find him in Neurology. But no, he won't be in till the morning."

Stunned, I call Mom from the hospital phone. I tell her about Rob's state as gently as possible, relieved I can at least reassure her that he is stable and that I will come back again in the morning to interrogate this Flanagan guy.

I find Barry and the girls asleep when I get home. I slink down the hallway to the kitchen and shut the door. I pour a large, cool glass of Bâtard-Montrachet and go sit at the end of the family room. Although I am looking at the view—a lovely panorama of the twinkling city at night and the Lions Gate Bridge adorned in strings of white lights—I see nothing. I drink my wine. I taste nothing. I try to process. After about fifteen minutes, I get sleepy and sneak into bed, being careful not to wake Barry.

In the morning, before I take Barry to Lions Gate, I call Acute Care at Vancouver General and am assured that Rob is still in stable condition.

Barry's skin is gray, matching his mood. We endure the protocol of being admitted, which includes repeating Barry's alarming symptoms for the admitting nurse.

"Extreme pain in my right leg," Barry says, while holding his right knee. He sighs, and on the out breath he says, "Headaches, serious night sweats, unexplained lumps."

I continue, "Fleeting pain all over," wishing inside I would just wake up and discover this is simply a nightmare. But the truth is tenacious.

Barry gets changed into a limp green hospital "gown." I have always thought that calling the hospital drape a "gown" is a gross misnomer. It is not a gown. It is an unattractive garment that abolishes any sense of modesty. And this is just the beginning. Soon his deepest tissues will be prodded and inspected and exposed. The entire experience is an attack on one's dignity.

Barry will be subject to a slew of examinations. He is going to be injected with highly toxic, radioactive liquid that will frenzy about his body, seeking out danger. This process apparently takes hours. I hate to leave Barry now, and I know he wants me to stay, but I have to go check on Rob.

"I have to go . . ." I say, but stop when he looks surprised. I thought he realized I would be going to VGH to see Rob.

I procrastinate: "I have to go to the bathroom." The ladies' room has always provided a badly needed respite. I've used it as an escape, a place of refuge, a break from whatever my current situation might be—be it the monotony of a boring dinner date or the unnerving anticipation of going live on air for a news report.

I wander down the hallway until I see the washroom and go in. As I touch up my lipstick, I ask myself, *How the hell am I going to tell Barry I'm leaving to go see Rob?*

Afterward, I find a phone to call Mom and tell her I'm heading off to see Rob. I let her know what's happening and then walk slowly back to Barry, searching for courage to tell him I'm going. He's sitting up in his hospital bed in a cubicle surrounded on three sides by hospital-yellow curtains. There is a young, blond, perky-looking nurse beside him. As she prepares to take his blood pressure, she asks, "You his wife?"

"Yes." I smile.

"Well, we'll just get this done and leave you two alone," she explains.

"Oh, that's okay. Thanks," I respond politely, secretly appreciating her gesture to leave as soon as she can, since I need to tell Barry when we are alone that I will be leaving.

Barry holds out his free hand and gestures for me to come hold it. I walk to the other side of the bed across from the nurse and take Barry's hand.

"How're you doin'?" I ask.

"Resigned . . . to becoming radioactive," he says, with a sigh and a smirk.

Before I can respond, the nurse says, "All done," as she undoes the Velcro blood-pressure band. "All normal."

"Could've fooled me," says Barry.

She turns and starts to leave, then says, "The technician should be here shortly."

We're alone. He's sitting in this hospital bed, in his green gown, white sheet pulled up to his waist, face ashen, staring at his ID bracelet.

The din of the hospital goings-on—nurses scurrying back and forth, patients being rolled by in gurneys, family members following close behind, doctors with stethoscopes—fills the silent space between us, along with an unspoken word: *terrified*.

"I-I-I . . ." I take a deep breath and search for the courage to tell Barry I have to go VGH to see Rob.

"You gonna go?" Barry asks, raising his eyebrows, and looking at me with abandonment in his eyes.

I look right into his green eyes, wait a few seconds, and say, "Yeah," relieved that he has brought it up. "I have to. I'm so sorry." I squeeze his hand. I'm anxious to go and leave this certain burden behind. *Burden? Did I really say that to myself? Burden? My husband, a burden? Fuck!*

"It's okay. I know this is tough on you," he says quietly, while slightly lifting our clasped hands together and squeezing mine.

"Thank you so much, hawney. I really appreciate your understanding," I say, as I bend down and kiss him on his lips. They're dry and limp. I let my hand linger in his as I turn to go.

"Hurry back," he says.

The words reverberate in my heart as I walk away.

Vancouver General is about nine miles and two bridges away from Lions Gate Hospital. As I head to the Lions Gate Bridge over spectacular Burrard Inlet, I turn on the radio and listen to the news, out of habit.

"The United States and its allies went to war against Iraq last night as hundreds of warplanes unleashed a massive bombing attack on targets in Iraq and occupied Kuwait."[1]

I drive over the bridge and into the Causeway, which slices through lush Stanley Park. Chaos is breaking out in the Middle East as I suffer my own brand of chaos on the west coast of Canada. I drive through downtown, numb to the international tumult, stranded here in my own turmoil.

"In Baghdad, witnesses reported that the moonless night sky was thick with tracer fire from antiaircraft guns and that a smoky pallor had settled over the city."[2]

I continue on Cambie Street Bridge to False Creek as the newscasters drone on.

I'm on the final stretch to Vancouver General.

I park at the hospital and head straight for the info desk, which is right past the gift shop. Maybe I'll buy Rob something later, or something for me.

Since I know Rob is okay, I decide to look for Dr. Flanagan first. The information officer is busy talking with an older lady who is having trouble hearing him. As I stand and wait and stare at them, I impatiently shift my weight from one foot to the other and tell myself to breathe deeply.

The info man has a droopy eyelid. He talks with a lisp as he tells the lady, "Neurology. Century Wing. Fourth Floor," and points down the hall.

The lady nods, mumbles, "Thank you," and shuffles away.

I move forward. "Where would I find Dr. Henry Flanagan, please?"

"The neurologist?"

"Yes. Would he be in Neurology?"

"Not necessarily." He looks down and starts flipping through a large binder of plastic-covered pages.

"Hmm . . ." He stops at a page and runs his finger down a type-written list. "There he is. He's downstairs." I fixate on the lisp of this info-desk man as he explains how to get to Flanagan's office.

"Oh, thank you," I say, less than satisfied with his answer, sensing this won't be as straightforward as he implies. I end up wandering through the seemingly endless maze of antiseptic hallways and door-ways, patients and medical faces and scrubs and whites.

Feeling a little lost, I ask a passing nurse, "Do you know where I might find Dr. Henry Flanagan?"

"I'm not sure if he's in," she says, "but his office is around the corner on the left."

I follow her directions. The door is ajar. I knock gently and peek my head in.

A gray-haired man sits at a desk with his back to me, reading one of the many pieces of paper stacked in messy piles in front of him. He's in a wheelchair.

"Dr. Flanagan?"

"That depends." He turns his wheelchair around so he can see me, moves his eyeglasses halfway down his nose, and looks at me over the rims. "Who are you?"

"I'm Rosemary Keevil. Rob Parr's sister."

"Oh." He sets his pen down and clears his throat. He needs both his hands to maneuver his wheelchair closer to me. Then he stops and gestures toward the small sofa in the office. He brushes his generous bangs off his forehead and says, "Have a seat."

"Thank you very much. I came last night, actually. Please tell me what happened to Rob. It looks bad. Is he going to be okay?" My gut instinct is to stand and fire questions at Dr. Flanagan, perhaps with a microphone in my hand, but I take a seat, both to be polite and to be at his height.

Dr. Flanagan explains in a measured tone, "Your brother fell in his apartment. A friend found him." He pauses, and I squint in an attempt to digest what I'm hearing. "The friend called the ambulance. He's doing a bit better today and will be able to go home in a week or so," he says dismissively, as if this will quench my desire for information.

"Why did he fall?"

Dr. Flanagan brushes his bangs off his forehead again and looks at me with his blue eyes, which seem more perfunctory than compassionate.

"He has a growth in his brain."

"What? B-but . . . w-why would he get a growth on his brain?" I protest. "The nurse said it was a tumor."

"We won't know until we do some tests. It could be an infection in the brain."

"How would he get an infection in the brain?"

"Well, it could be an opportunistic infection. It can happen when the immune system is compromised . . ."

Blah, blah, blah. I tune out. Opportunistic? Compromised immune system?

I stare straight into those cool blue eyes and say, "That's what happens to people who have AIDS, isn't it? Rob's gay."

He turns his wheelchair around enough to set his clipboard on the desk behind him and then turns back toward me and matches my stare.

"Obviously, I cannot keep this information from you." He leans forward, puts both elbows on his knees, and holds his hands together. "Your mother didn't want me to tell you, but Rob is HIV-positive. If this growth in the brain is an infection, Rob will have advanced to full-blown AIDS. However, it could be a tumor. We need to do further tests."

I sit straight up in my chair as if an electric current has shot through me. My shock jumps to anger. *Holy shit! Why, Mom? Why wouldn't you tell me Rob was HIV-positive? I'm his only family here. To protect me? Maybe to save face, too? And why wouldn't you tell me, Rob? Were you embarrassed?* It's like the two of them have been sharing covert information. Another fucking family secret.

I think back five years to when Rob was thirty-six and going out with Horace, a gorgeous, fun-loving, big black guy. He had a huge, always-ready smile that occupied his entire face. That smile could have competed with a full moon on a clear night. Horace died of AIDS a few years ago, and I have always wondered . . . but Rob has never said anything.

Dr. Flanagan says, "I'll be monitoring Rob, and the infectious-diseases specialist will see him." Then, as if I have broken through his distant demeanor, he adds, "Feel free to call me for updates." He moves back to his desk and takes a card from the stethoscope-shaped cardholder and holds it out for me. By this point, I have stood up. I stand beside him and take the card.

"Thank you, Dr. Flanagan. I really appreciate your frankness."

"Well, it was pretty damn obvious I wasn't going to keep this information from you." He looks up at me from his wheelchair. "Despite what your mother wanted. Besides, you're the one in Vancouver, and she's in . . ."

"Toronto," I say.

"Yes, the point is, she's not here."

"Mm-hmm," I agree. "Well, thank you again. I'll be talking to you."

"Yes." He smiles at me. "I'm sure."

As I make my way through the puzzling corridors of Vancouver General, I remain puzzled inside about this new wallop of information. But I don't have time to think about it. I have to find Rob. And then I have to get back to Barry. . . .

I'm so distracted, I haven't been paying attention to where I'm going. I stop in my tracks. Where the hell am I? I search for hospital signs. An older woman in scrubs stops and says, "Can I help you?"

"Yes. Where the hell am I?" I try to be funny, but she looks stunned. "Oh, sorry. Where are the elevators, please?"

I find my way to Rob's room and walk in. He's already looking in my direction. His eyes are half open and as red as burning embers. His head is swollen, but not as much as last night, and he looks a little more like my brother today. There is an IV tube attached to him and blood on the gauze where the needle is poking into his arm.

I walk to the other side of the bed. He opens his mouth, as if to talk, but nothing comes out. He mouths a few words, and then, finally, he mutters, "Thank you for being here." His delivery is labored, and he is not forming words very well, but he is understandable. "What happened?" he asks, and then his heavy, swollen eyelids close as slowly as the setting sun and he drifts off into delirium. After a minute, he regains consciousness and continues talking as if he never left the conversation: "Tell them I want a smoke. Oh, and I need you to get me sommmmme Winstons." Then he shuts his eyes yet again.

Just then, the nurse walks in, sees me, and asks, "How's he doing?"

"Well," I say, "he's asking if he can smoke, if that tells us anything."

The nurse is about thirty and hefty and in purple scrubs, reminding me a bit of the Purple People Eater. But I do like the color.

"When the patients get the okay"—she gives me a judgmental look—"they can go to a smoking spot outside. Dr. Flanagan has not signed that order for Rob."

"Thanks," I say. "I like your scrubs."

"Thanks." She smiles. "I've come to take his temperature, but I'll wait until he's awake. Are you staying long?"

"I'll be leaving shortly."

With that, she says, "Okay, I'll come back."

When Rob opens his eyes again, I try to get information out of him before he drifts off again: "What kind of Winstons? King size? And can I bring you anything else?"

"No, regular." Then a subtle smile appears as he says, "And maybe your chocolate chip cookies. That and your TLC will get me outta here real quick." His eyes shut again.

I am not much of a cook, but I make a mean chocolate chip cookie.

"Goodbye." I kiss his forehead and see that his lips are really dry, too. I'm a little uncomfortable being so close to his bodily fluids. "I'll be back later with smokes and cookies," I say to him, but he is oblivious.

The nurse comes back as I'm leaving and says to me, "We need his address."

Before I can reply, Rob opens his eyes and says, quite coherently, "Suite 403, 595 Beckers Street, Vancouver." He turns his head toward me. "Show me the escape hatch."

Back in the car, I turn the radio on and head toward the Cambie Street Bridge. Over the bridge and through downtown. All the while being deluged by more bad news.

"In a broadcast on state-run Baghdad radio five hours after the war began, a voice identified as Saddam's responded defiantly, calling Bush a 'hypocritical criminal' and vowing to crush 'the satanic intentions of the White House.'"[3]

Through the Park and over Lions Gate Bridge.

"The United States has moved under the code name Operation Desert Storm to enforce the mandates of the United Nations Security Council."[4]

Lions Gate Hospital parking lot. Sick of the news, I turn off the radio. I need to park. I need to buy a ticket from the meter. I need to find Barry. I need to be with him before he gets his results. He needs me. I rush into the hospital and up to the information desk. The attendant is free and gives me directions to Radiology. I maneuver through more endless medical hallways swarming with nameless doctors and nurses and patients and finally see the RADIOLOGY sign.

Barry, now in his civvies, is sitting on a chair in the waiting area. It's a small room with about a dozen seats, and he is alone. Barry looks up at me, and his eyes lock on mine; he's clearly longing for reassurance.

"Hello, hawney," I say.

As I put my bag on the seat beside him, I ask, "Did I miss any results?" I take off my coat. It's a lovely purple-and-khaki-green camel-hair coat that Barry bought for me when we were in Paris. My fucking world may be imploding, but I'm damn well going to look good as it happens.

"No, they've done the blood work and X-ray," he replies. I put my hand on his lap, and he continues, "I'm waiting for the CAT scan, and I've swallowed a nuclear plant for the gallium scan. How's Rob?"

I notice he appears fairly perky. "You seem in good spirits."

"Must be the radioactivity," he says. "Anyway, it's good to have these tests behind me, and it's good to see you. I missed you."

"Well, Rob is stable. I'll tell you all about it later. When will the results be ready? How long have you been waiting? Shall I find out when they're doing the scan? I'm going to call Bradley and see when we can get the results of the blood tests and X-ray."

"You've got a lot of questions," says Barry. "I'm having a hard time keeping up."

I smile and start to stand up, but Barry grabs my hand and stops me. "Thanks for being here and taking charge. I know it's tough with Rob and all."

As we are looking at each other, we hear, "Hello there. I thought I'd find you here." Dr. Bradley is walking into the waiting room in his white doctor's coat. He has an authoritative gait and a caring smile.

Barry smiles. "Good guess."

I stand and say, "I was just coming to find you. Are there any results?"

"Yes. I've come to share them with you. Shall we do it right here, or would you prefer a more private place?" Bradley asks, holding out the papers.

"Let's do it here," I say, overlapping Barry, who says, "Let's do this."

"We aren't too anxious," I add facetiously.

Bradley grabs a chair, and I note that he has a self-assured air about him that inspires confidence. When I sit back down, Bradley puts the chair in front of Barry and me, facing us.

"Well, first of all, there is nothing definitive," he says, as he sits and sets the file of papers in his lap and opens it to the first page.

I close my eyes, tilt my head forward, and rub my forehead with the middle three fingers of my left hand. Barry squeezes my right hand. I open my eyes and look up at him, and, without speaking, we acknowledge each other's feelings of impending doom.

"Okay, I'll get right to it," says Bradley. He holds up the first piece of paper and reads, "Blood tests negative so far, but we need to wait eight days for the culture."

He puts that piece of paper under the others and holds up the next one. "Chest X-ray negative."

He puts that piece of paper under the others and reads, "Brain scan negative."

He puts that piece of paper under the others and reads, "Gallium scan . . . hmm, not quite as straightforward. There is acute inflammation in the right knee and ankle and some other irregularities around the joints."

"But what does that mean?" asks Barry.

Putting the last piece of paper back into the folder and closing it, Dr. Bradley says, "We just don't know right now. Bone infection? Possible arteriosclerosis? Nuclear medicine wants to compare the leg X-rays to the gallium scan results. I know it's frustrating and worrisome, but you have no weight loss, you're not anemic, the chest X-ray is normal. I know you're in a lot of pain. They've decided not to admit you; they're going to let you go home. Let me know if there are any changes in your symptoms."

"Oh," I say, not quite knowing what to make of what he just said.

He puts his hand on Barry's knee and reassures us, "We'll get to the bottom of this. I can tell you that." He stands and leaves.

Back to the car, after ensuring that Barry is comfortable in the passenger seat, I start the fifteen-minute drive home. It's quiet. I don't turn on the radio. We need to think. I have the sort of tenuous equilibrium one would find in the focal point of a twister. If I don't maintain my balance, I will be sucked into the greedy, vertiginous chaos surrounding me.

4

"Up on the Roof"
Carole King

Monday, January 21, 1991

When I walk into the family room, Barry is sitting on one of the kids' large, colorful, wooden play cubes, his Les Paul guitar resting on his knees. Willow and Dixie are on the ground, looking up at him as he sings one of our family favorites, "You Are My Sunshine," making goofy faces and singing "gendarmes" when the words are supposed to be "in my arms." I notice he's not actually playing the Les Paul, and I wonder why.

"Hee-hee, Daddy," Willow giggles. "That's not how the song goes."

"Daddy's silly, isn't he?" I say.

He's entertaining the kids. A good sign. Music is such a big part of his life. I'm in awe of his talent. I have always wanted to play the piano. I recently took some lessons, and we set up a music room in the basement. I've already given up on the piano, but the kids haven't. Barry gets them playing on a regular basis. They bang away on the keys together, not exactly in harmony. Dixie bats away for a while: "Raining, pouring, bump, bump, bump . . ." she sings, then loses interest, slides off the piano bench, and grunts along in her amusing, two-year-old style. Willow, a couple of years older, has a little more staying power.

Dixie pulls on the neck of Barry's guitar, and he snaps, "Dixie, don't." He seems to have had enough of kids' play for the night.

"Hey, Willow and Dixie, let's get ready for bed." I try to shoo them away from Barry.

The doorbell rings.

"Saved by the bell, literally," I say. "That's gotta be Nana, just in time. She can help out."

The girls run down the hall to the front door.

"Nana, Nana," yells Willow, "were you, like, six in 1920?"

"I wasn't, *like*, six," Barry's mother says. "I *was* six."

I laugh. "They're learning about time and age in school."

"Yes, *old* age, probably," Nana says, in her soft-spoken way. She's seventy-seven years old, with an unassuming air about her. Barry has that, too.

Tonight, Nana is carrying the children's storybook *Angus and the Cat* in one hand and a pan covered with foil in another. She hands it to me, saying, "It's meat loaf, still warm. How's Barry?"

"Well, he's looking okay. Thank you so much for this. The kids say your meat loaf is the best ever."

"Nana, is that your meaty-loafy?" screams Willow, as she taps both hands on Nana's belly—she has a bit of extra weight on her.

Nana hands Willow the book. "Yes, dearie."

"Willow, settle down," I tell her, and gently move her out of Nana's way as I take the meat loaf and head into the kitchen. I set the pan on the wooden cutting board and ask Nana for her coat—a practical, dark blue car coat—just her style. "I'll go hang this up. Dixie and Barry are in the family room."

"Here, Nana, come with me," demands Willow, as she heads toward the family room, clutching *Angus and the Cat.*

Nana and Barry greet each other in their low-key fashion while

Willow holds up the book and yells, "Daddy, Daddy, look what Nana brought." Dixie runs up to Willow and tries to grab the book out of her hand. Willow has a secure hold on it and won't let it go.

"Give it to me. Give it to me," whines Dixie.

"No, no. I won't. I won't. I won't. I won't."

Nana butts in, "Now, now, girls, nobody can have it if you can't share. Let's go read it together."

She takes the book from Willow and coaxes them out of the family room.

"See ya," Barry says good-naturedly, acknowledging that he and Nana have barely said hello.

I turn to him. He's still on the chair in the guitar-playing position. "How come you weren't playing 'You Are My Sunshine' when you were singing it earlier?"

"I can't play the guitar," he mumbles, and hangs his head. "Parts of my right hand are numb." He holds up his hand, fingers limp.

I try to hide my shock, take a deep breath, and digest this development. *Numbness, numbness . . . that's neurological, isn't it?* I ask myself. *That means something's wrong with his* brain!

Barry's blood culture is negative. The electrocardiogram shows nothing. Bradley wants to send Barry to St. Joseph's Hospital in Bellingham for an MRI of his brain. Bellingham is just south of the border, in the United States, about an hour and a half drive from West Vancouver. Patients can pay $600 and get an MRI right away at St. Joseph's. In Canada, the wait is six months. There is an unspoken urgency to this quest for the cause of Barry's maladies, so we will pay the $600. I am so very grateful we can afford it.

Meanwhile, Rob, who has been in the hospital almost a week now, is improving, and I visit when I can. I even manage to make batches of chocolate chip cookies, which everyone—Barry and the girls, too—enjoys.

I delivered Rob's cigarettes on an earlier visit and am today able to make good on my promise to bring cookies. I walk in with a big smile on my face, carrying the basket of homemade biscuits, the smell of their fresh-baked goodness wafting through the air.

"Hi! Look what I brought." I hand Rob the handle of the wicker basket, which he puts on his lap. He unfolds the foil to reveal very chocolaty cookies. He puts his nose closer and sniffs.

"Mmm," he says. "Just what the doctor ordered."

Having resisted eating any on the way to the hospital, I ask, "Can I have one right now?"

"Yes, and can I go and have a cigarette right now?" he asks, his voice somewhat weak still and his big brown eyes glassy. He's got a good head of dark brown hair, which is all tousled.

"You don't want a cookie? Has Dr. Flanagan given the okay? Where do you go?"

Rob has put the basket on the side table and moved so that he is sitting on the edge of the bed, his feet reaching for his slippers.

"I can't go alone. I need to be accompanied. It's actually outside on the ground level. I have the directions." He stands up carefully and points to his worn dark brown leather jacket, hanging in the corner. "Let's go."

I hand him his jacket. He puts it on and then holds his elbow out for me to hook my hand into it.

Somewhat disgruntled with his tunnel vision—focusing on smoking and virtually ignoring me and my cheer—I take his arm, and we move slowly down the hallway. In fact, the pace feels too fucking leisurely, as I'm anxious to get the visit over with and get back to Barry. At the same time, I feel guilty that I am not more present for the visit with Rob.

He points straight ahead, instead of speaking. We come to an intersection of two hallways, and he points right.

We are at a bank of elevators.

"Not here," he explains. "We keep going to the next bank of elevators, to the left and at the end of the hall."

"Yes, sir," I manage. Even when Rob was well, he could be difficult. Dad picked on him growing up. He was the firstborn, and Dad was jealous, believing Rob took up too much of Mom's time. Then, when Rob came out of the closet, Dad completely rejected him. They've been estranged ever since.

Once we make it there, the wait for the elevator is long and the ride down the five floors excruciatingly slow. On the ground floor, we exit to a covered alcove designated for those sick people who are not sick enough to not smoke cigarettes. There is another couple there. An older woman in a wheelchair has her gray hair pulled back in a ponytail and black Poindexter glasses. She's wearing a parka and gray sweatpants and has a pink shawl spread on her lap. I assume the man standing beside her is her husband. He's wearing the same style parka—the kind with the fake fur around the hood.

"Hello," says the man, as he holds out an open pack of DuMauriers to his wife. "Nice place to be relegated to, eh? Do you have a light? Our lighter just died."

This guy is far too friendly for my crusty mood.

Rob says, "Oh, I forgot lights. Did you bring some?" Indeed I did. Thank God. When I bought the smokes, I figured I'd better get matches, too.

"You can have a package"—I dig into my purse—"if I can ever find them." As I rummage, I have a growing sense of anxiety as the smokers entertain the possibility that I can't find them. "There they are. They were in the front pocket." I hand one pack to Rob and one to the gentleman, who lights his wife's cigarette.

I watch Rob lighting his Winston, drawing very hard on it so the ember glows bright red, slowly burning up the shaft. He and the couple make small talk. I muster all the civility I can. I purposely stand downwind from Rob's cigarette smoke. Since I quit smoking some ten years ago, I occasionally get pleasure out of inhaling other people's smoke.

Rob exhales a lungful in the other direction, so as not to blow smoke in my face, and then puts out the cigarette in the ashtray provided, saying, "Time for another one."

"Oh, really?" I ask, disappointed and wanting to leave.

"C'mon, Peeface, this is my only chance," he says, using a nickname I was called when I was young and picked on by my peers for having a lisp.

"Okaaaaay, Fartface," I respond, fluttering my eyelashes.

When we finally return to the room, I'm about to seek out Dr. Flanagan to get an update on Rob's condition, when a doctor walks in.

"Hello," he says. "I'm Dr. Reeder, from Infectious Diseases. Uh . . ."

When he hesitates, I introduce myself. "I'm Rosemary Keevil, Rob's sister," I say, while Rob climbs into bed and settles into a sitting position. "Have you met Rob?"

"Not formally. I have the results of the CT scan."

"I'm so happy I'm here for this," I gush, thinking if we hadn't spent so long in the smokers' den, I would have missed this Dr. Reeder, who doesn't really look like someone who would be an infectious-diseases specialist. I guess I expected someone with his job to look more like Mr. Clean—sparkling white. This guy is about Rob's age—fortyish—with a casual air about him, wearing brown Blundstone boots, beige corduroy pants, and an open-necked shirt with chest hair showing under his white lab coat.

Reeder and I both stand beside the bed, forming a triangle with Rob. Reeder's one hand is holding his clipboard up. With the other, he scratches the back of his neck just under where his longish brown hair curls up. It's parted on one side and stuck to his head with some kind of hair product that makes it look a bit greasy.

"As you know, there is a mass in Rob's brain, and we've been trying to find out what caused it. But since Rob has been responding so well to the treatment in the early stages"—he puts his hand in his pocket, looks at me and back to Rob—"the mass is getting smaller, indicating that it is not lymphoma, which is what we suspected."

He pauses and checks his notes.

"It's getting smaller?" I ask.

"Yes, this is good. If this improvement continues, we can avoid doing a brain biopsy, a process that can be dangerous in itself—can cause injury to the brain, seizures."

Dr. Reeder takes a step back while saying, "It looks like he has toxoplasmosis." With that, Reeder puts down the hand holding the clipboard, as if this is all the information he has.

"How could he have gotten toxoplasmosis? What is it?" I ask

"It's an infection that you can get from cats and raw meat," Dr. Reeder says, "but Rob is more susceptible because of the HIV virus." He pauses, then continues, "Which, by all indications, seems to have advanced to AIDS."

Rob looks right at me, expecting a response. I stay stone-faced. Dr. Reeder interrupts the moment, suddenly turning very chatty, which seems somewhat jarring, considering the gravity of what he's just told us.

"Did you know how much of an emergency it was for Rob on Tuesday night at his apartment?"

"No," I say, anxious to hear what happened six days ago.

He looks at Rob. "You fell in your apartment. You had a seizure. By the time the ambulance got there, the paramedics had to cut off your shirt to get at you." He pauses, blinks his green eyes, and adds, "You almost died."

Rob and I are silent.

Rob closes his eyes and says, "Well, thank you, Dr. Reeder." He opens his eyes and continues, "And thanks to the paramedics, and thanks to Jean-Paul—he's the one who found me and called 911."

"Thank God he came by. It must have been really soon after you fell," I say.

"Yes," agrees Dr. Reeder, nodding his head, "it must have been."

"Thank you for all of this, Doctor," Rob says sincerely. "Can you sign the order for me to go for a cigarette unaccompanied?"

"No, I'm sorry," Dr. Reeder says. "Dr. Flanagan has to do that. I need to go now, but we'll continue to monitor you."

Rob turns to me as Dr. Reeder leaves. "Now you have the low-down. I'm a rare long-term HIV survivor. I've known since 1986. I knew this must be it—the AIDS taking hold."

Rob thinks I didn't know until now that he was HIV-positive, so I feign surprise. But now that it's out in the open, we talk about AIDS and the societal fear surrounding it. We talk about Lady Diana's courageous work in 1987, trying to dispel the myth that AIDS could be contracted through casual contact. Even though I try to appear unfettered by this paranoia about the deadly virus, I am secretly terrified of contracting it, too. It is known as a "gay man's" disease, and there is still a stigma around it that makes me feel like I need to be vigilant about my physical contact with Rob—and all gay men, for that matter.

"I guess we'd better talk to Mom," I suggest.

"Yeah, we've spoken—I'm able to call collect from here. We both feared for the worst. We kinda knew." Rob takes a long deep sigh of resignation. "Will you call her? She won't be surprised. Sal should know, too—I think Audrey's already warned her." Sal is our sister, and Audrey is Mom—Rob has called her by her first name for years. Just then, a nurse comes in to check Rob's vitals and he says to her, "Have I got the okay from the doctor for me to smoke unaccompanied?"

"No," the nurse says, as she wraps a blood pressure band around his arm. "You'll have to wait." She is older, with short, wavy gray hair and white scrubs, although she seems like the type of nurse who should be wearing a nurse's dress and nurse's cap. I have a feeling this is not the person Rob should be asking about smoking privileges.

"But how long do I have to wait?"

"Until Dr. Flanagan signs the form approving that." She pumps up the band.

"When will that be?"

"As soon as he does it."

"Can we hurry it up?"

"You'll have to wait."

"I can't wait."

She says nothing and checks the monitor for his blood pressure. "A little high but within range," she says, as she unwraps the band.

I squirm at Rob's impertinence.

"Did you know," she looks at me, "that Rob tried to leave the hospital Saturday night so he could go home and have a cigarette? We caught him in time. Good thing, too—next morning he had another seizure."

Rob appears nonplussed, like the nurse is talking about the weather.

"If he'd been at home, he would have ended up with permanent brain damage—or dead."

She puts the temperature gauge in Rob's ear, waits a moment, and takes it out, writing a number on the pad in her pocket.

Rob says nothing.

"Thank you," I say. "What's your name?"

"Maria."

"I'm Rosemary, Rob's sister."

"Yes, I know."

How does she know? I guess they're talking out there at the nurses' desk. I wonder what they're saying about Rob.

I explain to Rob that I need to leave to tend to Barry.

"Can I have another cigarette before you go?"

Shit, shit, shit, shit, shit. Really, Rob? Really? All he does is look at me like a dog waiting for his dinner. He does not acknowledge that he is being selfish.

With a deep sigh of resignation, I say, "Okay," and I do my best to act polite as I endure the brutally slow trip back outside. When we are finally back in his room and I am free to go, I tell Rob I will try to find Dr. Flanagan on my way out and ask about the cigarettes. I say goodbye with a timorous air kiss on his forehead, underscoring my discomfort with touching his AIDS-infected body—one of those actions, or inactions, that shrieks like sirens without making a sound. Both of us hear it.

"When will you be back?" Rob asks. It is clear that he is anxious to see me again only so he can go smoke.

"As soon as possible. And I'll speak to Mom and Sal."

"Thank you. As I said, she won't be surprised. She knows. Thanks for the cookies. Thanks for asking Flanagan about the smoking thing," he says. "Goodbye for now. I'm going to lie back now and rest my mass." We both smirk, and I walk out.

The next day, Barry and I head out to the hospital in Bellingham for his MRI. It happens that Vancouver General is on the way to the border, so I ask Barry if we can stop at VGH so I can give Rob a quick smoke break. He politely agrees.

I arrive to do my duty, and Rob is duly grateful as we head back out to the smokers' area. I strain to make congenial conversation with the other sick smokers, and even with Rob, who knows that Barry is waiting in the car for me so we can go to Bellingham for yet another medical test. I keep a watchful eye on Rob's cigarette as it burns toward the filter. Each puff makes the glowing ember creep closer and closer to my release. When it looks like there is no more tobacco and Rob is about to smoke the filter, he takes one last, lingering puff, relishing the hot nicotine as it gushes down his throat, through his windpipe, and to the farthest recesses of his lungs. As he stubs out the butt, I eagerly make a motion to leave—and he lights up another. I collapse inside. I drop my shoulders and tighten the corners of my mouth in resignation. *What the goddamn fucking hell? Jesus fucking Christ, Rob. Barry is waiting in the car! He's sick and desperate to find out what's wrong with him. I have two little girls at home who need me. What are you doing?*

I close my eyelids in search of civility, and when I raise them again, Rob is savoring another puff and looking back at me in a blank trance. I stand in a silent fury for the rest of his smoke break and the trip back to his room. My obvious but nonverbalized outrage does not affect him. I conjure up a polite goodbye before making my escape.

The visit to St. Joseph's Hospital is tough on Barry physically. The examination in the MRI machine is uncomfortable. He can barely eat his lunch in the hospital cafeteria. He is gray and weak and not hungry. We drive back to Vancouver under a disquieting pall.

That evening, I call my sister in Toronto for support.

She greets me with tenderness in her voice. "Hi, Rose."

"Hi. What are you doing?"

"We just got back from dinner with the kids at the club."

"Sounds so . . . so normal."

"Yeah. What's going on with Rob and Barry must be so tough for you. That's so sad about Rob and AIDS, although, I have to say, I already knew. Mom and I talked about it."

"Yes, I spoke with her. She seems pretty stoic, but I'm worried about her," I say.

"Let *me* worry about her. How's Barry? How're the girls? Do they know Daddy doesn't feel so good?"

"They're okay. They're acting up more than usual. Nana and Dianne have been helping out."

I'm anxious to tell Sal about what Rob did yesterday. I explain to her about the horrendous time I had with him at VGH, as Barry waited in the car, and then the miserable experience in Bellingham and the depressing ride home.

"I'm so worried about Barry, about what he's going through and about what could possibly be wrong. What do you think? I mean, man, when he started getting numbness in his fingers, I just don't know, Sal. And Rob and AIDS and all. I'm afraid to touch him. I'm being paranoid, but I can't help myself. I'm sucked in by all the paranoia around me. I'm even concerned about my gay hairdresser. And he's just washing my hair! I'm lying at the sink at the salon with the back of my neck on that cold, hard porcelain sink, trying to get comfortable, and I should be enjoying the scalp massage, but all I can think of is getting AIDS from him simply because he's gay! No, that's not all I can think of. I'm also agonizing over the plight of those poor families in the Middle East who are being bombed, their villages pillaged, the women raped. I'm worried about—"

"Whoa, slow down," Sal says. "You can't solve all the problems in the world."

"No, I can't solve *any* of them—and there are a lot."

"It has to be horrible for you, Rose." Sal's voice is gentle. "Mom and I will be there on the weekend."

"Yeah, Mom told me. That's so fantastic you're coming. Thank you. This has to be tough on Mom. I can't help but worry about her."

"She's holding up. You know her and Dad. Chin up."

"Yeah: 'Chin up, stomach in, shoulders back, and don't mumble.'"

We giggle at Dad's mantra. This laughter is a release that might otherwise be manifested in the form of tears or screams.

—

Mom and Sal come out West from Toronto on January 23. The moment they arrive at Vancouver International, my anxiety over Rob is diluted. I feel their comfort like warm rays of sunshine beaming down on me. Mom spends most of her time with Rob. Sal divides her time between Rob and Barry and me. I cherish the "normal" activities that I can do with my sister, like shopping on Robson Street, going out for lunch, getting our nails done, doing our swim laps together at my local health club—something that has been a self-care staple for both of us for years. It's a habit we got from Dad, who used to do lengths every summer morning in our backyard pool.

Having a pool was another contradiction in our lives. When we got it, I was in grade two and my friends at school asked me, "Are you rich?" But if this were true, why was my mother always fretting about the bills that came in the mail—which, in those days, were delivered twice a day during the week and once on Saturday? Mom insisted we hide the bills lest Dad come home and find them and have a conniption fit about how hard he worked and how we couldn't possibly ever pay them.

Dad did his laps nude, except for a bathing cap, for years—one of his many oddball habits. Once, he answered the door in his birthday suit and bathing cap when my boyfriend came to pick me up. I'm still surprised Dwayne didn't bolt. He must have really liked me. He told me he found Dad's behavior hysterical.

Sal's presence also enables me to pay attention to my career. I'm producing an educational special on the forest industry for the local cable station, and I'm also hosting a cable program called *The Associates*—an interview show where I talk to everyone from the local veterinarian (and his dog, who is brought in as a prop) to an arborist explaining why the cutting of trees to make way for views is such an emotional issue in Vancouver. I attend an acting class and do an audition for a Century 21 ad as well.

Mom and Sal can stay only a few days, as Sal needs to get back to her high-pressure financial job in Toronto. There seem to be some unuttered sisterly responsibilities being assigned here. Sal and Hal have been taking on much of the burden of our schizophrenic brother, Gavin, in Toronto. It appears to be my position, here in Vancouver, to undertake the care of our other sick brother, Rob.

Mom, meanwhile, cannot leave Hankey on the farm alone for long. (Hankey is what we now call Dad, as he hates his grandchildren calling him Grandfather; it makes him feel old. Hankey is a form of Dad's real name, Henry.) Mom and Hankey live on a two-hundred-acre farm in Collingwood, Ontario. They are not really farmers themselves, but they rent their fields to locals who grow alfalfa and such, and they rent the barns to people with horses.

There is no consideration whatsoever given to the idea that Hankey might come out to Vancouver. He hates change—and, of course, he does not particularly like Rob.

Shortly after Mom and Sal leave, the doctors tell me that Rob is well enough to go home. But will he be safe on his own? Does he need someone to take care of him? Who will that be? What about his medications?

When VGH does release Rob, they give me little guidance. I have a handful of prescriptions for him, so we go to the corner drugstore to get them filled. The pharmacist looks closely at the prescriptions and gives them right back to me, explaining that we have to go to a special drugstore to get AZT, an AIDS-specific medication. Gee, thanks, VGH.

With a bit of research, I find a Persons with AIDS, or PWA, support group in the basement of St. Paul's Hospital. I learn that St. Paul's is *the* AIDS hospital, and that sheds some light on why VGH could not wait to get rid of Rob. I've always thought of PWA as Pacific Western Airlines, but now it has a new association. The other acronym that has changed for me is CBC—which, to me, has always stood for the Canadian Broadcasting Corporation that would never hire me but now means complete blood count. The helpful PWA people tell us where to get Rob's slew of prescriptions filled and how to keep them in order. He needs a dossette, a pill organizer that separates all the pills according to time of day. A social worker will come to his place twice a week to help organize his medication and provide assistance.

The people at PWA also direct us to Dr. Andrew Katses. Every one of the patients in his waiting room is a gay male, and when we meet Katses, I feel instantly safe. This blond-haired man oozes authentic kindness through his soft blue eyes and wholesome smile. When I explain my situation—that my husband is also suffering from a potentially serious illness—he consoles me, "Rosemary, you are in crisis management right now. And you are doing an admirable job." It's reassuring that Rob is under the care of what feels like a genuine protector—a saint, in fact. Having the social worker in place to help Rob out with his meds and other needs around his apartment is comforting as well.

It is late in the evening, and silence reigns in the household. I am the only one awake. I check on both children. They are in their beds. Asleep.

I check on Barry. Asleep.

Dianne is staying over. She is in the guest room. Asleep.

This kind of silence is different than any other. It carries with it a glorious but tentative sense of relief. I know this quiescence could be as fleeting as a hummingbird's visit to a feeder.

I slide into my bed, trying not to disrupt Barry's slumber. I lay my head down on my pillow. My body, thirsting for rest, sinks into the mattress under the fluffy duvet.

The phone blasts its presumptuous, vociferous ring through the house like thunder. I lunge for the receiver near the bed, hoping the family doesn't wake up.

"Hello?"

"This is Emergency at Vancouver General Hospital. May I speak with Rosemary Kibble, please?" My last name, Keevil, rhymes with the word *evil*.

"Yes."

"Is this Rob Parr's sister?"

"Yes."

"He's in Emergency here. Please come to the hospital."

"Oh my God," I say, my pulse quickening. "Oh my God. Is he okay? What happened?"

"He hurt himself—on purpose. He's quite stable, but we need you here."

"How did—"

"We need you here now, Mrs. Kibble," the voice says.

"Yes, I'll be there. Goodbye," I manage, and hang up.

I pause to gather my thoughts and strength. I wake Barry to tell him I have to go. I throw on exactly what I was wearing before I changed for bed and grab the car keys, a newspaper, and an apple and cheese. I've learned that you never know what's going to go down, and I may need sustenance.

As I get into the car, I realize I'd better tell Dianne what's going on, too, but I don't really want to wake her. I think about it and know I have no choice. I go to her room and gingerly nudge her shoulder. "Dianne. Dianne?" She opens her eyes slightly and sits straight up when she sees me.

"I'm so sorry to frighten you. I have to go to Vancouver General for Rob—something's happened. Okay? Everyone is asleep."

"Oh, oh, okay, Rosemary," she says, rubbing her eyes. "I'll go sleep on the couch in the family room so I'm closer," she offers, as the guest room is somewhat removed from the other bedrooms.

"*Wow.* God, thank you, Dianne."

I rush to the car and race across town as safely as possible, figuring if I get stopped I can tell the officer it is indeed a real emergency. I fantasize about getting a police escort to the hospital.

It disturbs me that Rob was taken to Vancouver General, instead of St. Paul's. But I figure that's all about geography—Rob lives closer to VGH than to St. Paul's.

When I arrive, I am immediately directed to Rob's curtained cubicle. He's lying propped up in the gurney, fully awake. When he sees me, he spreads his lips slightly to form an enigmatic grin. Blood is seeping through bandages on his wrists and his ankles.

"What the hell happened, Rob? Are you okay?"

"Yeah, I guess?" It's more a question than an answer.

As I get closer and he turns his head farther toward me, I see that his neck is wrapped in bloody bandages as well. "Rob, what did you do?"

"The roof. On the roof," he says. "I did it on the roof." I assume he means the roof of his four-story, redbrick, walk-up apartment building.

"With what?"

"Scissors."

"Why, Rob? Why?"

I can't get much information out of him; he gives me only monosyllabic answers.

I need to find a doctor to tell me what condition Rob is in. All I can find is the damn attendant at the main Emergency counter. She looks like all the others I've seen over the previous weeks—another faceless uniform. This one tells me to take Rob home.

"Pardon me?" I ask, not believing what I'm hearing.

"We don't believe it was a bona fide suicide attempt," she says. "This may sound . . . well, you know, well . . . we need the bed."

"Ah," I say. "Can't he be admitted?"

"As I said, he's stable and well enough to go home," she shrugs.

"Well, he's wrapped in a helluva bunch of bandages, and even if he were stable physically, as you say, he is obviously not balanced mentally," I say. "He needs help."

"It was a pretend suicide attempt," she says. "If you want him admitted, his doctor has to request that."

"You mean the neurologist? Dr. Flanagan?"

"Yes."

"It's midnight. Is he on duty?" My anger is building. "This is nuts. I need to take care of my husband, who's seriously ill. I have two young children at home, and my brother is in Emergency at your hospital, covered in bloody bandages, having just tried, or pretended to try, to kill himself."

I stop and try to gather my thoughts. I can feel the blood rushing to my face, my hands clenched, tears welling up behind my eyes. I feel as if I could implode. "What difference does it make if he tried or pretended to try? Whichever it was, he clearly needs help and would need someone to stay with him if he were brought home. Don't you understand I cannot possibly do that? Isn't it obvious that he needs medical supervision?" I stop again, stuck for words. "This can't be happening."

"You can use that pay phone to call Dr. Flanagan," she says nonchalantly, and gestures to the wall behind me.

"Call him now? He won't answer his phone at this time of night."

"You can leave a message."

Fiery inside, I attempt to compose myself and walk to the phone. I leave a message on Dr. Flanagan's phone to please call Emergency and give the admission order. I know that the chance of this actually happening is unlikely. I may not be able to connect with Flanagan until the morning. I stay by the phone, with my back to the desk, for a moment and allow myself time to think. I know what I need to do right now—grant myself a breakdown, lie down, let those tears surge forth, wallow in the anxiety and fear, indulge in defeat, eventually conjure up a plan of action. But first, the fucking lady at the desk!

I march back there and see the emotionless woman sitting behind it. I refrain from saying what I really feel—*Are you out of your fucking tree, you fucking bitch?*—and instead say, "Of course, I did not reach Dr. Flanagan. I left a message, but I don't imagine I'll hear from him till morning. I have to go say goodbye to my brother now and go home to my family, who need me. I have no choice."

A different nurse notices my distress and steps in. "He'll be fine here overnight," she reassures me. "He's stable."

"Thank you," I say. "I'll be back in the morning."

5

"Midnight Hour"
Wilson Pickett

Thursday, February 7, 1991

"Well," says Dr. Bradley, upon feeling the lump on Barry's right rib, which has grown to the size of an egg. "I believe it's time to remove this and get it biopsied."

Bradley is sitting in a chair directly in front of Barry, who is sitting in a chair facing him, holding his shirt up so Bradley can feel the lump. After Bradley removes his hand, Barry touches the lump and gently moves it a little back and forth. Then puts his shirt down, scowls, and opens his mouth to talk, but Bradley continues, "I will do this in Emergency this afternoon." He stands up, walks to his desk, and checks his schedule: "One thirty."

Barry and I look at each other, mirroring shock, and both check our watches. "It's noon. I guess we'll go have some lunch," I say, standing up and straightening my skirt.

Barry stands as well and says to Bradley, "This sounds serious."

Bradley nods slightly, walks to Barry, looks him straight in the eye, and says, "Could be." Bradley grasps Barry's right bicep with a reassuring shake. "Let's wait. We'll have the results tomorrow. See you at one thirty."

With that, Barry and I give our thanks and leave Bradley's office. We go to the cafeteria at the hospital. Neither of us is very hungry or talkative. Barry has tomato soup and crunches up a bunch of saltines to put in it. "Comfort food," he explains. I simply have tea, my fallback.

When we reappear for the biopsy, Bradley explains to Barry that it will be quick and fairly painless. He will have the results tomorrow and will call us.

That evening, Barry is sullen and irritable around the kids. I try to act normal, but it's hard not to be distracted by angst about what might be.

The next morning, Dr. Bradley calls to say there is a diagnosis and we should come see him right away at his office. On the way, Barry and I barely say a word, but our mutual fear is deafening.

When we enter his office, Bradley gestures to the two chairs in front of his desk. "Take a seat."

He sits, puts both hands down on his desk in front of him, takes a deep breath, and says calmly, "We have a diagnosis. T-cell immuno-blastic non-Hodgkin's lymphoma." He pauses and looks from Barry to me and back to Barry again. "I know you will have a lot of questions, and it's best to get the answers from Dr. Charles Kasheemo, the oncologist at the clinic at Lions Gate. He's in now and expecting you."

Barry and I stare at Dr. Bradley, who has not actually uttered the loaded word, *cancer*, but clearly Barry has it. He has lymphoma and is seeing an oncologist.

I open my mouth to say something, but all I can manage is, "Uh, um, what does this mean, Dr. Bradley? How bad, how bad, a, um, a cancer is this?"

"Well"—he clears his throat, then continues in his consistently compassionate tone—"it's quite aggressive. But Barry is young, and you have one of the top lymphoma experts in the world in Kasheemo."

As we walk the short distance to Dr. Kasheemo's office, we are holding hands so tightly that my blood flow becomes restricted. I reassure Barry that he is going to be okay no matter what, and that I am right beside him and always will be.

At the clinic, we are directed to Dr. Kasheemo's office. My heart is beating more quickly and loudly with every step, so loud I'm sure Barry can hear it. Maybe it's his heart I'm hearing. It is as if we are about to enter a burning house that is engulfed in flames.

Dr. Kasheemo is indeed expecting us. He is stern and sterile-looking in his crisp white medical coat. He doesn't smile and tells us to sit down. There are no windows, no pictures, little furniture, and many files—and, above all, a paralyzing sense of foreboding.

"You have been diagnosed with T-cell immunoblastic non-Hodgkin's lymphoma," Dr. Kasheemo says. "This form of cancer is aggressive and requires aggressive treatment. At forty-one, you are fairly young to get cancer. Younger people are less likely to get malignancies, but when they do the cancer is generally an aggressive one. Chemotherapy treatment, provided you decide to go this route, will start on Monday."

Dr. Kasheemo may be a brilliant oncologist, but he has zero bedside manner.

We both stare at him, speechless. I am too terrified to ask *the* question: *Is it terminal?* Instead, I start in safer territory.

"But why would he get this?"

"This cancer is not genetic, and they don't know what causes it. It's just bad luck." He hands us a thick pamphlet entitled "You Have Been Diagnosed with Non-Hodgkins Lymphoma" and says, "This provides a great deal of information. We'll conduct more tests on Monday. We need to test your bone marrow and spinal fluid and do ultrasounds of your abdomen and a CAT scan. The chemotherapy is done here in the clinic."

But how aggressive is it?

Can this go into remission?

What's the prognosis?

I can't bring myself to ask any of these questions out loud.

"I would plan for an intensive eight-week chemotherapy treatment," Dr. Kasheemo says. "There is an 80 percent chance you will respond well."

These words clang around my head, colliding and smashing into each other, striving desperately and hopelessly for a place to land. What does that mean? It is what this emotionless doctor has left unsaid that is most petrifying. *How long does Barry have?* I ask myself. I hold Barry's hand and look at him. His eyes are closed. I put my other hand on his leg and squeeze gently. He is quivering. "Barry?" I whisper.

He opens his eyes slowly and looks at me with sheer terror. He turns to Dr. Kasheemo. "Ah, ah . . ." He sighs deeply. "What's the prognosis with and without chemo?"

"You could respond well to the chemotherapy, and you would have under a year," Dr. Kasheemo says. "Without chemotherapy, you would have six weeks."

The answer stuns me. Barry has just been diagnosed with cancer. Terminal cancer. Under a year to live—even with treatment. I can't believe we have an oncologist whose name rhymes with the treatment he administers. Kasheemo who does chemo.

God, please release me.

After grave conversation and discussion, Barry and I decide to proceed with our weekend plans to go to Whistler. I have to pack up the food, the supplies, and the kids. Dianne comes with us. We grab drive-through McDonald's for dinner, but Barry barely eats.

When we arrive at Whistler, Barry goes straight to the bedroom and lies down. I unload and get the place organized. I ask Dianne to busy the girls and set them up at the dining room table with a puzzle and coloring books. I put the food away, put the tea on, light the fire. Lots to do.

I have no idea what to expect with Barry. I have no idea what to say or do. Where's the instruction manual for this? I arrange fresh flowers and take a vase of orange and yellow gerbera daisies to our bedroom.

"Can I get you anything?" I ask him, as I set the vase down. "We're having a snack. Cheese and crackers and pickles. You know, the regular happy-fizzies tray."

"Happy-fizzies tray?" He seems somewhat interested. But this brief spark is soon extinguished by a dismissive, "I'm not really hungry."

I sit beside him and kiss his forehead. "You feel warm. I'll take your temperature."

I go to get the thermometer, and when I come back, he is holding his right shoulder.

"My shoulder hurts," he says, "and so do my knee and hip. My hand is numb."

"Oh dear, sweetheart. I'll get the Tylenol as well." I set the thermometer down on the nightstand and retrieve the Tylenol. When I return, I look at my husband with tenderness and sit beside him and hold back my tears. He needs me to be strong.

"I'm afraid, hawney," he says holding my hand and looking into my eyes. "I'm dying."

"We'll fight this. You'll be the miracle. I know it," I say, not knowing what else to say.

"I sure hope so."

I set the Tylenol down beside the thermometer. I lie down and snuggle him. We hold each other. We cry.

"Maybe a glass of wine would be just as good as a thermometer and Tylenol," Barry suggests after a while.

"Sure," I say. "I'll open that lovely Bâtard-Montrachet."

"This would be as good an occasion for Bâtard-Montrachet as any."

"You could call it a Bâtard-Montrachet kinda day." I do my best to smile.

Relieved to be able to do something that feels useful, I bring us two large goblets of the chilled chardonnay. Barry is propped up in bed, looking out the window. The trees provide a peekaboo view of the lake, which is lit up by the full moon.

"I'm thinking about Dad," he says. His father died in 1989 of multiple myeloma. "I always wondered how he got through the diagnosis, the prognosis, that nefarious word *terminal*. I remember trying to understand how he coped with it all. I sure hope I can maintain the kind of strength he had."

"You know," I said, "I really feel his spirit at his island in Seratami, with that copper carving of him in the rock and his ashes in the lake."

"Yeah," says Barry. "That ceremony up there was really special."

I nod. "It was powerful. Watching his ashes come out of the seaplane over the sunset and then swimming toward them from his island. The girls were so young, especially Dixie. I don't know if they have any memories of him, but Dixie and Grandfather had some tender moments together near the end. I think they both have wise souls."

My mind wanders. Is this really happening to my husband? Can it be reversed, maybe? I stroke his head. "We'll be okay. You'll fight this. You'll be the miracle." This is my mantra. I have to believe it. There is no choice. If you ain't got hope, you ain't got nothin'.

Barry stays in bed most of the weekend. I spend time with the kids and visit him regularly. He is weak and headachy.

The girls gaily come and go; they think their dad is just a little under the weather. He tries to muster up some energy for them, but Dianne and I mostly keep them occupied.

"We're going out for a walk down by the lake," I say on Saturday afternoon. "Do you want to come?"

"No, I don't feel up to it," he says. "Do you think the kids are okay?"

"Yeah, they're just going about their antics. They're okay. It's you I'm worried about." I walk over to the bed, sit down, kiss him on the lips, and say again, "You can be the miracle, honey."

He smiles mutely.

His skin is gray.

By the end of the weekend, his hair is thinner.

His body is thinner too.

He is an old man already.

He is dying right in front of my eyes.

Monday morning, Barry is admitted to hospital and bombarded with more fucking tests. The ultrasounds of his legs and abdomen show evidence of lymphoma. The bone marrow biopsy is negative for lymphoma, which sounds like good news, but we're not sure what it means. He receives an intravenous injection of a contrast material, followed by a CAT scan of his head. A lumbar puncture is performed, and fluid is extracted from his spine.

Barry's spinal fluid tests positive for lymphoma. This is clearly very bad news—and, we soon learn, means that Barry needs to have a reservoir put in his head so the chemo drugs can be injected right into the cerebrospinal fluid, since the IV chemo does not infiltrate the spinal fluid. Therefore chemotherapy is going to be administered in two ways: intravenously into his veins and through the reservoir in the head. It's called intrathecal chemo.

The operation to install the reservoir is scheduled for the next day. The IV therapy starts today. Barry and I are told to go to one of the gurneys in the clinic. They are not in separate cubicles, divided with curtains, but rather lined up, as if on a ward, about five feet apart.

The other patients seem to be at ease with the entire procedure, lying about, attached to IV tubes, chatting with one another and the medical staff. We, on the other hand, are entering this foreign land with great trepidation. The foreign language includes words like *neomycin* and *cyclophosphamide*.

Barry lies down on his gurney, and in less than a minute he is hooked up to his IV and chemotherapy drugs are being pumped into his veins with vigor. I sit in the chair beside his bed, and we stare at each other, acknowledging our mutual bewilderment. Then we both burst into laughter. What the hell is so funny, I do not know. It must be a survival mechanism—if we weren't laughing, we'd be reduced to lifelessness.

But this is barely the beginning. We do not even discuss Dr. Kasheemo's decision to send Barry for brain surgery. Kasheemo is the cancer God, and we accept his decisions as if there is no other option.

Barry has surgery on Tuesday, the day after the first IV chemo treatment. After the operation, a nurse rolls him into his hospital room on a gurney. I am startled by Barry's appearance, as his head is swaddled in white bandages, but what exactly did I expect after brain surgery?

Dr. Hunter is accompanying Barry. Barry's eyes are open, but he looks groggy.

The doctor, as if acknowledging my shock, explains, "I have inserted a reservoir into Barry's skull. This is so the spinal fluid can be easily accessed to insert the medications."

"Why isn't it done through the spine?" I ask.

"The spinal fluid is a unique part of the human body," he says. "It's hard to infiltrate. It protects itself. We don't know that what we insert into the spine actually makes it to the brain, and vice versa. Dr. Kasheemo will likely administer chemotherapy drugs into the spine, as well as through this reservoir."

"When does this start?"

"I think Dr. Kasheemo will start using the reservoir chemo today."

"Did you hear that, Barry?" I ask, turning to my husband.

He opens his mouth to talk, but nothing comes out for a few seconds. Then he delivers an emotionless "yeah."

"Do you have any other questions before I go?" asks the doctor.

"How long do the bandages stay on?"

"They'll come off later this week. Then there will just be a small patch on his head covering the reservoir. He can shower like normal."

"May I call you if I have any other questions?"

"Of course," Dr. Hunter says. "Here's my card." He hands it to me, and I tuck it into the front pocket of my purse.

When Dr. Hunter leaves, I go to Barry's bedside and gently put my hand on his. He is bandaged up like a mummy. How the fuck is this possible?

"How are you doing?" I ask.

"Miserable, shitty," he says. "I have just had some *thing* installed in my brain. It feels like there's a Mack truck stuck in my head." The content of what he's saying belies the monotone of his delivery.

I wince. "It must be horrible, hawney. I'm so sorry you're going through all this. You had all that chemotherapy yesterday afternoon, and now this operation . . . and more chemo today. Kasheemo is going to use the reservoir this afternoon. It's called intrathecal chemo."

"Great," Barry says sarcastically.

"I don't blame you for being grumpy," I say. "This is so absolutely atrocious. Look at what you're being put through—a petrifying diagnosis on Friday; that slew of tests, more tests; needles in your spine, hip, and arms; swallowing gross liquid; photos of your brain and stomach. Then the onslaught of chemo drugs yesterday and brain surgery today. This is a fucking shit show."

"I know you're trying to be helpful," Barry mutters, "but it's not working." He glances out the window and says with resignation, "I guess it's time to tell my mom and the others."

It's as if his harsh words shoot a bullet through the small bubble of stamina I have been coveting. But I need to hang on to the mere ripples of energy I have left in order not to fire back at him and to leave him alone.

"Ah . . . Yeah, ah . . . Sorry, sweetie," I say. "It's hard to know what to do. Yeah, I'll take care of telling your family."

I am living with my throat swollen and my eyes puffy from tears. Barry is in the hospital. I love him so much. I cannot remember what I am doing from one moment to the next. There is too much to do. I don't keep it together telling Barry's brothers and sisters what's going on over the phone. They are all shocked and concerned and offer to help. Barry is very private in his despair and expresses explicit desire not to have his siblings visit. I call on Nana and fall on her lap in anguish. She comforts me while dealing with her own feelings over this devastating news. She is so concerned about me, she says she is going to call about getting a social worker to come and speak to me.

The following day, I am able to lie in the hospital bed with Barry, and we both cry.

"I love you so much, hawney," he says to me.

"I love you, too, hawney. You're so special."

"I love you," he says. "You're everything to me."

"This is a nightmare," I say. "But you'll beat this." And I try to believe it.

—

As the week progresses and we move into an acceptance zone, I am able to help more. I go to Quadra Stone to collect samples of marble for the Whistler kitchen counter and take them to Barry so we can decide which one we want. This is a positive distraction and gives us a project to work on together. I do the banking, which he normally takes care of. He arranges for the bank accounts to be amalgamated, telling me, "So if I die tomorrow, it will be easier."

The phone rings constantly. Willow asks, "Why is the phone ringing so much?" I complain to Barry that the fucking phone calls are constant. I know it is only because a lot of people really care about him, but I don't know what to tell them. He suggests something to say: "Barry has aggressive lymphoma, is under good care, and has the best doctors in North America, and we appreciate the concern. He does not want flowers or gifts, but cards are good."

I drive Willow to the hospital to see her daddy, thinking that taking one child at a time is wise. Turns out there is nothing wise about it at all. She acts distant. It feels like she is mad at him. She probably is. Barry is depressed—not his usual self with her—and she doesn't understand what's happening.

Nana did arrange for me to see a social worker, who says the girls need to know that they are going to be okay and that Daddy is sick but has really good doctors. She says to keep our routine the same. It is important to stick to as many traditions as possible. Get them to draw and paint, try to express feelings that way. Unfortunately, she says, children feel the stress in situations like these and tend to act up more.

By Friday, some levity has crept into my conversations with Barry. I lie down beside him in his hospital bed, and on the little television we watch *Dallas*, a series that we have been following since we met. It's our second-favorite show, next to *Seinfeld*. In this episode of *Dallas*, a relative appears at Southfork, claiming to be a Ewing, and Bobby wants out of the oil business. It's refreshing to be immersed in something so mindless.

Dear God, I pray while lying beside Barry and looking at him watching TV, *please help Barry.*

Barry is released from hospital at the end of the week, but things are hard at home. Sometimes he doesn't want to see the kids. I go to the kitchen to get something, they whine and nag, and then I go back to the bedroom to sick Barry.

Dear God, please help Barry.

On Monday the week after his chemo started, we go in for his outpatient dose of intrathecal chemo and then to Robertson Lighting to choose fixtures for Whistler. We go to the family restaurant, the White Spot, for lunch. We often bring the girls here; Barry loves the burgers with special Triple-O sauce. But it's really crowded and noisy. Barry looks like he has a Mohawk haircut, and he has a big lump and a bandage on one side of his skull. I can tell the waitress is trying to avoid looking at his head, as if everything at this table were perfectly normal. We may not look normal, but we're doing something normal!

On the way out of the restaurant, some guy turns to me and says, "Daw, what happened to that guy, car accident or somethin'?"

Asshole, I think.

We're fortunate enough to be able to hire a second nanny. I find Meredith, an eighteen-year-old student and artist who tutors elementary-school children and has lots of experience with younger siblings. Her references are good. She wears her curly, dark hair in a big ponytail on top of her head, Pebbles from *The Flintstones*–style. She has large, handsome features and an ample, warm smile. My trustworthy, motherly instinct tells me the children will be safe and have fun with her. I guess she reminds me of me.

Dear God, please help Barry.

On Tuesday, Barry goes to the office for a few hours and gets very cold. We think he overdid it. He develops a fever in the night and throws up. I take him to Emergency, and they admit him. Although neither of us says it, I think we are both relieved. I was so worried about him at home and had no idea what to do. "Thank you for taking care of me," he says more than once. I need to hear this. I need to know he appreciates what I'm doing. Being bombarded by sick, grumpy, dying men is stripping me of all my spirit, my life. Barry's showing thanks feeds me morsels of energy that sustain me.

Poor Rob. I feel bad that I can't see him more often. I take him to his important appointments and try to squeeze in some time for him. One day, after I take him to see Dr. Katses, we have lunch at an outside table at a café on Broadway. It is cold, but he can smoke outside.

As I enjoy my hot tea, he says, "Rose, I need to talk to you about something."

"Okay," I say, putting down my mug and paying attention, noting that he is looking much better, his thick mop of brown hair clean and combed neatly, even a bit of color in his cheeks.

He takes the last bite of his BLT and pushes the plate away. Arms crossed, elbows on table. "This thing's gonna get me. I've got to make plans. I'm worried about Audrey's extreme grief. I'm worried about my personal stuff. I need to address my pension to make sure Audrey will get whatever money is coming."

"Whoa, whoa, slow down," I say, putting my hand on his arm. "We can take care of things, but we don't need to do it all at once, Rob. At least let me finish my tea." I pick up my mug and lean my head back so I can take the final gulp, as we both chuckle. "Listen, why don't we start by going to your apartment and going through your things?"

"Most of it will go to the Salvation Army, but not the grandfather clock. That was in my room when I was growing up,"

"Rob, this must be so hard for you. I can't imagine being in your shoes."

As if he doesn't hear me, he switches the topic. "Most people with AIDS are cremated. What about my pension papers?"

It's like he's jettisoning tennis balls at me from a ball machine and I barely have time to react to one thought because I have to deal with the next. But this is all so important, I need to focus on one issue at a time.

I tell him how positive the experience with Barry's dad's ashes was, but he doesn't want to talk about the spreading of ashes.

"But you want to be cremated?" I ask, confused about where he wants his ashes strewn.

"Audrey will know what to do."

"You know," I say softly, "I picture you in an aura of light." I put my hands up in front of him and hold them out like I'm holding a fragile glass ball slightly larger than his head—just as an aura would look. "Later," I say, instead of, *After you die.*

He says bluntly, "It'll be a relief. This life has been a big struggle, and when I die I'll be released." He pauses, looks away into the distance, and says, as if to himself, "I'm afraid of the pain, though."

Then he starts talking about the expense of flying people out to Vancouver from Toronto for the funeral service.

"There will be no rush," I reassure him. "They can fly out on discount fares. Why don't we tackle one thing at a time?" I manage to assuage his anxiety somewhat by putting a bit of a plan in place, starting with sorting out his personal belongings. I think if I'm overwhelmed by all these heavy topics, what must it be like for him?

Afterward I get in the car, put my forehead down on the steering wheel, and cry and cry and cry. So tired. So tired. I check the time: 5:05. Dianne is at the house with the kids. I could go the club and do some lengths in the pool. I do just that, and as I breaststroke back and forth, I'm still crying, but the harder I swim and the faster I swim, the more I'm fortified and the less I cry. By the time I do my after-swim stretches and have a shower, I'm ready to attack any of this shit that is being thrown at me. I cling to my current fragile tranquility.

Dear God, please help Rob.

So many people need me. Willow has an ear infection. Dixie had one before her. Meredith is having serious headaches. Dixie has to have day surgery at BC Children's Hospital to remove a cyst from her temple near her right eye. Poor little Dixie. When she wakes up from the surgery, she says, "Mommy, Mommy, the bandage, the bandage, please," trying to tell me to take the bandage off her eye.

A crown on one of my teeth comes off; I need to see the dentist. I'm so tired. And so sad. I have died and gone to hell. I fall apart—no time to do anything. Barry is in and out of the hospital. The girls are misbehaving. They're getting up earlier than usual. But amid all this, Barry and I are planning another trip to Whistler—which means I have to organize for that. I call Mom and have a good cry.

Barry comes home from the hospital with a bit of energy but not a lot of patience. It's Friday afternoon, and I'm loading up the car for Whistler. I go into the bedroom and grab my weekend bag. But Barry is slipping his runners off, which seems curious, as we are leaving, not staying. Then he collapses on the bed. Lying on his back, he says, "I don't think I have the energy to go, and I have severe pain right here." He rubs his stomach under his ribs, then touches his throat. "And my throat is a lot worse, quite bad."

I set down the bag and say, "It sounds like we'd better go to the hospital." I check my watch. "Damn, it's late. It's Friday. Kasheemo won't be around, but we should have you looked at. I guess we'll have to go to Emergency. We can't possibly go to Whistler."

"What about the kids?" he asks. "They'll be disappointed."

"Well, ah . . ." I breathe deeply and let out a big sigh while I think up a plan. They're with Meredith right now in the family room. "I'll go talk to them. Don't you think about that. I'll deal with it, and then we can go to the hospital. Do you want anything?"

"I just want to feel better."

I go to his side of the bed and feel his forehead. "Maybe we should take your temperature. I'll get the thermometer before I go deal with the kids."

"Mommy, Mommy!" Willow bursts into the room. "Daddy, what are you doing in bed? I thought we were going to Whistler."

"Well, we have to change plans because Daddy isn't feeling so good," I say. "I'm going to take him to see the doctor. I thought you were playing a game with Meredith."

"We were, but Dixie had a fit because I won the candy and it was my candy to begin with and I want it back."

"I'll go see what's going on." I feel my own temperature rising.

"Willow, why don't you get me the thermometer?" Barry suggests, as I hustle down the hall to Meredith and Dixie, who is crying.

Meredith is being her creative self and trying to get Dixie to sing "Blame It on the Rain," by Milli Vanilli, and do hand movements mimicking raindrops coming down from the sky.

I give Meredith a look of confused exasperation.

"Oh, it's okay, Rosemary," she says. "They were fighting over that lollipop, but it's over now."

"Well, easy for you to say. Willow doesn't think so," I retort. "And there's been a change of plans. We aren't going to Whistler." I sit down beside Dixie on the couch and wipe a tear from under her eye.

"Daddy has a bad tummyache and a sore throat, so I need to take him to the doctor."

Dixie starts to cry again. She climbs into my lap, and I hold her tightly. I apologize to Meredith for being so short with her. She is sympathetic and says she understands that I am under a lot of stress.

At Lions Gate Emergency, Barry and I wait and wait, until finally I go up to the nurses' station and explain that my husband is suffering severe pains, is a patient of Dr. Kasheemo's, and has non-Hodgkin's lymphoma.

Barry is uncomfortable and distraught. We read the papers and try to discuss the news, but nothing distracts him very long from this predicament. He is pale and fidgety. I keep glancing at the nurses' desk to try to catch the eye of the nurse I spoke with.

But even after my pleading, we wait another hour before they finally take him into an emergency cubicle—and then we wait again. Blood tests are finally ordered. We wait for the results. And wait.

Finally, results! His blood counts are way down. The doctor orders a blood transfusion and admits him.

They put Barry in a room with four beds. There are three other men who are very old and horizontal. One is snoring, and another is groaning.

Barry, who by now is in hospital garb, climbs into a sitting position on the bed, glances around at his surroundings, and looks at me with desperation, as if to say, *Do something about this room, please, hawney.* He's telling me he needs a private room, that I need to make him more comfortable. I can't believe this is happening. But I don't allow myself to indulge in thoughts about the crush of worries trying to shackle me. I'll save that internal conversation for my next breakdown, which I hope to be able to hold off until it is convenient. Yes, I'll have a convenient breakdown, later. For now, I'm on a mission. I need a private room, but first a tea and a phone. I see a pay phone right beside the elevator. I call my sister in Toronto.

"Hi, Sal. It's me," I mumble weakly.

"Oh, hi, Rose. What's wrong?"

"Well, Barry and I and the kids had planned to go to Whistler, but he felt so shitty that I took him to Emergency at Lions Gate Hospital instead. His blood counts were so low that they admitted him, and he's feeling really bad, and he's in this room with a bunch of sick, groaning old men. It's so depressing, and we're waiting for a blood transfusion, and I can't reach Kasheemo, of course; it's late on a Friday. What are you doing?"

"Oh, Rose," she says. "It must be so hard on you, and you have Willow and Dixie to worry about. Hal and I will be there in a few weeks for Easter. That'll help."

I hear noise in the background. "Do you have people over?"

"We're just having a dinner party," Sal says.

"A dinner party?" I burst into tears. At the pay phone. In front of the elevators. On 6B at Lions Gate Hospital. "I so want to do something so normal like that. I need to say goodbye now. I need some tea and a better room for Barry." People are getting in and out of the elevators and looking over, but I don't care.

"Oh, I'm sorry, Rose," Sal says. "That was insensitive of me. I'm so sorry. You're going through such a difficult time. Please call anytime."

I hang up the phone, stand there with my back to the elevators, and weep, allowing myself a mini-breakdown. After a few minutes, I get it together. I go to the cafeteria for tea. I talk to enough people at the hospital that I finally get a commitment. Barry can have a single room. But it won't be available until Sunday afternoon.

6

"I Shot the Sherriff"
Bob Marley
Friday, February 22, 1991

In an attempt to keep a routine going for the girls, as the counselor recommended, I take them to church on Sunday morning. I am not all that religious, but church on Sunday morning was a habit Mom got us into growing up. I like the designated time to commune with God, and some of the formal worship. I also find the Bible stories interesting and educational. The kids enjoy the Sunday school, and I figure it can't hurt for them to meet God and Jesus and all that—especially now, given our circumstances. Personally, I am turned off by too much Jesus talk, but they can decide for themselves.

Since we met, Barry has cheerfully participated in my church-on-Sunday-morning thing. We used to go to a charming little church near the cute country place we had in Hockley Valley, just north of Toronto. The church must have held about fifty people, and the minister actually played the guitar during the service and used words like "goodly." The church we attend in West Vancouver, St. Francis-in-the-Wood, is not quite as quaint, but it is enchanting. It's nestled into lush and tiny Tiddly Cove. The church, which holds about two hundred, has a distinct old English style to it, as do the surrounding homes and leafy gardens. The minister, Reverend Asherbey, is folksy and easy to take.

After the service, I struggle with the goddamn car seats and look forward to the day when I can kiss these suckers goodbye. Once we're in the car, I tell the girls we're off to the Park Royal Hotel for Sunday brunch. This is another tradition. The hotel is beside the Capilano River, and the maître d', Guy, always greets us with a big smile and gives us a special table with a view of the garden, the trees, and the fast-moving river.

"Will Man be there?" Dixie asks.

I laugh and exchange glances with Willow. "You mean Guy?"

That evening, Nana helps with bedtime. I wonder how she is dealing with Barry's diagnosis. She seems like such a rock, but I have no idea what's going on inside her head.

Nana gets Willow ready for bed while I help Dixie with her teeth. After I tuck Dixie in, I go into Willow's room and read *Goodnight Moon* to her. I set Dixie on my lap in the rocking chair in her room, and I read her *Amelia Bedelia*.

I put her in her crib and kiss her.

"Butterfly kiss," I flutter my eyelashes on her cheek. "Eskimo kiss." I rub noses with her.

She titters gleefully in anticipation.

"Monster kiss." I nuzzle my face into her neck, snort, and pretend to bite. "Good night. I love you."

"Don't go, Mommy. Tell me a story."

I breathe a deep sigh.

Willow is at Dixie's door, listening.

"Mommy, I'm all ready for bed."

"I'll be right there."

"Go away!" Dixie cries.

"Nana, I need you!" I yell out the door, and before the words are out of my mouth, she's at the door, too.

"Can you help me settle Dixie, please?"

"Well, well, what's wrong, deary?" Nana walks up to the crib, grabs a big stuffed panda bear, and nuzzles it into Dixie's face. Dixie is distracted enough to not protest when Willow grabs my hand and leads me into her room. We sit on the side of the bed together, her in her sweet Winnie the Pooh pj's. I pick up the book on her bedside table.

I read, "Goodnight room. Goodnight moon. Goodnight cow jumping over the moon. Goodnight light, and the red balloon . . ."

When I am almost finished, she asks, "Mommy, is Daddy going to be okay?"

"Well . . ." I set the book down. I think about what the social worker said, which was to tell the truth but not the whole truth. "He's not well." I cradle her right cheek with my left hand and look into her innocent hazel eyes. "But we have very good doctors, and we're getting the best help possible, so he's okay now."

"Is he *going* to be okay?" she insists.

"We don't really know," I say. "We do know he has the best doctors in North America, and he really is doing okay now. We are fortunate."

"Will you tell me a bedtime story?" Thank God for the short attention span of five-year-olds.

"What kind of story?"

"How about the first-kiss one?"

I smile. "Okay. You lie down, and I'll tell you that one. Remember, I met your daddy at that gig his band had in the country."

"What's the name of the band, again?" She asks, as she reclines on her back and lays her head on the pillow.

"Haven Tweezer."

She laughs at the name.

"He and his bandmates just took out a dictionary one day," I say, motioning my hands as if to open a book, "and opened it up and chose two words at random because their band needed a name."

"What does 'random' mean?"

"Random means, like, just out of the blue—no reason, really. And they came up with Haven Tweezer."

She grins. "That's silly."

"Yes, Daddy is silly sometimes."

"Then what?" she asks, while rolling from her back to her side to get more comfortable.

"Well, after the gig at the barn, a few of us stayed at Daddy's little country place in a place called Hockley Valley. It was nearby, and when we were leaving the next day, he offered to drive me home. We were the last to leave, and his car wouldn't start. Gophers from the fields had gotten into his engine and destroyed the radiator, and so we had to stay together, alone, at his farm."

"What are gophers?"

"They're kind of like squirrels."

"So, you're together because squirrels ate his engine?"

"Sort of."

She giggles. "What about the kiss?"

"Well, Daddy and I walked through the fields in the dimming daylight to a wooden bench that looked over the large valley of beautiful trees painted gold by the setting sun. It felt like we were at the top of the world. Then the full moon stepped in for the sun."

I look up, as if into the sky.

"The stars dazzled us, and we looked for satellites, just like we do now on the boathouse deck in Seratami. Well, I was *pretending* to look for satellites. I was a little distracted by the handsome man beside me. We were talking, and it was kind of uncomfortable, because we didn't know each other very well, and I didn't know if he wanted to kiss me, and I wasn't sure how close to sit to him, and then he just put his arm around me and leaned over and kissed me. I felt excited and safe at the same time. That bench is so special, we kept it when we sold that little place at Hockley Valley, and we took it to Seratami. That's the one we sit on to watch the sunset."

Willow is nodding off. Thank goodness.

I kiss her forehead. "I love you so much, sweetheart. Good night. Don't let the bedbugs bite."

I walk into the family room, which is right next door to Willow's room. The house is ranch-style, so all the bedrooms are on the same floor as the dining room, kitchen, and family room.

Nana is on the couch.

"Would you like a glass of wine?" I ask.

She shakes her head. "I'll wait until I get home and have my nighttime scotch."

I pour a very large goblet of cool white wine for myself and flop down beside her. She looks worn out.

"I'm sorry they're so much work, Nana."

"Don't you be sorry," she says. "It's hard on everyone." She puts a hand on my knee. "I couldn't help but overhear your conversation about your first kiss. That's very romantic."

I take a huge gulp of wine. "It was. He's a romantic fellow, that son of yours. And he's brilliant, funny, talented, energetic . . . What's happening, Nana? What has happened?" I set the glass down on the coffee table and rub my eyes. I get carried away and really rub them, so my makeup is all smeared. "There, how's that? That felt so good. What do I have to lose at this point?"

We both have a badly needed chuckle.

"You're doing remarkably well," she says. "Keep on doing what you're doing, as hard as it is. The girls will be okay."

"Thanks so much for your help. But what about you? It has to be so painful to see your son deteriorate like this. You seem so strong."

She says nothing. We are at one in our bewildered and fearful state.

I let my mind wander back to the day of the first kiss. It was a remarkable day—Friday, June 17, 1983, the same week I interviewed for the job at CFTO TV. I had been living in Vancouver and working at CKVU TV—which, I thought, was not promoting me the way it should, so I'd taken a two-week vacation to look for a job in Toronto. Reporting for CFTO would be a dream job—and then I met Barry, who was pretty dreamy himself. The stars must have been aligned for me that week: I got the job and the guy.

That was just eight years ago, but it seems like decades—a heady time when I was working at an exciting job and dating Barry, who was managing a record company. Then he decided to practice law (he already had his law degree), because when he met me, he said, it was time to "take life more seriously." Life was full and busy and interesting and we were madly in love and he proposed to me and we got married and our future sparkled in front of us.

What happened?

I collapse onto Nana's lap and erupt in a spasm of tears.

7

"Eye of the Tiger"
Survivor

Spring 1991

Rob gets stabilized on his meds and is plugged into the Persons with AIDS group. I take him out to Granville Island for lunch every week. We even manage to have a few laughs, especially when I trip on my maxi-length coat walking up the stairs to the restaurant and almost splatter my tray of mushroom soup, crackers, and tea all over the staircase, which is in the central part of the market, in full view of dozens of shoppers on the main floor. I buy him cigarettes and ready-made foods, like roasted chicken and spinach bagels, and give him $50 each visit.

One day while we're having lunch, he says this weekly Granville Market outing is something he really looks forward to. He also looks forward to spending time with his buddy from PWA and a couple of other friends who have been helping out.

But then on another visit he's very depressed. We're in the car, driving to the market, and he stares out the window blankly, not noticing all the stores and restaurants along Broadway whiz by.

"There's nothing to live for," he says. "You just get sicker and sicker, and you die."

How do I respond to that? Well, I don't. Instead, I think about what *I* look forward to: my glass—or two, or three—of white wine every night. I am jogging and swimming whenever possible, too. It is invigorating. But I am short on help: Dianne can't handle the stress in my household, so she works just two days a week now, and Meredith is a student and has only so much time.

Meanwhile, Barry is receiving his IV and intrathecal chemo treatments. The level of his blood counts has become of paramount importance. We have learned that the white blood cells should be above 4,000 and the hemoglobin above 140. If they get too low, he needs to skip a treatment. It is the potent chemo drugs being pumped into his system that cause the blood counts to plummet at times, because they attack both the bad cells and the good cells in the body. If the blood counts go really low, he runs a serious risk of infection and needs to be hospitalized for IV antibiotics.

By mid-March, Barry has been hospitalized twice. He's often morose and moany and will not let anyone but Nana and me visit him. "I don't know what to say to anyone else," he says. His siblings would very much like to see him, but Barry remains standoffish, just fielding the odd phone call.

It's trying when he's in the hospital. It's trying when he's at home.

On his first visit home, the girls do not acknowledge his arrival. Willow acts aloof. Knowing the pain this causes Barry puts a knot of sorrow in my gut.

On the drive home from his second visit to the hospital, Barry says, "I hope Willow comes down the hallway like she used to, yelling, 'Daddy, Daddy.'"

I desperately want to go in ahead of him and give Willow instructions. In anticipation of the worst, I feel my shoulders seize up and my breath catch in my throat, restricting the flow of oxygen as we walk in the door . . .

"Daddy, Daddy!" Willow *does* come running down the hallway.

Barry crouches down and holds out his arms in anticipation of this cherished affection from his firstborn baby girl.

"Willow, gentle!" I exclaim, and she tempers her landing just before falling into his embrace. I lean against the wall and drop my heavy purse, which has become laden with I don't know what. It lands with a thud, and I almost collapse with relief. I realize I have no fucking control over absolutely anything. Life is buzzing around me like a swarm of angry of bees whose nest has just been whapped with a stick.

I have an appointment with Dr. Bradley, the diagnosing doctor, to see how I am handling Barry's illness. Apparently, not very well. Of course, I am crying as I explain how stressed I am, with Barry being so sick and demanding and the kids acting up and the juggling of part-time nannies and basically *everything*. He asks how I am coping. I tell him all the things I'm doing: running, swimming, calling my mom, calling my sister, drinking wine, drinking more wine. I mention my career, or lack thereof, but realize that is not a priority at the moment.

He looks at me intently and hands me the box of Kleenex from his desk. I grab two or three tissues and then decide to take the whole damn box. I have a big nose blow and rub my eyes with a wad of damp tissue, abandoning any attempt to preserve my dark eyeliner and supposedly waterproof mascara. Whatever makeup that's not on the Kleenex is now smudged under my eyes.

Dr. Bradley tells me: my reaction is normal; my career needs to go on hold for now; I should get more help with the kids; and I shouldn't drink half a bottle of wine a night. He gives me the name of a psychologist who specializes in grief.

Meanwhile, the girls are not sleeping well. Willow has continuing nightmares about the "yellow eyes."

"They're at the window, Mommy," she says. "They creep up from the ground: even when the curtains are closed, they look in at me. Between me and the eyes is a whole bunch of blood, and above there are a bunch of scary wires that kill you when you touch them. I have to choose which way to get to the eyes—I have to drown in blood or be killed by the wires."

She says sometimes the blood is pee, and sometimes huge yellow wasps take the place of the electrical wires. She also talks of a place where the yellow eyes take her, where ". . . there are a whole bunch of Daddies lined up with a whole bunch of Dixies on their shoulders, and I have to choose which one is the real one, and if I don't choose the right one, the real one is just, just . . . *gone*."

I talk to the pediatrician, who offers practical suggestions, such as sticking to a bedtime routine and making it light and fun, discussing the nightmare during the day, and coddling Willow when she wakes up from the dream. I try to rock her to sleep and am so scared for her that I don't want to leave her room. I realize it is time for her to see a child psychologist.

At home, Barry rarely has a good day. He is plagued with ailments—sore throats and severe headaches—and has lost his hair. Willow says he looks like "a ghost with no hair," and he finds her honesty refreshing; he knows he does not look good. He is stuck in the bedroom much of the time, and whenever I walk through it to the dressing room and office, which is on the other side of the bedroom, he says, "What're you doing?"

Some days I feel like shouting, *Leave me alone!*

I gently try to let him know I am a bit bothered, and he says he's sorry, but he can't do anything about it. Barry wants me to devote my entire life and energy to him. But what about the kids? Rob? Me? I want someone to take care of me for once.

—

"I'm sad Daddy can't play with me anymore," Willow says one night as I'm tucking her in.

"I'm sad, too," I say. *He can't play tennis or golf, ski, or go to dinner and the movies with me, either,* I think.

"I wish grown-ups didn't have to die before us," she says.

"Like Grandfather?" I say. "Are you afraid Daddy is going to die, too?"

Of course, she is. I want to fold her all up and put her in my heart to protect her. I know I can't wait too long to answer her, and I think again about what the social worker advised. I lie down beside her, take her in my arms, and rock her gently. "Daddy's not going to die really soon, and I will be here forever." I squeeze her a little harder. "We have to hope and pray Daddy gets better." I myself am clinging to this hope. If we ain't got hope, we ain't got nothin'.

Oh, God, please make him well. We are going to have nice dinners again and play golf and go on holidays. We are, we are, we are, we are, we are. He needs me too much. I miss him so much, my healthy, energetic, do-everything-with-ease Barry. Please, may I have him back? I need him. I have only so much strength, Lord. I need my husband back, please.

Sal and Hal were supposed to come visit on Easter weekend at the end of March. We wanted to take them to Whistler to show off the new house, which is almost complete. I am disappointed when they have to cancel their visit because Barry feels too unwell for company. But Barry and I are still planning a long weekend at our new home to celebrate Easter with our traditional Easter egg hunt and turkey dinner, so I focus on that.

The Thursday before Good Friday, Barry is due to have his IV chemotherapy treatment. When the nurse checks his blood counts first, as they need to be robust enough for his system to sustain the next onslaught of chemicals, the results come back, and his counts are low. We are hoping Kasheemo will cancel the session, since Barry feels the worst just after his chemo and we are concerned about our long-weekend plans being thwarted by his feeling too shitty to enjoy anything. But Kasheemo is very reluctant to miss a chemo session and says Barry's counts aren't low enough to cancel it altogether; he decides to administer a lesser dose of drugs instead.

"Does that mean Barry won't feel as rotten as he does with the standard dose?" I ask.

"Maybe," Kasheemo says. "No guarantee."

We go to our new home at Whistler that night and take Dianne with us. The next day, Barry is feeling very unwell, of course. I've lugged some personal belongings from the old condo to the new house in an attempt to cozy it up. It's spacious, with lots of room for the kids to play, but Barry says it doesn't feel like home yet. Even deciding where to hang a picture seems too onerous a task.

Saturday, the girls and I go to the village for pancakes and peach juice. Fun. Too bad Barry can't join us. Sunday morning, I play Easter bunny and create an Easter egg hunt. Barry is not doing well. He is tired and can hardly handle going up the stairs. He has mouth sores, so eating is difficult.

He's doing so poorly, we decide to drive back home to West Vancouver. It is actually a beautiful day for a drive on the Sea to Sky Highway, the white-tipped mountains providing a majestic background for the glistening waters of Howe Sound.

Barry starts shifting around in his seat, opening the window, closing the window, reclining his seat a little, then returning it to its upright position.

"You having trouble getting comfortable?" I ask Barry.

"I'm feeling worse and worse," he says. "I can barely move without feeling like I'm going to throw up, and every movement is painful. My mouth sores are throbbing. I'm not sure I'm going to make it through the day."

"Oh dear," I say. "It sounds like we'd better take you to the hospital."

He concurs.

When we arrive at home, Barry waits in bed while I unload the car. Then we head straight out to Lions Gate Hospital. The emergency people don't know what the hell they're doing. We know he needs antibiotics; we even know which antibiotics he needs. But they're saying things like, "How did the disease present itself?" *What? Are you kidding? Give me a fucking break, and give him some antibiotics.*

Then the nurse takes it upon herself to do some counseling. She takes my hand. "I know you're both scared. I can see it." *Oh, fuck off.* This is even more upsetting than the fact that nobody seems to know what they're doing.

However, at least they took a blood sample.

Finally, a specialist—Dr. David Bolder from Internal Medicine— is called into our emergency cubicle, where Barry is on the gurney in the familiar position, sitting up, legs stretched out in front of him.

Holding up a clipboard, Bolder says to an ashen-faced Barry, "I see you're a patient of Dr. Kasheemo. And you've been sick for a while."

"Thank you so much for coming to help, Doctor," I say. "We know Barry needs antibiotics, and the staff here just didn't get it. All the while, Barry is feeling worse and worse. We've been quite anxious."

"Well, feeling rotten is to be expected. You're going through quite an ordeal," he says, looking at Barry. "When were you diagnosed?"

"February eighth," I say, at the same time Barry says, "February." I ask, "Do you have the blood results?"

"Yes, you're right—you need antibiotics and a blood transfusion, which I will book for tomorrow. You'll be admitted."

Hearing the word "admitted" is like having a warm blanket wrapped around both us. We're going to be okay.

"You're a saint, Dr. Bolder. We can't thank you enough."

—

When Barry comes home later that week, he is feeling better because of the blood transfusion—*like a vampire*, I think—and also because he did not have his scheduled weekly chemo treatments, which always trash him. He was in such poor condition a few days ago that Kasheemo decided to skip this week—what would have been week six of eight in Barry's chemo agenda.

Given these two developments—fresh blood and no chemo—Barry is actually pumped up a bit. I, however, am panicking, as we're about to enter a three-day stretch from Friday to Monday with no nanny. I haven't had time to find more help, and I don't want to rely on Nana too much at her age. The girls, like any two- and four-year-olds, are even more trouble than normal these days, just as the social worker warned me they would be. They both demand attention at the same time. Dixie throws tantrums and likes to bug Willow, who is so sensitive that she breaks down at the slightest provocation.

Miraculously, it turns out to be a successful weekend. We even manage to pepper it with a couple of traditions. On Saturday morning, we all go to the family restaurant, White Spot, for breakfast, and then we take the girls to Ambleside Park by the beach. Willow rides her bike, and Barry walks Dixie down the pier—he actually has some strength. Back at home, the girls and I make chocolate chip cookies, another tradition, and we all enjoy them. At long last, some normalcy.

A week later, Barry starts treatment again—week six—and promptly starts feeling as if, as he describes it, "a heavy, bristly, putrid-smelling blanket" has been laid over his entire body, including his head. The kids are fighting. Thankfully, Meredith is on duty and is as resourceful as ever—she's often able to dilute the drama by getting the girls to sing and dance.

I, meanwhile, lose it easily. I grab a carton of eggs from the fridge one day, and when they fall onto the floor, I scream, "Somebody help me!" I cannot function. I want to disappear from everyone's radar, like those planes that vanish into thin air. I crawl into the love seat at the end of the family room, assume the fetal position, and cry.

Barry finds me and says, "Is this about something in particular, or is it just a general meltdown?"

We laugh and hug, and he says, "I need you beside me in bed."

I am always running out of time. I go for a run. I feel better. I feel overwhelmed. I drink wine. I feel better. Time with Barry. Time with kids. I have no time. Food shopping. Doctors and Barry. Doctors and Rob. The kids and the dentist. Go for a swim. Errands. Running the household. It all seems endless. Glass of wine. Another glass of wine. Need a holiday. Want to go to Hawaii, but Barry is too sick.

God, please give him back to me.

I am just as concerned about how the girls are going to be through all of this. Barry tells me he does not want his daughters to remember only their daddy dying, but I can't save them from that. Dixie is more shielded from the pain and worry than Willow is because Dixie is only two years old. However she certainly notices the stress and reacts to it. At the same time, they can be so cute and so funny and have so much personality that I am crazy in love with them.

Dixie is up a lot in the night crying. I try Dr. Ferber's method of letting her cry for five minutes and going in to her, then letting her cry for ten minutes and going in to her, letting her cry for fifteen minutes, and so on, but it wears me down.

One night, Dixie does not stop crying.

"Everyone in the house is asleep," I say to her, trying to settle her down.

"I just don't care," she replies—which is actually amusing, as she says it in exactly the same tone in which she has heard *me* say those exact words.

Lord, help me through this. Give me courage, strength, balance, and also the ability to guide my children through this unharmed.

I make my way back down the hallway to our bedroom, and by the time I walk into the room, I am a blubbering mess. The light is on, and Barry is awake, lying in bed, listening to his Discman. He takes off his earphones, hands them to me, and pats the mattress beside him. "Have a seat, and have a listen," he says, disregarding the late hour.

I put my two pillows against the headboard and lean back. He is lying down beside me with his hand resting on my thigh. I put my hand on his.

"It's the CD Heather gave me—*Avalon Sunset*, by Van Morrison," he says. "Every song, almost without exception, is surprisingly appropriate. There's even one called 'I'd Love to Write Another Song,' which I'd love to do for you, but my fingers are too numb." Heather and Dave are dear friends with whom we have a lot in common. They are also building a house at Whistler, and they enjoy golfing, too.

Barry does sing me love songs. The first time was in Seratami, the summer we met. He sang Eric Clapton's "Wonderful Tonight" to me with his guitar in the bedroom when I was getting ready for dinner with his friends, the self-proclaimed Bozos (he and his three lawyer buddies gave themselves that name, maybe in an attempt not to take themselves too seriously). I still remember what I was wearing: a white, backless sundress with bright, embroidered flowers on it that I bought when I was working in Tahiti.

He sang that song to me at our wedding, too.

I tell him that Bradley asked me in my appointment if I missed sex. "I explained to him that I don't miss sex," I say. "It's replaced by a profound and intimate tenderness." I lean over and kiss Barry's forehead gently. He gives my thigh a squeeze and closes his eyes. I put the headphones on and press PLAY and close my eyes, too. Van Morrison's hypnotic, alluring voice absorbs me instantly, and I am astounded at how appropriate the lyrics are on this album right from the get-go.

Each song penetrates my soul more deeply. "Higher Ground" is about being turned around and then lifted up to higher ground. "Have I Told You Lately" is about filling someone with happiness; by the end of this ballad, I am in tears. I grab a Kleenex from the bedside table and realize Barry is asleep, his hand still on my thigh. I move it off me as gently as possible, trying not to disturb him. As the CD continues, I succumb to the lyrics of every song; I am convinced each one was written for us right now.

I drift off to sleep in a mire of sorrow.

8

"I'm Tired Joey Boy"
Van Morrison

April, 1991

By the end of April, Barry has finished the eight-week chemo-therapy protocol Kasheemo first laid out. Barry's blood counts hit rock bottom, and the heavy, bristly, smelly blanket lowers itself upon him yet again. He's back in the hospital. He's lying down in the bed and I'm standing beside him when Kasheemo comes in to talk about the possible next step—the "augmented treatment." It would take place at the British Columbia Cancer Agency, which is across town near VGH, and would involve three days of continuous IV chemo. After that, Barry would stay at the BCCA for three weeks to recover—but Kasheemo has concerns about how Barry will handle the toxicity of this treatment. He explains that the BCCA oncologists will basically be replacing all the blood in Barry's body and it will be horribly unpleasant.

"They are going to push you to the brink of death," he says.

Thanks for that, Dr. Kasheemo. Barry dwells on these types of statements from the doctors.

This procedure would treat the "lumps and bumps" in Barry's

lymphatic system, but not the spinal fluid of his central nervous system. It is as if he has two cancers—one in his lymphatic system, the other in the central nervous system. This central nervous system involvement is not uncommon in T-cell lymphoma. The two are being treated separately but parallel to each other. This aggressive treatment is aimed at ridding the body of the lymphatic system cancer—not the central nervous system cancer.

The spinal fluid is the real battle," Kasheemo says. "At the moment, there is no sign of cancer cells in the fluid. That cancer disappeared quickly, but it doesn't mean it won't come back. If it does, it'll happen within six weeks, and then Barry will have about four weeks."

"To live?" I ask.

"Yes," he says. "Now it's up to you to decide whether you would like to take this next step."

With that and a curt goodbye, Kasheemo leaves the hospital room. Barry and I stare at his backside as he disappears into the hallway. The doctor is being only too true to his brutal bedside manner; he's been the same since Barry's initial diagnosis, on February 8. He seems to think that the fact that he is one of North America's best experts on non-Hodgkin's lymphoma excuses all his harshness.

We turn and stare at each other in abject fear. What the holy fuck! The blood drains from Barry's face, and he turns gray. I grab his hand and squeeze it. Maybe if I squeeze it hard enough, we will awaken from this nightmare. I feel my knees start to buckle, so I crumple onto the bed and cuddle into the very narrow space beside Barry. We hold each other and rock and cry.

Although we take time to discuss it, Barry and I both know we will opt to go ahead with the intensive treatment. But we're terrified. The whole idea seems to be that you have to get it right the first time around, or you lose.

Please, God, please. I need my hubby back. We're going to do it. I know. We have to.

—

Thursday, May 2, Barry is admitted to the BCCA. The next day, he has an operation to install a portocath close to his heart. They put three tubes into the portocath to administer the toxic drugs.

The treatment starts on Saturday. Barry lies there with three tubes pumping three huge bags' worth of chemo drugs into his chest for three days in a row.

Surprisingly, he is actually not in terribly bad spirits—until he gets a roommate who looks like a sumo wrestler and who's barfing and having diarrhea all over the place, that is. Barry is so upset, he resorts to swearing about his situation—and, unlike me, he is not a swearer.

"Get Dr. Conrad in here to do something about this fucking situation!" he hisses. "I can't stay here like this. They keep piling shit on me."

Dr. Jason Conrad is one of the doctors treating Barry at the BCCA. His other doctor is technically Dr. Sarah O'Hare, though we haven't met her yet. Both are as highly regarded in North America as Kasheemo, and we are lucky to have them. I seek out Conrad and tell him I have never seen Barry so grumpy and that it is imperative we find him a private room.

I am heartsick to have to leave Barry in such a frantic state, but I have to go. I have to breathe. I have to have some space. I have to scream. I have to cry. I have to see the girls. I have to collapse.

When I return on Saturday, I can't find Barry and am hoping he has a better room. I ask at the nurses' station, "Has Barry Keevil been moved to a private room?"

"Your father has been moved to a private room. Nine. It's over there." She gestures down the hall.

"He's my husband," I reply matter-of-factly, thinking, *Really? How can you be so stupid in your position? Fucking idiot.*

Over the next couple of weeks, life is a blur of juggling kids and nannies and hospital visits and trying to address the normal mechanics of life, like the kids' doctor and dentist appointments, and my own maintenance, such as getting my hair and nails done. I insist on taking care of myself, and hair appointments are sacrosanct. I don't forget to feel grateful that I can afford to take care of myself during these times and am not struggling to handle a job along with everything else.

When I visit Barry, I have to be super meticulous about germs—when I arrive at the hospital, I put a robe on and wash my hands before going in to see him. He's miserable; this heavy-duty treatment has really wreaked havoc on his body. He does look like an old man—no hair, skinny face, droopy eyelids. His fever is bouncing all over the place. He's had platelet transfusions and blood transfusions. He is on major antibiotics and who the hell knows what else. There are tubes all over the place.

He is always so relieved to see me. "Where have you been?" he asks. "I couldn't feel worse. I may as well be dead now. This is horrid. I was so desperate last night, I almost walked out of this nasty place."

Yes, it *is* horrid, and I just want to leave—which I do, after spending what I consider a sufficient length of time to satiate his need for me without my detonating in a fit of anger and frustration and fear and sadness and pain.

He always calls afterward. "I'm sorry. I love you and cannot tell you how much I appreciate everything you do. I know it's hard for you. And you're dealing with Rob, too."

By mid-May, when Barry has been in the Cancer Agency for two weeks, I feel a need to have a break with the girls—a getaway—before he's released from the hospital near the end of the month. I decide to take them to Henderson Lake Resort and Spa, a lovely place an hour-and-a-half drive from Vancouver, situated on one end of Henderson Lake, with a view of the deep blue water right in front of the hotel and the snow-tipped mountains in the distance.

At Henderson, we go to Flintstones Bedrock City, then come back to the hotel to swim and play with pool toys and explore the grounds and lobby. In the main foyer, everyone says hi to my cute little kids. They say, "Hi, what's your name?" in return.

One couple engages them in conversation. "I'm Jack, and this is my wife, Freda."

Dixie latches on to this and repeats, "Jack and Freda. Jack and Freda. Jack and Freda," as she takes off toward the big couch by the inviting fireplace and plops onto it. "Jack and Freda," she calls from her perch.

We have meals in the family dining room, and the girls are fairly well behaved. We talk about Barry.

"This is so nice," I say. "But what's missing?"

"Daddy!" Willow exclaims.

I nod. "Did you know that we were here with Daddy and Nana three years ago, when you were very little and I was three months pregnant with Dixie?"

"Was Daddy sick then?" she asks.

"No, sweetie." I reach my right hand out and cup her left cheek.

It feels so right to be here in this relaxing environment with the girls—somewhere I can cater just to them and actually have some fun myself. It's a healthy distraction for all of us. We have a divine two-day reprieve from the conveyor belt of demands awaiting us at home. But then we have to return to reality.

Back in Vancouver, I continue my daily visits with Barry. By Friday I'm spent, and when I get home from the hospital, I'm tired and hungry and cranky, and it only gets worse when I learn that Willow has been naughty at preschool—disobedient and lethargic.

"I think she misses her daddy," her teacher says.

She does. I try to give her more time and attention at bedtime that night. We have a routine that makes her feel very special—if she waits patiently and lets me tuck Dixie in first, I will give Willow a scoop of ice cream. I am not above bribery; tonight I make it two scoops and rock her to sleep.

As soon as I leave Willow's room, the phone rings. *Oh, shit*, I think. *Now what?*

I go into the kitchen, shutting the door behind me so the girls won't hear. It's Barry, in a panic.

"Rosemary, something is desperately wrong. I have double vision."

"Oh dear, this has never happened before," I say, as I sit down, alarmed that it may have something to do with his brain and therefore his spinal fluid. I don't say this out loud but assume he may be thinking the same thing. "All we can do is speculate. Best not to jump to conclusions. Have you told the doctor?"

"There's no doctor around, of course. I've spoken with the nurse." He coughs. "But it's not very reassuring."

"What did she say?"

"She claims it could be a reaction to the drugs, but I'm not buying it."

"I'm sure you can see Conrad or another doctor in the morning," I say. I pour myself a glass of wine while I'm talking to him. "I think we should listen to the nurse."

"But maybe she's just saying that."

"When did it start? Has it gotten worse?"

"About fifteen minutes ago. All of a sudden, everything is double. It's so frightening."

I have a sip of wine. "Yes, I'm sure it is. But let's listen to the nurse," I insist, not knowing what else to say. "You know how you hang on to the doctors' words like gospel? Maybe give the nurse some trust. Anyway, there's no sense brooding on it tonight."

"You're right," Barry mutters, and then there is silence.

"I'll see you in the morning. Let's get some sleep."

"Thanks for being so kind and loyal and putting up with me," he says, with deep sincerity.

It is so sweet, I cry. "Remember the evening you asked Dad if you could marry me, and he told you I was a 'classy, loyal dame'?" I ask.

"Yes, and you are, hawney," he says. "Classy and loyal. You're the best. I love you."

The following day, I take the girls to Story Time at the West Vancouver Memorial Library. We have lunch at Café Take Away, where we sit at the counter in front of the window and people-watch and make up stories about who they are and where they're going. Dixie is particularly creative. Then I leave Willow at home with Meredith and take Dixie to visit her dad.

Neither of the girls has seen Barry for almost three weeks, since he went into the BCCA for the intensive treatment. It would have been too complicated and too scary to take them before now. We'd have had to wear hospital gowns, and Barry was attached to a bunch of tubes. Besides, he was in no state to be hosting rambunctious little girls. Now that he is over the intensive treatment, there are no tubes and we don't need to sterilize ourselves.

When little Dixie walks into the room and sees Barry, she squeals, "Daddy!" and he squeals, "Whistlin' Dixie!" She wants to sit beside him on the bed. I am uncertain this is a good idea, but Dixie is insistent, and when I check with the nurse, she says it's fine—she even encourages it.

I lift Dixie up and set her beside Barry. "Be gentle with Daddy," I caution, and I hover over them, lest Dixie gets too rough.

They are oblivious to my discomfort with the situation. Dixie starts eating the chocolate pudding I brought for Barry, and he dabs some on her nose. She giggles that carefree gut giggle that only gleeful little children have. She somehow seems to know not to wiggle around too much, as two-year-olds are wont to do. It has always seemed to me that Dixie is an old soul—and right now, on some level, she knows to stay low key. But I listen to my own inner voice and make the visit short, as things could go pear-shaped at any time.

The next day, it's Willow's turn to visit Daddy. She doesn't seem excited, but it's so hard to read what she's thinking. In the car on the way, I ask her, "Are you looking forward to seeing Daddy?"

"Yes," she mumbles.

"Do you want to bring something to him, like a chocolate bar?"

"No."

"Willow, talk to me. Are you upset? Are you mad that Daddy's sick?" I rest my right hand on her left knee for a moment.

She is silent, and I am full of trepidation.

I don't know what the hell to do, so we continue with the plan. We go to the hospital. I hold Willow's hand as we make our way to Barry's room. She is shuffling along, dragging the toes of her shoes. I feel devoured by sorrow. This is so sad—for everyone.

"Do you just not want to visit Daddy today? That would be okay, sweetie." I stop and bend my knees so I'm on her level. "Do you just want to go home?"

Willow looks down at the ground and shakes her head softly, her pigtails moving back and forth. So she *does* want to see him. But she's probably terrified, and I can't protect her.

When we enter Barry's hospital room, he gives her an enthusiastic greeting and puts his arms out for her to come in for a hug. But Willow just stands at the end of his bed.

"You don't want a hug, Willow?" Barry asks.

"No."

"What about a kiss, Willow Mellow Yellow?"

"No."

"How's school?" I flinch a bit at this one, as she was just caught acting up.

"Good."

Barry asks her a few more questions, and she continues with the monosyllabic answers. It is not a complete disaster, but it's not what we hoped for.

After a little bit, Willow turns to me and takes my hand. "I want to go, Mommy."

Barry and I exchange knowing glances. His lips are pursed, his eyelids heavy. I kiss him, tell him I'll be back, and leave with Willow.

On the way home, Willow is goofing around with her seat belt and unfastens it.

"Willow, smarten up," I scold her. "It's actually against the law not to wear your seat belt. There's a reason for that. It's for your own safety. If anything happens, we need to be secure in our seats. Do you understand?"

She starts to cry. I look at her and start crying, too.

"I'm so very sorry. I should be more patient. It's hard seeing Daddy sick, isn't it? It's hard for all of us." When we arrive home, I give her a big hug and tell her how much I love her. I leave her with Dianne and Meredith and go out for a long jog, which helps, as does the wine that follows.

It's the end of May, and Barry is due to come home. I have mixed feelings about this, as I have been independent while he's been in the hospital for three weeks, and his presence at home will crush that. At the same time, I do want him home, and he seems to have perked up now that the intensive treatment is behind him.

When he arrives, he's feeling all right and able to participate in life. It's just become June, and summer is on the bud. We go on walks with the girls and have lunches out. He is able to calm Dixie down right away when she awakens at midnight.

I make my weekly trips to see Rob. I take him to his doctors' appointments. I'm relieved when Mom comes to visit, as it takes the pressure off me to care for Rob. It's hard for me to lean on Mom for support, since she's going through the same thing with her son as I am with my husband, but it's also hard for me *not* to lean on my mom, who has always been there for me. Sal visits along with Mom sometimes. Sal's great with the girls and so warm, and they love their Auntie Sal. This is tough for Sal and Hal. Barry is a dear friend, and Rob is Sal's brother too.

Hal and Barry talk on the phone regularly. I overhear one of their conversations. "I have a list of things I'd like to do," Barry says. "Like play in the band again—Haven Tweezer's Final Tour—go to Hawaii, see a Blue Jays game in Toronto, go to Seratami."

Yet another surge of sadness powers through me as I take note of what Barry says he wants to do, and I wonder if I can make any of it happen. I don't think he'll be playing in the band again. Hawaii may be a bit ambitious, but a trip to Toronto for the Blue Jays and Seratami—we might be able to do that.

Barry tries hard to be social. He joins me, Sal, and the girls for lunch at the Park Royal Hotel one day when Sal is visiting, and he also goes out for a meal with his mom and some of his siblings. There are nine of them. They sincerely want to help out, but there is not much they can do. They appreciate being able to visit with Barry, but he tires easily.

Barry is able to give Willow and Dixie a fair bit of attention. I catch him once as he's leaving the kitchen after talking to the girls, and he has a tear in his eye.

"What is it, hawney?" I ask. "What are you thinking about?"

"My daughters," he says.

We hug, as we do a lot these days. I'm careful not to squeeze his fragile body too tightly.

"It's so cruel," he says.

I nod. "You're so smart, talented, energetic, and special."

"It's not fair, is it?" he asks. "I don't know how I would have gotten through these last months without you. You've been so strong. I had the strangest dream last night when I did finally get some sleep. Everyone I ever knew, even people I haven't seen since law school, was giving me herbal recipes to cure my cancer. Sean Connery gave me some as well and said, 'Your nerves in your stomach are going to cause you problems.'"

"Well, I wonder if Sean Connery is one of the best lymphoma specialists in North America," I say with a chuckle.

By the end of June, Barry's condition is deteriorating further. He is not sleeping well. He is weak. He has headaches. He cannot pick up Dixie or cut his steak. Somewhere in all this, he contracted Bell's palsy, and it partially paralyzed the left side of his face. His left eye is stuck almost closed, he cannot blink, and the left corner of his mouth doesn't move well; it gives him this lopsided grin, which is actually quite cute.

Kasheemo does some tests and calls us to his office to talk about them. As we walk through the door, I have dreadful flashbacks to previous conversations where he dictated the possible life spans available to my husband.

"Nature is playing tricks on me," he says when we sit down. "You have no lumps and bumps. Your blood tests are negative, as is your spinal fluid. But you have the Bell's palsy and other symptoms of progression that someone with your disease would normally have. Sometimes we don't find the cancer cells in the fluid we take out of your brain and spine, but it may mean we are looking in the wrong spot. The fluid doesn't move around very much. I'll continue to test for physical evidence of the disease, but you need to be prepared for the worst. I would say you have four to six weeks left."

I feel my entire body slump as if I weighed five hundred pounds. I can barely lift my hand to set it on Barry's lap. He grabs my hand with both of his, raises it to his mouth, and sets his lips on the back of it, not moving, benumbed.

Kasheemo continues as if he were talking about the weather.

"You'll get weaker and more fatigued. Eventually you will not be able to get out of bed; a commode and bedpan will be necessary. But there'll not necessarily be a lot of pain," he says, in an apparent attempt to soften the news, "and I'll give you a prescription for morphine."

This is not happening. What the hell is he talking about? Dear God, help us. Kasheemo's terrifying words are racing around in my head, desperately trying to find a place to land, but it's too chaotic in there.

I look at Barry. He has his head in his hands. He slowly puts them down, locks his eyes with mine momentarily, then turns his head to Kasheemo.

"I don't know much about dying," he says weakly. "Will I have to be in the hospital?"

"People can die at home."

"I was hoping to get to our cottage this summer," Barry says. "Is that not possible now?"

"Well, we can try another round of chemo, if you're up for that. Once you get over the initial setback, it might pick you up enough to go on a trip."

I sniff back my tears and say, "Barry, do you want to try that? Could you stand another round of chemo?"

He lowers his head in resignation. "It's worth a try."

—

The kids are out with Meredith when we get home. Barry and I sit down beside each other on the love seat at the end of the family room. We hold hands and look out over the city.

"I guess you'll be helping me more and more," he says.

I assume he's talking about the commode and the bedpan. "That's why I'm here," I say. "That's all I want to do. I'm also praying for a miracle."

I feel consumed by grief. It attacks my insides like acid, burning its way to every cell of my soul. It's surprisingly physical. Even the memories hurt. We'll never go back to the Mauna Kea Beach Hotel in Hawaii and Michel's restaurant. Will we never get back to Seratami, either? Maybe Kasheemo can make that happen. I lay my head on Barry's shoulder, and I can't stop crying. I feel myself getting hysterical.

Barry holds me close. "You have been so incredibly wonderful, hawney. Thank you. Thank you. You're one special woman, and I'm extremely lucky to have you."

I'm practically shaking with fear now. He kisses my forehead and gently rocks me in his arms. I'm able to calm down, put my head up, wipe my tears away, and look at him. He brushes my hair out of my face and says, "My beautiful wifey, what will you hapless females do without me?"

What *will* we do without him?

How will I finish Whistler without him?

How will I sort out all the pictures? Barry always does that.

How will I get Dixie to be quiet at bedtime when she calls out at night?

How will I help the girls through this tragedy?

How will I do anything?

How will I manage the finances?

What will I do?

Oh, God, please help. Give us courage and strength.

The conversation with Kasheemo keeps going through my head.

"*Commode and bedpan.*"

"*Four to six weeks.*"

"*Prescription for morphine.*"

"*People can die at home.*"

I decide to light a lavender candle; the scent is supposed to be relaxing. It's going to take a little more than a candle to ease this distress, but it's worth a try. I go to light it, but I can't find any matches. Then I notice a white package of matches from our wedding day sitting behind a photo of the kids on the mantel. I pick it up and read the inscription.

Happy Birthday, Barry. October 20, 1984.

Barry and I got married on his thirty-fifth birthday, almost seven years ago.

9

"Helpless"
Neil Young
Monday, July 1, 1991

Before his next round of chemotherapy, Barry develops a lump on his right rib. The doctors aspirate it, and it is indeed recurrent lymphoma. Kasheemo tells us when we meet that the prognosis may be closer to four weeks now but that Barry has rallied before and very well could again. I know both Barry and I are thinking about Seratami. Does this development mean going there is out of the question?

Barry and his siblings spent every summer in Seratami growing up. Their father started a lumber company there in the 1950s. Today it is a global lumber company.

It's hard to determine exactly what gives Seratami its allure. It's probably a mélange: picking blueberries outside the kitchen door for morning pancakes with real Canadian maple syrup; skinny-dips in the cold, cleansing lake; serene canoe paddles in the setting sun's tranquilizing rays as the loons' haunting calls echo across the lake; the inherent spirituality of the rocky, treed land, inspired by natives who were the only inhabitants of this godly country before the whites infiltrated; the enigmatic northern lights dancing brightly in the dark night sky; the wind rushing through the tall, majestic pines, carrying the promise of an explosive storm; seeking safety inside, with a fire crackling in the large stone fireplace, with marshmallow-topped hot chocolate and a family game of Clue.

I make my appeal: "This trip to northern Ontario needs to happen, Dr. Kasheemo. This place, it's not just a summer cottage." I shake my head and gaze directly into his eyes. "It's, it's . . ." I take a deep breath. "It's his *soul* country."

Kasheemo hesitates and then actually offers Barry some hope. "Let's do an extra dose of chemo to attack the recurrence, give you time to recover from that, and then package you up to take this trip."

I exhale. "Thank you."

"I want to beef up your treatment when you get back, though," he says to Barry. "The disease is simmering."

Kasheemo then informs us that he's going away for six weeks, so Barry's next chemo treatments will be done at the British Columbia Cancer Agency instead of at Lions Gate. Barry is distressed that his king of chemo is leaving town, but Kasheemo tries to assure us that Barry will be in good hands with Dr. Joe Conrad, whom we know and trust from Barry's intensive treatment in May, and with Dr. Sarah O'Hare, whom we still have not met.

Barry has the expected debilitating reaction to the chemo but recovers surprisingly quickly. We go on our Seratami trip. He bears up well during the five-hour flight, and the kids actually act reasonably well, too. It helps that we've taken Meredith along with us.

When we get to Toronto, we stay with Hal and Sal for a couple of days. The kids play with their cousins, who are about the same age, while Barry and I go to see Dr. Kurt, a lymphoma oncologist, at St. Margaret's Hospital in Toronto.

Dr. Kurt confirms that we have expert care in Kasheemo, and now Dr. Conrad at the BCCA.

"Chuck and Jason are top notch," he assures us. "Their treatments are state of the art and beyond." Kurt suggests other possible treatments, such as a bone marrow transplant and radiation for the whole spinal-fluid area. Although this approach would clearly make Barry feel simply ghastly, it sounds like it might buy us some time.

When we get back to Hal and Sal's, we call Kasheemo and ask him about the transplant and radiation.

"The bone marrow transplant would be redundant after the intensive treatment you had at the BCCA," Kasheemo says. "And the radiation would do you in."

In Seratami, we feel Barry's dad's reassuring spirit looking over us. When he was alive, he had a commanding presence—tall and lanky, combed-back red hair, big hands, a wide and mischievous smile, an eye for lovely ladies, a brilliant brain, and a zest for life. His ashes were scattered in the lake near our cottages during a divine sunset. In death, his potent presence lives on, especially in Seratami.

We have no phone on our island, but there is one on Grandfather's island, where the family's original house is. However, it's a party line—four families use the same one—so it's not always available when you need it. On top of that, it's a radiophone, meaning that even when you get to use it, the connection is unreliable. This telephone situation in itself is enough to make Barry anxious. He needs to know he can connect with his doctors.

It doesn't help that he's feeling awful. He has severe headaches and back pain, despite the painkillers he's downing, and he can't sleep, despite the sleeping pills he takes every evening. His facial paralysis is getting worse. He's so concerned about his inability to communicate with his doctors that he's considering returning to Toronto and leaving us here. I pray he can stay.

Barry wakes me one morning at six thirty with a gentle kiss on my cheek. He's lying beside me, resting on his left elbow.

"I have to leave, hawney," he says. "I think I can get the ten-fifteen flight from North Bay to Toronto, stay with Hal and Sal, and see Kurt again at St. Margaret's."

I sit right up. "Are you sure you're okay to take the flight on your—"

"It's only an hour, and I feel better knowing I'll be closer to expert medical care," he says.

I can tell there's no way to convince him to stay, and we both know it's best for the kids if they remain a bit longer at the cottage with me and Meredith.

"The thought of being here without you at this stage leaves me . . . well, my insides are, I dunno, like . . . sinking," I mumble. A few tears roll down my cheeks, and I wonder if my tear ducts may just run dry one of these days. More disappointment.

The twenty-minute boat ride to the landing where we park the car is rough; a north wind is churning up the water. Barry is feeling even worse. I drive the car onto Lumber Road—a windy, bumpy gravel road that leads to the highway—and we get stuck behind a slow car that spews dust at us, making it hard to see. Gravel stones bounce around the car.

Barry complains that my driving is making him feel more ill.

I say nothing but fear that if I have to contain my hurt and anger any longer, I might shatter.

He's saying something else now, and he's hard to hear over the rumble of the car tires on the gravel.

"Speak up," I snap. "I can't understand a word you're saying." Immediately, I'm regretful. "Oh, I'm so sorry." I put my right hand on his left one. "I'm just tired and stressed and worried and don't want you to leave."

"I don't want to leave, either. But you know I can't stay."

"I know."

We don't talk. For the next few minutes, all we hear is the rumbling gravel beneath us. We finally make it to the highway, and I feel a sense of relief as the car tires hug that black pavement.

"I understand," he murmurs, and then raises his voice to ensure that I can hear. "You must be exhausted, too. You're so wonderful in the night when I can't sleep and keep cuddling you. I know I'm keeping you up, but you don't say a thing."

"It's okay, sweetie. I love you. It feels good," I reassure him.

He gives me a gentle smile, then stares out the window at the granite cliffs that jut out from either side of the road. Symmetrical lines run through the pink-and-gray stone where the powerful road-making equipment blasted right through it to build the highway. As he turns his head back to me, he says, with a melancholy smile, "At least we got our kiss on our bench." This transports me back eight years to Friday, June 17, 1983, about five thirty in the evening, to our first kiss on that wooden bench, and I think how romantic he is to have transported that bench all the way from the farm to the cottage.

"Yes, sweetie, that was so precious," I say. "That made the trip."

As we embrace at the airport, we meld together into a timeless cloud of muddled emotion. I never fully understood the famous Aristotle quote, "The whole is greater than the sum of its parts," until this precise moment.

When I get back to the cottage, the kids are all over me. I go to make myself some tea. Although Dixie is immersed in drawing with Meredith, Willow keeps nagging at me: "Can we make chocolate chip cookies? Can we make cookies? I want to eat cookie dough."

"Maybe you and Meredith can do that," I say.

"I want to make cookies with *you*," she whines. "I want to make cookies with *you!*"

"Shut up!" I yell—and immediately feel like a piece of shit. I bend down and hold her hurt little face in my hands. "I am so sorry I got angry, sweetie."

"Are you sorry you got angry? Are you sorry you got angry?"

She keeps repeating herself. It's driving me crazy.

"Yes, I'm very sorry I got angry," I say, forcing myself to stay calm. "But it might happen again if you don't stop repeating yourself. Now, please, stop doing that."

"But can't we make cookies, Mommy?" she whines, pulling on my hand.

"Okay, dear, but I need to go to Grandfather's island first, to call Daddy. I need to be sure he made it to Hal and Sal's okay."

I'm able to get through to Barry, who is feeling much more secure now that he's only a few miles from the expert medical care of Dr. Kurt and the staff at St. Margaret's Hospital. I, in turn, am feeling much calmer with the simple knowledge that my husband is feeling calmer. This seems to give me immediate permission to let go. My crashing waves of emotion give way to the rhythmic ripple of the peaceful lake.

Finally, we are able to slip into life at our unpolished Lake Seratami cottage. Here, we keep things simple. Strips of city formalities are peeled away, including clothes. As Willow tells Dianne on the phone, "We don't need underpants or undershirts or anything." Barry and I like to bathe in the lake, but the kids are still young enough to need their bedtime baths. Oftentimes, we pee in the woods. We even toilet-trained Dixie in the woods last year. "Dixie pooed in the woods again. Dixie pooed in the woods," Willow would report.

My mood sets the tone for the kids. Once I'm calm, the days are filled with swimming in the revitalizing lake, catching frogs, exploring the islands, picking blueberries, canoeing by Sunset Rock and into Loon Bay, going on motorboat rides up the inlet toward Babika Bay, roasting marshmallows at night on the fire on Rosemary Rock Point, and generally having no agenda. The girls actually settle quickly at night in the same room; Dixie looks at her books until she gets sleepy.

These are bittersweet days. I miss my darling husband. *I miss you so much*, I think. But the truth is that I miss the healthy Barry. He's the one I yearn for.

We spend a few more days at the lake, and on Saturday, July 13, we go to Toronto and join Barry at Hal and Sal's. Barry leans down weakly to greet Willow, who gives him a reticent hug. She steps back and looks at him. "I thought you'd be all better, Daddy. But you still look weird," she says, probably referring to his crooked, partially paralyzed Bell's palsy face. Dixie, however, shows no sign of this ambivalence. While Barry is still leaning down with Willow, Dixie butts in, hugging his neck and smothering his face with kisses.

As soon as I'm alone with Sal, I break down. "It's just so frustrating not being able to make any plans. They keep changing because of Barry's health. Oh, Sal, Barry and the kids, they need me so much. I wish it were five years from now and that whatever is going to happen would have already happened." I grab an apple from the table. "Can I have this?"

Sal hugs me. "Have whatever you want." She lets go, grabs the kettle, and says, "Want tea?"

"If in doubt, make tea." One of our sisterly jokes. I almost manage to smile.

"You must feel smothered, Rosalee," she says gently. "Maybe you can have a couple of days here, and Mom and I can give *you* some support."

But that is not meant to be. As good as Dr. Kurt is, Barry is uncomfortable not being in Vancouver with our expert medical support team. He is feeling abysmal as well. We decide to return to Vancouver the following day, Sunday, July 14—three days ahead of schedule.

Back in Vancouver, I'm on my own with the kids and interviewing nannies, as Dianne is able to help out less and less and Meredith has quit in order to get ready for art school. I have an avalanche of tasks to take care of: making Barry comfortable, doing a major food shop, arranging summer-in-the-city plans for the girls (swimming lessons, play dates). And I need to organize Willow's fifth-birthday party, her first-ever birthday not held in Seratami. It requires much more work than a cottage event held on the boathouse deck. And Willow is still thinking her father is going to get better, so I need to learn how to address that. I feel trapped.

Dixie's gone wild. She's pooping in her pants and biting her sister. Apparently, Dixie's toilet training—or, should I say, woods training—has gone all to shit.

But then, after days of this, we have a breakthrough. I hear Willow squeal, "Dixie pooped in the potty. Dixie pooped in the potty!"

I run to the bathroom and join her and Willow just in time to watch Dixie put her poop from her little potty into the toilet, flush it, wave at it, and say, "Bye-bye," as it swirls around and around and down the drain.

She looks up at Willow and me, and we all burst out laughing.

"Well, just when I thought you'd be pooping in your pants until you were sixteen!" I pick her up and give her a big smooch on her cheek.

I cherish this good news as much as I cherish the frivolity that is in such contrast with the pervasive gloom that has come to characterize our lives this year.

—

One evening when I'm having trouble settling Dixie and all I want to do is sleep myself, I decide to leave Dixie crying for a bit and hope she will calm down on her own. I'm headed down the hall to our bedroom, when I hear Barry call out in pain. "Ohhhhh."

I rush into the room. He's in bed, lying on one side but propping himself up with his right elbow so he has a direct sight line to the door.

When he sees me, he says, "Hawney, I'm dying."

I rush over and sit beside him. "You really are in so much pain, aren't you? How can I help? Can you lie all the way down?"

"No, it hurts to move," he says. "My head is screaming, and I can't sleep."

"What can I do? Shall I get some more painkillers? If I run you a bath, could you sit in it? Would it help?"

"I dunno. I dunno. I just took some tramadol." He gingerly starts to move onto his back, and I help to lower him. "Oh," he says, "that's a bit better. My head isn't screaming as much. It's settled to a dull roar."

"Maybe a bath'll help."

"Thanks so much, sweetie. I love you," he tells me. "I'm glad you're on my team. You *are* my life."

Amid this affection, I feel a breeze of tenderness waft over me. We freeze in the moment, gazing at each other in love and sorrow.

I run his bath and help him in. Barry is in less pain now. The bathroom has a solarium at the side that faces the city. There is a ledge in front of it the same height as the tub. I sit on it to chat with him.

"It's a good thing we're going to the hospital tomorrow," he says.

"Yes, hawney, and don't forget—you're going to be the miracle," I say, because we need hope. I'm afraid he'll stop fighting if he feels me giving up on him. "We girls need you. Willow and Dixie love you so much. I love you so much."

My extreme adoration of my husband takes hold, but its grip is tenuous. That very adoration incites a grief-stricken anger that makes me want to blurt out, *Why did you have to let this happen to you? You had a sore knee, other symptoms they couldn't diagnose, and you were so worried you had cancer, you talked yourself into it!* But I remain rational.

"It *is* a good thing we're going to the hospital tomorrow," I repeat.

Dr. O'Hare has kind, wise brown eyes and shoulder-length gray hair that makes her seem older than her real age, which is about forty. She sits before us in her office at the British Columbia Cancer Agency in her white doctor's coat, her stethoscope hanging around her neck, and flips through Barry's chart as she talks to us. She asks Barry how he has been feeling and exudes professional, but seemingly authentic, compassion as he tells her about his severe headaches, the pain and weakness in his left hand and right leg, his occasional double vision, his inability to sleep, his anxiety.

"There clearly hasn't been adequate pain management," Dr. O'Hare says. She looks at Barry and turns her head to me. "We can do something to right this. We can address the pain. But, and I know you know this"—she looks at Barry while she sets down her file—"it appears the large dose of chemotherapy that Dr. Kasheemo administered in early July was effective only in dealing with the lump. Your blood and spinal fluid tests are negative, but the disease is showing signs of progressing. The lymphoma may be clinging to the nerve cells in the brain and hiding in places we can't aspirate. It's likely the disease, and not the toxic drugs, as was considered at one point, that's causing the deterioration. There's really no cure, but there's no reason we can't do the best we can to make you as comfortable as we can at home. The goal right now is to maintain as good a quality of life as possible."

"How long will this go on?" Barry asks, once again scrambling for a concrete prognosis.

"I would say it's a matter of months," Dr. O'Hare says. "As I say, you can have a good quality of life. That's the aim."

"We were told a matter of weeks," Barry says.

Dr. O'Hare just looks at us, and I can't read what she's thinking.

"What'll happen eventually?" Barry asks.

I know he's referring to when he does die. I swallow and nervously push my hair away from my eyes and behind my ear. It's a topic he and I have only really skirted around, too difficult to address. It must be fear that drives that. Talking about it makes it so real.

Barry folds his arms at his chest, which he often does at times like this—as if he's protecting his heart from the news.

O'Hare leans her elbows on her desk and puts her hands together in front of her, almost in prayer position. She continues at the same pace and with the same comforting tone. "It will be relatively quick when it happens, and there's a possibility of a semiconscious state because of the spinal-fluid involvement," she says. "But you won't necessarily be that uncomfortable, especially with adequate pain management."

Dr. O'Hare makes us feel safe and taken care of. She has an uncanny way of stating the bare truth while peppering it with hope, even if it's only for a fulfilling—and minimally painful—final run. Her manner is the antithesis of Kasheemo's.

This visit buoys Barry. He's so grateful to Dr. O'Hare, he actually writes her a note saying, "You have given me a sense of control that was elusive to this point. I fully expected to be an invalid and doped out on morphine by now. Thank you very much."

On the morning of Willow's birthday—Thursday, August 1—I am up at five o'clock, wrapping presents, writing Willow's card, preparing burgers, blowing up the new pool toys, icing the cake . . . the amount of preparation seems endless.

I go to check on Barry. He's also awake, being his insomniac self, and sitting at his desk in our office. He gives me a cheery, "Good morning, hawney," and seems to be feeling somewhat upbeat. He's holding a photo of him and newborn Willow and me. We are in the hospital. Barry is in hospital scrubs, posing with Willow in his arms; I'm snuggled right in there with them.

"This was taken five years ago today, probably to the minute," he says. "You were a bit out of it on morphine, which I may well be soon enough, and not happy with your hospital room. I went to get you a single room, which you have done for me several times this year."

Barry and I discuss his general perked-up state, and it bodes well for the day ahead, as well as for a trip we're taking to Toronto in a couple of days. He's planning on visiting with the his lawyer friends, the Bozos; going to a baseball game; going to dinner with Hal and Sal and other friends at his favorite Toronto restaurant, Centro; and maybe even visiting my parents at their farm in Collingwood. Now that he's feeling much better, it seems like all this will be possible.

Willow has a blast at her birthday party. Barry has enough stamina to start making the burgers on the barbecue, but then he needs to retire to his room to rest.

The following day, I have an opportunity to audition with the famous casting director Sid Kozak for a movie role—a "baseball wife" part. I actually think I can make the audition, as Barry is feeling better and Dianne is here for a few hours.

I shower, wrap my hair in a towel turban (which we call Queen of Sheba style in our family), put on a fluffy white robe we brought home from one of our trips to the Mauna Kea Beach Hotel in Hawaii, and go into the bedroom.

Barry is in one of the two chairs facing the TV. "You look beautiful, my beautiful wifey," he says.

"Oh, I've no makeup on or anything, but thanks, sweetie," I say, as I go over and touch his knee in appreciation. I walk back into the bathroom, lean over, towel-dry my hair, flip my head back up, and grab a comb. As I'm walking back out, running the comb through my hair, I say, "You know, you've created a beautiful life for your two beautiful daughters—a beautiful house and vacation spots—and for us." I sit in the chair beside him. I'm remembering what the social worker told me about how to talk with him so he feels good about his life. "You're brilliant and creative and talented and an incredible father."

"Well," he says, looking down at his body, "I seem to have taken a turn for the worse."

I blanch. "Really?"

"It hurts to pee, and there's blood in my urine. I have severe pain here, in my right leg"—he holds his right thigh—"and, surprise, surprise, I've got a fever."

"Oh, dear God," I say. "What do you think this means about the Toronto trip tomorrow?"

"Yeah, I dunno," he says. "Let's go to the hospital and see what O'Hare says."

"But you've been doing so well," I say.

He pauses, looks at me admiringly, and says, "I so appreciate you. It must've been so lonely for Dad to go through this alone. I'm worrying. I'm worrying about everything. I'm worried about not seeing the kids grow up. The poor girls, losing their daddy. They're so precious. Last night in the middle of the night, I went to check on them in my wandering-insomniac mode. Willow stirred, and when I asked if she was okay, she said, 'No, Daddy, I want you.' I told her it was sleep time and that I loved her, and she said, 'I love you, too, Daddy. I love you very much.' I went in to Dixie, and although I didn't want to wake her, I kissed her forehead and my heart melted."

"How wonderfully sweet. They do love you so much," I say, knowing full well I can't very well jump up now and start getting ready for my audition. It's just not going to happen. I give in to this more quickly than I would have a few months ago. Something else is controlling my life right now. I have basic survival obligations. I will have to knock Sid Kozak's socks off some other time.

We head out to the hospital. I drive us down the mountainside and over the Lions Gate Bridge. We aren't talking, both immersed in our own thoughts. I drive over the Cambie Street Bridge, the final stretch, and Barry breaks the silence: "I want more time."

There is no appropriate response to this. It's all too heavy.

When we arrive at the BCCA, Barry's fever is rising and, just as we suspected, his blood counts are way low. He's diagnosed with a bladder infection and admitted. He's in the same bed on 6W as he was for his intensive treatment three months ago. It's Wednesday, August 7. We were supposed to go to Toronto tomorrow. Although this is depressing as hell and all too fucking familiar, I also feel some relief. I always do when I can hand over his care to the professionals and he can get the attention he needs.

Dr. O'Hare comes to talk to us in Barry's room.

"How do you feel?" she asks.

"Daunted and scared," Barry says. "We had hoped to go to Toronto to visit friends and family tomorrow."

"I can see you're feeling desperate," she says. "No wonder, with the low blood counts and a bladder infection. We'll give you a high dose of antibiotics and some intrathecal methotrexate, up the steroids, and see if we can't get you to Toronto soon, but definitely not tomorrow."

"When?" Barry asks.

"Perhaps two weeks." Dr. O'Hare always gives us hope. "I'll go get these orders in place."

"Thank you," we both call after her as she leaves.

Barry and I look at each other, and I see that he is already resigned to the fact that our trip is postponed.

He picks up the glass of water from his bedside table and takes a long drink. "Do you think my strength and spirit will bounce back and we can make the trip in two weeks?" He sets the glass back down and continues, "With things so uncertain, I have this sense of urgency to do things we want to do right away."

"Yes, hawney," I say, and sit on the edge of the bed beside him. "You'll be good. Maybe we tried to take on too much this last week. It was so hectic."

"But it was sure good while it lasted."

"It was."

"You've been so unselfish and strong and supportive throughout this whole ordeal." Barry takes my hand. "I can't tell you enough how much I love and appreciate you. Thank you for standing by me almost constantly these last seven months, all the while being a support for Rob."

"Thank you," I say. "You're worth every second."

"I need you and feel closer to you than ever and can only hope and pray that . . ." He looks down. "I'm feeling more scared than ever right now."

I stroke his left cheek with the back of my right hand. "You'll bounce back, and we'll go to Toronto in couple of weeks, just in time to catch the Blue Jays game on August twenty-fifth. You'll see."

10

"Face the Music"
Donna Summer

Saturday, August 10, to
Tuesday, September 17, 1991

By Saturday, August 10, the second Saturday in August, Barry has been released from the hospital and admitted again.

He's at home barely long enough for Willow and Dixie to ask him if he's "going to play with them lots" when he gets better. Willow proclaims that he now looks like "a monster with a bit of hair." Barry figures this is probably better than before, when she called him "a ghost with no hair," and admits he must indeed look like a bit of a monster, with his face crooked from the partial paralysis, head puffy and legs spindly from the steroids, and body scarred.

Back in the hospital, Barry's situation is looking increasingly dismal. His mouth sores are returning, it's getting even more painful for him to pee, as he has cystitis, and he's coughing constantly. His stay includes more tests—a cystoscopy to see if it is the disease or the toxic drugs causing the cystitis, as well as a test for pneumonia. If he has that, it will mean a three-week stay in the hospital, which will nix the Toronto trip.

—

I meet up with Rob for our weekly Granville Island outing. We start filling his shopping bag with bananas and fudge, and all the while I'm trying to explain to him the string of bad news Barry and I have had recently. As we're standing in the lineup for fresh bread, I say, "I'm just surprised I haven't had a hysterical grief fit lately. . . . I'm going to get a loaf of the whole wheat. What do you want?"

"First, pray tell, what the hell is a hysterical grief fit?" he asks. This makes us laugh hysterically.

We have to settle down to order our bread, and then I explain, "A hysterical grief fit is simply physical grief—shaking, unrelenting tears and nausea, like I've been in a small boat buffeted about by huge swells in a thunderous storm in the middle of the ocean."

Rob makes a face. "That's very descriptive, and horrid."

"Yeah, it *is* horrid." I know I'm embellishing a bit, but it feels so good to laugh. "Let's get some french fries," I suggest, "and sit over there on the dock and feed the obnoxious seagulls."

"Thank you for all your help, Rosepots," Rob says, using a nickname from our childhood. "You know, I've been depressed for some twenty years, and, ironically enough, although I can certainly still be depressed, at times now I feel like I'm actually coming out of it."

On Tuesday, August 13, three days after being admitted, Barry is allowed to return home from the hospital with some good news: he does not have pneumonia, the lymphoma has not caused the cystitis, and his mouth sores are subsiding. With tentative optimism, we plan another trip to Toronto for Thursday, August 21—my thirty-seventh birthday. I know, without Barry's telling me, that he desperately wants to say his final goodbyes to his close friends, and to Hal and Sal.

But the next day he wakes with a stuffed-up nose and sore throat. All the while, Willow is coughing, even though she's on antibiotics for bronchitis. I can't take any more distressing news. Fighting a complete collapse, I go for an aggressive swim at the club, hoping to defuse the anger, pain, fear, and anguish strangling me.

Shit, man, give me a goddamn fucking break. As I plow myself through the water, I fervently plead to God for Barry's sore throat to disappear and for Willow's cough to fucking stop. *And while you're at it,* I think, *why don't you also stop the onslaught of all the other shit, too, and give me a respite from this nightmare?*

Over the next couple of days, Barry's throat gets sorer and his coughing increases. On Friday, August 16, he's admitted, once again, to the BC Cancer Agency. His blood counts have plummeted from 7,500 to 1,200 in a week. Normal blood count is somewhere between 4,000 and 11,000 per cubic millimeter of blood. Barry questions out loud whether he has the strength to go on fighting this insidious disease, with all its complexities.

When Dr. O'Hare visits us in his hospital room, she detects that Barry is nearly inconsolable. "I suggest a major dose of antibiotics," she says. "That could be what it takes to get you well enough to possibly go to Toronto within the week."

The trip to Toronto does happen. We'll be gone from Wednesday, August 21, to Tuesday, August 27. The plan is for the girls to stay with Hal and Sal, where Mom can also help out, so Barry and I can have some alone time at the apartment Barry's family lumber company owns. Barry figures we might feel some of his dad's spirit in the place, as he lived there for a time.

Over the next few days, Barry is social and courageous. He doesn't look well, but he shows incredible stamina despite his weakened state and legion of trips to the toilet because of his bladder infection. He buys me a flowing purple crepe-and-lace dress for my birthday, and I wear it to our dinner with Hal and Sal and other friends at Centro Trattoria, where we imbibe copious quantities of Tuscan Antinori Tignanello red wine and eat too much scrumptious Italian pasta and gnocchi.

Barry goes to a ballgame with his three Bozo buddies. Afterward, he remarks how differently people react to the bad news that he's basically on an end run here. The Bozos have a "just act natural" approach, which Barry is more comfortable with than he is with the intensity of another buddy he has drinks with, who remarks, "Oh, man, how horrendous it must be to be so close to the end. It's just not fair." No matter what their attitude, however, his friends obviously care very deeply. Barry says it's one of the things that keeps him fighting.

The next day, we have lunch with two of my dear friends, Liz and Hutch. Barry takes a trip to the bathroom, and Hutch pushes her plate aside, folds her arms on the table, looks straight at me, and asks, "How *are* you, really?"

"Just very, very sad," I say, and look down at my tea. I take a sip and look back at Hutch. "We love each other so much. I thought we were going to grow old together."

"You two have always had such a special relationship," she says.

Barry and I have an enchanting time in Toronto without the girls, the doctors, the chemo treatments, the nanny scheduling, and all the other details that bombard us in Vancouver. It's him and me and our friends and family. I believe we have been granted a miracle. We even fly home on schedule—on Tuesday, August 27. But during the flight Barry's spirits are low, and I, too, sense a comedown from our adrenaline-fueled high.

As we're eating dinner in front of the TV that night, I turn to Barry. "What's on your mind, hawney?"

He stares blankly at the screen in front of him, then turns slowly to me. "Well, I guess we have to face the music. The endless summer, as Van Morrison calls it, is coming to a close."

Within two days of our return to Vancouver, as if on cue, Barry takes a turn for the worse. He is so weak that he falls over in the night while trying to get to the bathroom. He's nauseous, he has severe pain in his joints and bad headaches, and the left side of his face is now completely paralyzed.

I'm am trying to take care of him while being inundated with other obligations, like finding at-home nursing care, preparing for the new school year, and interviewing nannies. The nanny situation continues to be challenging, as Meredith has quit and Dianne, who is an old 65, simply can't help out anymore—she struggles too much with the intensity of the situation in our home.

I end up hiring twenty-one-year-old Katy, who is taking a year off school. She reminds me of Meredith—a confident air, a ready smile. She cannot start until Monday, September 2. She'll move into our extra bedroom and work the Monday-to-Friday shift, have the use of our Subaru to ferry the kids about, and get a credit card to buy groceries and other necessities. It will be a relief to have full-time help, although I'm still interviewing for evening and weekend help. I know I am spoiled to have all these options, and I try not to be too far from gratitude.

On Friday afternoon, August 30, Barry is doing so poorly that he may need an oncologist, but they're impossible to reach on weekends. And—minor detail—Barry could die—literally any time now. What would I do with his body if he did? I realize I don't even know whether he wants to be cremated. Don't I need to know that if he dies? How soon do I need to know that?

Obsessed with this worry, I go grocery shopping after dropping the girls off at a friend's house and I'm so preoccupied that I forget to pay as I hurry out with my cart of food. The grocery packer has to come chasing after me as I rush away from the checkout stand with my cart full of food.

"Ma'am, ma'am," he calls. "You forgot to pay."

I turn around and look at the young, pimply-faced teenage Safeway employee, who seems to be panicking. I break into a smile and say, "Oh, that! Details, details."

We laugh, and it's a release of tension for both of us.

Still, no amount of distraction can stop me from thinking about what I'm going to do about Barry's body if he dies this weekend, and I figure I'd better call the lawyer who drew up the will. But it's four forty-five, and I have to phone by five. I see a pay phone near the Safeway, and I actually get through to the lawyer.

Initially, I'm proud of myself for being so composed—but it lasts only about two minutes. *Oh, God, here they come.* I can't stop the fucking tears. *Shit. Just don't break down completely. Save that for bedtime.*

"I need to know . . . um, Barry is really not well, not at all." I stop and take a deep breath. "What if, what if, like, this weekend?" I manage.

There is silence.

Then I continue, "Well, I need to know about instructions . . . about if he, he . . . doesn't make it through the weekend," I say, wishing this lawyer would just tell me what the fuck I need to know. *Don't you know what I'm trying to say? I need to know if there are instructions for Barry's dead body. I don't even know whether he wants to be cremated.*

"Oh, yes, there are instructions," he says. "I'll give you my colleague's phone number. There's a memo to the will, which is what you need, and he can bring that to you if you need it. He lives in West Vancouver as well."

I thank him, say goodbye, hang up the phone, and fall

apart right here in the mall area outside the Safeway, beside the butcher and the florist and the newsstand and the deli and the Japanese restaurant and all the accompanying bustle of a late Friday afternoon of Labor Day weekend. Then I worry some more.

What if this colleague guy isn't home when I call?

Barry makes it through the weekend but continues his grim downward spiral. On Tuesday, we get in touch with the cancer clinic at Lions Gate Hospital. Kasheemo is due back tomorrow, Wednesday, September 4. It's suggested we get tests done so Kasheemo will have the results when he returns.

On Wednesday at noon, we find ourselves sitting in front of Kasheemo once again—Barry's face bloated, his eyes bloodshot, his face cockeyed, his mood dismal. Kasheemo is his efficient self, behind his desk in his sparsely decorated office, wearing his white doctor's coat.

Dismissing pleasantries, Kasheemo starts up.

"Well"—he looks down at papers on his desk and then up at Barry—"all the tests are negative for lymphoma. It leads me to question whether the chemo has killed the cancer and you are in fact in remission."

Before we have a chance to have a taste of realistic hope, Kasheemo leans into the desk so his head is closer to us. "There still needs to be a reason why you're deteriorating so rapidly. There are three possible explanations. One, it's a treatable virus. Two, the chemotherapy has caused irreversible drug damage. And three, the lymphoma cells are there but eluding all tests."

As Kasheemo is downloading this mishmash of possible scenarios, I feel like we're being battered about on an infinite bumper-car ride. What if it is a treatable virus? Will Barry recover? What if

Barry is in remission? What if the lymphoma is indeed lurking in the recesses of his body, waiting to pounce in a final ambush?

"Dr. Kasheemo," I say, moving my chair closer to Barry and putting my arm around him, "what is the most likely scenario?"

Barry clears his throat and adds, "If it's a virus, could I recover fully?"

"I don't know, and I wouldn't get your hopes up. I suggest an MRI of your brain. This will help figure out what's going on. The wait for an MRI here is months. I suggest you go to St. Joseph's Hospital in Bellingham again."

It is simply understood by all three of us that Barry and I will be taking the trip to Bellingham, just south of the Canada-US border, and we'll be doing it as soon as possible.

I'm dreading the trip. Barry is so sick, he doesn't fare well on long car rides, and my bad memories of the last trip to St. Joseph's are still fresh.

I drive Barry to St. Joseph's Hospital for the MRI on Friday. He's so weak that he can't walk, so I push him in a wheelchair. The MRI is a miserable experience, as Barry needs to lie flat and still while this large metal machine hovers about his head like a spaceship about to land, all the while making loud, eerie clanging noises.

We're done by one thirty. We need to get the MRI films back to Kasheemo before five, but Barry insists we have enough time for a bite at the cafeteria. We sit at a table with our snacks. His arms are feeble and shaky; he struggles to get his cookie to his mouth and slops his coffee on the table.

I try to assist him, but that only makes him cross. He pushes my hand away. I know the people around us are looking at my near-helpless husband and wondering what is making him incompetent.

Where is the instruction manual for dealing with the despair I feel witnessing Barry in such dire condition? I'm bereft of resources. I imagine myself squished into a jar, compacted with stress. My stresses and fears keep accumulating in the jar until they hit the lid, which won't budge. Nothing moves. I'm stuck. My emotions are frozen. There is nowhere else to go.

The route back takes us through the US-Canada border in Friday-afternoon rush-hour traffic. The border queue ends up taking only about half an hour—surprisingly short—but then I get us lost trying to find a return route more efficient than the regular Highway 1. Suffocating in my stress jar, I fantasize about driving the Jeep right into the concrete barrier separating the north and south lanes at ninety miles an hour.

We eventually make it to familiar Granville Street, and I see a phone booth on the corner of Granville and Nanton. It's almost-four twenty; I doubt we'll make it to Lions Gate Hospital before five o'clock. I pull over to call Kasheemo to see if he can wait for us. While on hold, I glance out the window of the phone booth and realize we're right beside St. John's Shaughnessy Church, where Barry's dad's funeral was two years ago.

Unsuccessful in my mission to reach Kasheemo, I jump back into the driver's seat. "Of course, Kasheemo's not available. I left a voice mail. Oh, dear God, give us a fuckin' break."

"That doesn't help matters much," Barry says.

"I can't believe how calm you stay throughout all this," I say, giving his hand a squeeze. "It's amazing."

It's just after five by the time we get to Lions Gate, and I let Barry stay in the car while I rush in with the MRI results in my hand.

I don't see Kasheemo, so I corner a nurse. "Where is Dr. Kasheemo?"

"I think he's gone for the day," she says.

"What? He needs these MRI films. He's expecting them. They're of my husband, who's dying. Can you please help me?"

I seem to be drawing attention to myself, but I don't care. Another nurse overhears our conversation and comes over.

"Dr. Kasheemo said he might be coming back," she says. "I'll take the films and make sure he gets them."

"Thank you. Thank you. Thank you."

At home, Katy, who started working this week, makes us a dinner of smoked salmon, broccoli quiche, and banana cream pie. We have an angel in our midst. She even agrees to stay and help with the children this weekend.

At about nine o'clock Saturday morning, Barry is still in bed and the girls and I are having breakfast at the kitchen nook. The phone rings.

I jump up. "Hello?"

"It's Dr. Kasheemo."

My God, I think. "Yes, good morning."

"Well . . ." And then he pauses. This is often how he starts his explanations. "The MRI films show viral encephalitis."

"Viral encephalitis?"

"That's inflammation of the brain. There's also significant atrophy, considering his age."

"Atrophy?"

"Degeneration."

I'm stupefied and baffled and feel my eggs churning up in my stomach.

"However," Kasheemo continues, "there is no sign of the lymphoma."

"What does this all mean, Dr. Kasheemo?" I ask, baffled.

"I've spoken with Dr. Sutherland, the neurosurgeon," he says, "and he thinks the brain is in good enough condition to biopsy the front right side."

Oh God, I think, *another operation?* I close my eyes and cringe. I can't imagine this happening to Barry right now.

"If you're in agreement," Kasheemo says, "we'd do the craniotomy on Monday."

"What would you be looking for?"

"If it shows lymphoma, then radiation is possible."

"But Barry is in rough shape, Dr. Kasheemo. I don't even know if he'll make it until Monday."

"Check with Barry that he wants to go ahead with this," he says, "and if he does, I'll send an ambulance to get him to the hospital as soon as possible. We'll do the craniotomy today."

I lie beside Barry on the bed as we wait for the ambulance, my right arm around his waist. I can practically feel the will draining from his body. What little hope we have left is infused with futility and an impending sense of doom. Without words, we know we both feel exactly the same way. We are communicating via a type of telepathy.

Willow and Dixie are looking out the front window as the ambulance pulls into the driveway, mesmerized by the big white-and-red vehicle with a red light on top—which is not flashing—that has come to take their daddy away. My motherly instincts make me desperately want to shelter them from all of this, but I can't. I can't cushion them from this harsh reality.

I watch them watch the ambulance attendants readying the gurney. I see two little girls grappling with a tangle of new emotions, and I know that their innocence will shield them for only so long. This is something none of us can escape from, and it will leave an indelible mark on our souls.

It's almost as difficult watching them flounder as it is watching my husband die. What must this be like for their little two-year-old and five-year-old minds and hearts? What are they thinking?

As if she hears my ponderings, Willow looks up at me and says, "Is Daddy going to die today?"

Flustered by her brutally honest curiosity, I can muster up only "Well, sweetie, we really don't know what's going to happen."

Right then, the paramedics knock on the door.

I open the door for the two male attendants. One looks a little old to be working in such a physical job, and the other is a young, clean-cut man. I lead them to Barry in the bedroom. I can tell by the way he looks at me that he wants me close as the paramedics maneuver him onto the gurney. I go over and kiss him. "Goodbye. I'll see you at the hospital shortly."

"Where do I meet him?" I ask the paramedics.

"He'll be in Emerg."

"Thank you."

After they roll Barry out the front door, I close it and join Willow and Dixie by the window. We all stare at the ambulance as it drives away.

After I arrive at the hospital and meet up with Barry, we wait . . . and wait . . . and wait for the surgery to happen.

Finally, Dr. Sutherland arrives and speaks with us before the craniotomy. He tells me, "You don't need to wait. I will call when the operation is complete."

Again, I watch Barry being rolled away, this time for brain surgery. I slump into the uncomfortable hospital chair and forage deep inside myself for more energy to carry on. I sit there in a stupor for a good half hour, staring blankly at the goings-on in Emergency, all too bloody familiar.

I pick up some groceries on the way home but don't dawdle, anxious to be home for Sutherland's call. I check my watch: four thirty, not too early for a large goblet of chilled chardonnay. I take the leftover quiche from the fridge and cut a slice of fresh sourdough bread that I just picked up at Safeway. I stand at the counter to eat, but before I can put anything in my mouth, a wave of grief washes through me. My legs get weak, my stomach tightens, my throat swells up, and my eyes overflow—and then the phone rings, shocking me so much, I drop my wineglass. It smashes onto the tiled kitchen floor, but I can't care about that; I'm too desperate to get to the phone, as it is likely the surgeon.

I step over the mess and answer the phone. It is indeed Dr. Sutherland.

"There were no complications," he says. "We were able to cut one cubic centimeter from the right side of Barry's brain, by the ear."

"Was there any lymphoma?" I ask.

"I don't know; the brain matter still has to be tested. But here's what I do know: there is widespread, advancing degeneration of the brain, and it has atrophied. The brain has a protective wrapping around it, but Barry's brain has shrunk away from its wrappings."

I don't know what to say. Even though I wanted the results, I wonder if he needs to be quite so graphic.

"What does this mean?" I ask. "What does this tell you?"

"Dr. Kasheemo will know more for you at the beginning of the week, after some tests are completed," he says. "Is there anything else I can do, Mrs. Keevil?"

"No, no. Thank you very much for calling," I say. "I so appreciate it."

I lower the phone slowly onto its cradle and leave my eyes fixed on it. My hawney's wonderful brain. My brilliant, creative, witty, special guy. *What did they do to your brain? What if the drugs caused this? Let's have a miracle that leaves you cured and not half-cured.* As if I can be fussy about my miracles.

Sobbing, I sweep the big pieces of broken glass into a dustpan, get down on my hands and knees with a wet tea towel, and try to gather up all the tiny pieces that could cut the girls' bare feet. I dump the towel full of glass shards into the garbage and go down the hall to my bedroom, carefully locking the door behind me—and then I stomp through the bedroom into the office and slam that door. I figure if I have both doors closed, the girls won't be able to hear the impending rampage.

I open the office door again and slam it shut and continue to open it and slam it shut, open it and slam it shut, open it and slam it shut, screaming the entire time, until I'm hoarse. My intellectual brain recognizes that this rage has been percolating under the sadness for too long. The rage has been seeping through the sorrow, commanding more and more attention, and for now the rage has conquered the sadness.

The day after Barry's operation, Sunday, September 8, I go to the ICU to visit him. A nurse is checking the bloody bandages wrapped around his head when I walk in.

Upon seeing me, Barry says, "I don't need you here, Rosemary. Go away."

The nurse apologizes for him, explaining, "Brain surgery can temporarily affect the temperament."

I feel another bawling session brewing and order myself to wait until bedtime.

The next day, Barry's mood is much more civil, but he's still somewhat aloof. I'm so blue I can't hide it from him. The visit leaves me torpid and numb. What to do next? When will this be resolved? I'm getting so worn out. The uncertainty is gnawing at my brain and heart.

Almost as if a divine force senses my waning strength, when I visit the next day, Tuesday, September 10, Barry's personality starts permeating the hole in his brain and the anesthetizing morphine. He can once again carry on a simple conversation—certainly enough to repeatedly tell me how much he appreciates me. Although his mood gradually improves over the week, he's extremely weak and needs the morphine for the pain.

On the morning of Friday, September 13, before my daily visit to Barry, I'm at home in the kitchen with the girls. Willow pours milk in her cereal, holds out a spoonful to me, and offers me a bite.

"Weeellll, Cap'n Crunch is not my favorite, but—" I suddenly notice that the middle finger on her right hand is bruised and bent. "What happened to your finger, Willow? What's this? What happened?"

"Well, you see Willow and I—," starts nanny Katy, but she's interrupted by Willow.

"My finger got caught in the car door."

"What? When?" I ask, incredulous. "Katy?"

"Oh, it's nothing," Katy says. "It just happened yesterday, and—"

Again, Willow speaks up. "No, it didn't. Yesterday was Thursday. It happened on the way home from Nana's on Tuesday. I know it was Tuesday because I always go to Nana's after school on Tuesdays," she says matter-of-factly. "And Dixie goes on Wednesdays after school."

"Tuesday? Katy, why didn't you tell me? Why didn't you tell me?"

"I didn't think it was that serious," Katy says, "and I didn't want to bother—"

"She told me not to cry and not to tell you or I wouldn't get my treat from 7-Eleven," Willow says.

"That's not true, Willow. She's making that up." Katy takes Willow's empty cereal bowl to the sink and starts doing the dishes with her back toward me.

"Katy, turn around and talk to me." I poke her shoulder. "This looks serious." I guide Katy to Willow who is still sitting at the kitchen counter. "She needs to be seen by a doctor. What were you thinking? What *are* you thinking? C'mon Willow, we're going to Children's Hospital emergency."

—

An hour-and-a-half hour later a nurse is inspecting Willow's finger.

"She'll need an X-ray to see if the finger is broken," says the nurse. "When did this happen?"

"Tuesday," I say.

The nurse looks shocked.

I realize this looks bad. It's Friday. A child with possibly a broken finger is not brought to the hospital until three days after it happened? I wonder what the nurse is thinking. Neglect? Child abuse? At best, irresponsible. *Shit!*

The wait for the results of the X-ray seems interminable. It feels as if I'm awaiting a verdict deeming me an unfit mother. Finally, the doctor enters our curtained emergency cubicle and explains that Willow's finger is badly sprained but not broken. She won't need a cast, just a splint.

There is some grace after all.

That evening I crawl into bed around eleven thirty only to be woken two hours later by a knock on the front door.

What the hell? I jump out of bed, grab my robe, and go to the front window to check out who's there. It's the police, with Katy. I open the door.

The burly police officer doesn't say hello, instead he asks accusingly, "Are you her mother?"

He points at Katy, who is standing beside him—or rather, trying to stand, as she is clearly drunk, her eyes bloodshot, her mouth perched in a Mona Lisa–esque grin.

"She's the nanny," I say.

"We picked her up on Taylor Way speeding. She seems to have been drinking, too. Is that your Subaru she was driving?"

"Yes, is it okay?"

"Yes, you'll find it parked on Clyde at the bottom of the hill, just off Taylor Way. Here're the keys."

The officer gathers information about Katy and myself.

"That's all for now, ma'am. We'll be in touch. Goodnight."

I thank the officer and show Katy to her bed. She flops on it. I'm running out of emotion, and childcare. Fuck it all. I'll deal with this in the morning.

When Katy strolls out of her bedroom at noon the next day, I ask her to go retrieve the credit card and any petty cash she has. When she returns I tell her we need to chat and walk her down to the end of the family room. We sit on the love seat facing each other, and she gives some feeble excuse for her abhorrent actions—something about hanging out in a pub with some friends who were visiting from Scotland. I'm so appalled it's hard to be civil, but I tell her in a calm and authoritative voice that she is to pack her things and leave.

Luckily, Mom has come out from Toronto to visit Rob and help me out, so I'm not totally screwed. I go to the hospital daily. Barry is getting weaker and weaker, and parts of his body are going numb. He says he's afraid to go to sleep. "I don't know what my body will be like when I wake up," he tells me. "Like, this morning, my whole right leg was numb."

Tuesday night, September 17, when I'm lying beside him in his hospital bed, Barry is dozing off but keeps opening one eye to see if I'm still there. He's sweet and tender. With droopy eyelids and a squeeze of my hand, he says, "Hawney, perhaps I'm ready for the big sleep."

My heart aches to hear this. Is he ready for some peace? Oh, my hawney.

Barry needs morphine regularly for his pain, and it sometimes works for only twenty minutes. He's nauseous. His hearing is going. He can't get up to use the washroom. He vacillates between agitation and composure. He can still enjoy a baseball game on the hospital TV, which swings around as close to his face as he needs.

The following night, I lie beside him in his bed, and we watch *Seinfeld* together on that TV. It's the episode where George becomes very uncomfortable about the fact that he got a massage from a man. George tells Jerry that he thinks "it moved" during the massage and starts to have doubts about his sexual orientation. Mindless. Just what we need.

The show ends, and as I lean up to turn off the TV, Barry says—at least, I think I hear him say—"Grandfather's waiting."

He's talking about his father, who died two years earlier.

It's now definite. He's very close to death. What am I going to do? He doesn't want to die in the hospital. He needs to be at home.

I hardly sleep that night, haunted by a sense of urgency. Early the next morning, I am panicky; I can't get to the hospital fast enough. Barry might die before I get there. I must talk to Kasheemo. I must tell him we know Barry is dying. It doesn't matter what the tests say. He wants to die at home. *Please do something. Please help us.*

I find myself thinking the most horrid thought in the world: *If he is going to die, dear Lord, please let him die. This lack of resolution, the possibility of his living in a wheelchair, this not knowing, this fear of living with an invalid . . . Please, may this be over?*

I'm a horrid person. Am I really wanting my husband to die? Am I really wanting him to die, instead of for him to live with permanent impairment?

Kasheemo and I go for coffee in the hospital cafeteria. As we fill our cups from the dispenser, I rehearse in my head what I'm going to say when we are face-to-face.

We sit down across from each other, and the moment is suddenly upon me. Kasheemo takes a sip of coffee, and I stare down at mine. I shake my head, look up, and say, "I don't even drink coffee, Dr. Kasheemo." I sigh and continue with what I want to tell him. "We feel Barry is losing the battle. This is such a trial for him, being in the hospital. We want him home. We need him home. We need him home as soon as possible." I pause and realize Kasheemo looks a little confused. "Dr. Kasheemo," I say, "Barry knows he is dying. I know he's dying. I feel it right down to my core, in my very marrow, and . . . and . . . he wants to die at home."

Kasheemo says, "Okay." He puts both his hands on the table in a gesture of decisiveness. "We'll do a set of extensive tests immediately. Maybe this will give us something. Plus, the results of the brain biopsy should be ready today."

It seems like he's looking for a scientific sign that will confirm what Barry and I already know. The battle is over.

11

"Whenever God Shines His Light"
Van Morrison
Thursday, September 19, 1991

After my conversation with Kasheemo I spend most of the day in Barry's hospital room. He drifts in and out of sleep, but when he's awake, he's alert and suffering from waves of nausea and extreme weakness, so much so that he can't lift his legs off the bed or his arms above his head.

A nurse arrives and tells us they're about to come with a gurney and take him out for a number of tests—more tests to try to determine what is causing Barry's swift degeneration. The tests include a bone scan (yet another fucking bone scan), an X-ray of his chest (yet another fucking X-ray), and an ultrasound of his abdomen (yet another fucking ultrasound). As the nurse continues, my mind retreats—or maybe it's my heart. I'm suddenly not present. I'm recoiling from all this overload of medical information and intrusion into my once-normal and promising life.

Within a couple of hours, Dr. Bradley enters the hospital room.

"Hello, Dr. Bradley. Good to see you. Pleasant surprise."

"Yes, Dr. Kasheemo has been keeping me in the loop, and it

sounds like you're having a difficult time of it. I have the results of today's tests. He's, uh, well, all clear," he says hesitantly, as he holds up medical papers in his right hand. "Gallbladder, liver, kidneys, spleen, pancreas. The heart's good. There is no sign of lymphoma cells anywhere. Either Barry is in remission or the lymphoma is eluding all tests. And the bone scan—well, the bone scan has not changed for months. Some inexplicable abnormalities. There's nothing new here." He shakes his head and looks at Barry and then at me. "Nothing to explain the rapid decline."

"That was quick, getting those results. Thanks, Dr. Bradley." *But, I think, I'm not sure no news is good news.*

"We're still waiting on some results—for the bloodwork and the chest X-ray and the brain biopsy," Bradley says. "I'll let you know when we have those."

He forces a little smile and leaves the room. I turn to Barry, and before I can say anything, his eyes are closed and his head seems to settle more deeply into the pillow.

The next morning, Friday, September 20, I'm in the kitchen, getting the kids ready for school, when the phone rings. It's Barry, and he's in a frenzied state.

"I had a seizure," he says. "I woke up. I woke up with my arms and legs all moving uncontrollably. I couldn't breathe or swallow."

"Are you okay?" I ask. "Are you sure it was a seizure? How horrifying."

"I know it was a seizure. The nurse confirmed it."

"Are you okay now?"

"I think I'm okay, but I need you here, hawney. Can you come right—"

"Of course, sweetie. I just need to . . ." I was about to explain that I need to get Willow ready and take her to school, but I don't need to bog him down with details. Mom is visiting, and I can let her take over. No nanny this morning. "I'll be there as soon as possible. There are a couple of things I need to do with the kids, but I'll be there as soon as possible."

I tell Mom what to put in Willow's lunch and to remember that her school project is due today.

"I think she might need a sweater; it could be windy," I say to Mom. "Are you sure you know how the car seats do up? The buckle on Dixie's is sticky, so make sure it clips tightly."

Mom is listening intently. "Remind me the route to the school again, dear."

"Oh, of course," I say, but hesitate, thinking that explaining it will almost take longer than driving Willow to school myself. Besides, I don't have the patience to go through the details of the circuitous route. "You know, I'll take her this morning. Can you just help get her ready and then stay with Dixie?"

Mom is able to help by brushing Willow's teeth and distracting Dixie as I pack up Willow's stuff. Willow wants me to take a popsicle to her dad, and I suggest she gives him something that won't melt. We settle on a few Oreo cookies, which they both like.

This all means, of course, that I'm later getting to Barry than he wanted, and he's short with me when I get there. "Where were you?"

"Oh, Mom didn't know the route to get Willow to school, and . . ." I sigh. "So I did it. I'm here now."

Bradley enters the room. "Hello. Hear it was a rough morning. How're you feeling, Barry?"

Barry explains his seizure to Bradley, who listens sympathetically and then says, "Well, the results of the X-ray are here, and your lungs are clear and there are no chest wall abnormalities. For some reason, the blood biopsy isn't ready yet, but I'll keep you posted."

"Thanks so much, Dr. Bradley," I say. "You've been great."

Barry's mom and a sister and a brother visit throughout the day, and he's relatively perky—when he's not asleep, that is. He's now okay with having a few family members drop in. I think he's relieved he hasn't had another seizure. He's able to sign some papers for work that his brother brings in. I suspect this may have to do with life insurance. Barry even eats part of the McDonald's burger his sister delivers.

I head home in the afternoon and at about four o'clock start making phone calls to prospective nannies. One, Lainey, seems appropriate and is willing to come into a household in the state of stress mine is in at the moment. She's twenty-one and looking for a full-time position while she takes evening courses to qualify for nursing school. I'm interviewing her on the phone and taking notes when I hear the call-waiting signal. I worry it could be Barry or a doctor, but Lainey is in the middle of telling me how she helped out at her mom's daycare, and I'm trying to wait until she takes a breath, but she doesn't stop and I hear the beep two more times.

"I was always the one who played games with the little ones on—"

I hear another beep and cut in. "I'm so sorry to cut you off, Lainey, but I'm getting another call and I really have to go. It could be a doctor I need to talk to. Can you start Monday? I'll call you back."

"Oh, that's—"

I hear another beep and hang up on her. *Shit, she probably doesn't even want to work for me now.* But, God, who would? Kind of a heavy situation to parachute into: two little girls with a dying dad and other family members floating in and out. Fuck.

It's Dr. Bradley calling, and I am so relieved not to have missed his call.

"The white-blood-cell count is in, Rosemary." He stops.

"Yes, yes. What is it?"

"Rosemary, do you know the normal range?"

"Yeah. I think around four thousand?"

"Yes, well, between four thousand and eleven thousand." He stops again.

"What are they, Dr. Bradley? Just tell me, what are they?" I say, unable to hide the irritation in my voice.

"Forty thousand, and half of them are malignant."

My head goes down, and my left hand loosens its grip on the phone handle as I swallow hard. I lift my right hand to my forehead and cradle it, my right thumb on my right temple, my forefinger and middle finger on my left temple. I squeeze hard and rub, as if maybe if I rub hard enough and tightly enough, I will erase the last eight months.

This is a categorical confirmation that a multitude of lymphoma cells have been hiding in Barry's body for months.

"Rosemary?" Bradley says, startling me. "I know this is tough, and it's been really rough."

"He doesn't have much time, does he, Dr. Bradley?"

"It could be a few days."

"Does he know the blood results?"

"Yes, I just told him."

"Well, I need to make the arrangements to get him home," I say.

"Anything I can do, let me know."

I thank Bradley and say goodbye.

Frantic, I grab my purse, run down the hall, update my mom on what's going on with Barry, and ask her to check Lainey's references and then call her back and hire her. Then I speed to the hospital, my mind racing through what needs to be done right away. I must get Barry home. But how? What about the wheelchair, the commode, the shower stand, the morphine, telling the rest of his family? I'm bombarding myself with unknowns.

At Lions Gate Hospital, I run up the seven flights of stairs again, rush to Barry's bedside, place my lips on his cheek, which is wet with sweat, and keep my mouth there for what I wish could be forever.

Freezing that moment in my mind, I take my lips away, but I stay standing there with my face inches from his. I put both hands on his cheeks and stare into his eyes. The one eyelid that is not paralyzed shut is droopy, the eyeball glassy, the white a murky mix of yellow and red. His eyes pop out of his sunken, gray face. I pray his body can hold out until I can get him home, which I can't organize until tomorrow.

"Oh, hawney," he says, "I need to come home. I don't know how to die. I don't know how to die."

"I know, my darling," I tell him, not letting go of his face or losing eye contact. I can practically see the blood draining from his face, the life draining from his body. He's slipping away, as if this final test confirming that he's indeed on the way out has given him permission to stop fighting. He's letting go.

"You can hang in there, hawney. We need you at home."

Rosemary, I tell myself, *keep it together.* But I don't. I start to whimper, the precursor to a collapse. *Rosemary, control it. Wait until bedtime.*

"This is no time for a hysterical grief fit, my beautiful wifey," he says, easing the tension slightly. And he's right. There is too much to do.

"We'll get you home tomorrow," I say. "There's lot to get in order, but I'll get you there, hawney. Don't doubt it." I convince myself as well that we'll get him home in time to die there, not at the hospital.

"I know. I'm okay for now, hawney," he says, granting me the time to do what needs to be done. I feel as if he's really saying, *You do what you need to do. I'll hang on.* "But I need to sleep and I'm afraid to sleep. I might have another seizure."

"It must be terrifying," I say. "Janey is coming to stay here with you tonight." Janey is Barry's oldest sister.

"Where?"

"I think they'll bring a cot in. Your sisters love you very much. Your family loves you. Your friends love you. I love you so much, hawney."

His eye slowly closes as he drifts off to sleep.

I head home, pour myself a huge goblet of chilled Bâtard-Montrachet, go lie down on my bed, curl into the fetal position, and collapse into a ball of sobs and shakes like an electric kettle of water that has been stuck at near boiling for too long and has finally broken into its full, committed growl.

On Saturday morning, September 21, I wake up knowing that before I do anything else, I need to go for a jog to anchor myself, to fortify myself, to review in my head exactly what needs to be done—how I will approach the day and get my husband home to die.

I run along the West Vancouver seawall, between the beaches and the seaside parks, squealing children on swings, owners walking dogs big and small, waves splashing on the shore. There's a cool September breeze coming off the ocean, and I take a moment to admire the seductive view of the Gulf Islands—bathed in the morning sun's soft glow, the hills layered and extending into the distance, just like in a Toni Onley painting.

This is comforting territory that provides a safe backdrop for me to go inward and focus. *Mom and Nana can look after the kids. Maybe they can clean our sheets so Barry can come home to a bed that smells of the Sunlight detergent he likes. His sisters Samantha and Janey can get the wheelchair—and I need to remember to ask them if they can get a commode and shower stand, too. Someone needs to make dinner. And what about the morphine? Maybe Mom can get that.*

I need to get to the hospital as soon as possible to be with Barry. I need to call the woman at the nursing agency to get an on-call nurse for the weekend.

As I rhythmically pound one foot in front of the other, my brain sharpens, my heart strengthens, my spirit brightens, and my body rejuvenates. I am empowered. I am ready.

—

When I arrive at hospital room 714, Janey, Barry's sister, is massaging his feet and he's smiling.

"Find out how to do this, Rosemary," he says. "It takes the pain away."

I kiss him and give Janey a little air hug around her neck as she continues her massage.

"Loving kindness is a profound source of healing energy," Janey says.

"I talked to Janey earlier," I say to Barry, putting my purse down on the hospital chair. "She said you had a difficult night."

"I woke up with a start, not able to breathe, and then when I finally caught my breath, I had sharp pains in my ribs," he explains, as he lifts both hands to hold his chest. He is talking slowly and almost slurring his words. I can see him tire as he speaks.

"He called the nurse a number of times," says Janey, as she stops massaging his feet.

"But no seizure?" I ask.

"No," he and Janey say in unison.

"But he would wake up and smile at me," she says.

"I kept forgetting she was here," Barry says.

"Thanks so much, Janey," I say, and then I talk them both through the plans for bringing Barry home. "I'll stay with him for a bit, and perhaps you and Samantha can take care of picking up the wheelchair and commode in your truck and check in with my mom at home to see if they need anything. The ambulance to take him home is ordered for six thirty. Right now, I need to get back and meet the nurse there."

I make it home minutes before the nurse, who is a little early. Her name is Nina. She's dressed in blue hospital scrubs. She has a glowing smile and a shiny, dark ponytail.

I show her the bedroom, and Willow rushes in to meet her. "What's all that stuff you're putting on the dresser?" she asks, as Nina starts to lay out medical supplies.

The phone rings, and when I go to answer it, I hear Willow saying to the nurse, "My daddy sleeps on that side of the bed."

It's my mom calling from the pharmacy; she can't buy the morphine there. The pharmacist gets on the phone and says we need to go to a special pharmacy.

Why didn't anyone tell me this? Jesus Christ. I kick the bottom of the kitchen cupboard and immediately regret it when I feel the resulting pain coursing through my foot. Dixie walks into the kitchen just in time to witness my freak-out.

"We're not supposed to kick the cupboards, Mommy."

"Yes, dear, yes, dear, you're perfectly right. We're definitely not supposed to kick the cupboards," I say, in as controlled a voice as possible. "Here, have a lollipop," I tell her, grabbing a sucker from the candy jar. "I have to call Dr. Bradley right away."

I call Bradley, who always seems to come through. He talks me down and says he'll call in a prescription at a pharmacy that stays open late near the hospital. It'll be waiting for me.

Willow comes into the kitchen as I hang up the phone, and she tugs at my hand. "Daddy's coming home tonight?" she asks, and I nod.

Dixie jumps up and down, echoing, "Yeah, Daddy coming home! Daddy coming home!"

"Hey, I want a lollipop, too," Willow exclaims.

My fucking God, I'm going to explode. I hand her a sucker.

The doorbell rings. It's Nana, whom I'm expecting.

"Oh, Nana, just in time. Come on in," I say with relief. "I'm just explaining that we're bringing Daddy home in an ambulance tonight. He's not doing too well, but he'll be home. In fact"—I check my watch—"it's five forty-five. I gotta go."

Nana looks at the children, who have followed me to the front door. "Lollies for appetizers, eh? Well, I hope that won't spoil your appetite for my meat loaf."

I pause and look into Nana's blue eyes. "I really hope you're doing all right in the middle of all this," I say. "You've been such a rock. Thank you. Oh, and mom will be home soon. I'm sure she'll love your meatloaf too. You don't need to stay. Thank you again."

I kiss them all goodbye and fly out the door.

Twenty minutes later, I'm at the special pharmacy, picking up the morphine, then racing to get to Barry before the ambulance comes to pick him up at six thirty. I park the car and run into the hospital, and when I think about the fucking slow elevators, I decide to run up those seven flights of stairs again. It's six thirty on the nose, and I begin to panic that the ambulance people will take Barry away before I get to see him.

I reach the seventh floor, pull open the door, and run down the east-wing hallway, clipping a doctor on my way down. "Sorry, sorry, I'm sorry," I call over my shoulder, not even looking back.

I can't. I can't. I can't let them take my husband away without my being there for him.

I rush into the room—and I see my terror was all for naught. He's simply lying there, his good eye partially open. When he sees me, the corner of the good side of his mouth turns up. But he seems dopey and not totally there.

I kiss his forehead and hold his hand. "We're waiting for the ambulance, hawney."

He nods his head slightly, but I'm not entirely sure he understands exactly what's going on. A nurse comes in, and I ask if he knows what's happening.

"A certain amount," she says. "His behavior can be attributed to the morphine or to the disease, likely both."

Then we wait, and wait, and wait, and wait.

The ambulance is late. How fucking late can the ambulance be? I'm desperate to get Barry home.

The paramedics finally arrive at 714 East at 9:00 p.m., two and a half hours late. As they transfer Barry to the gurney, I hurry to my car to try to beat them home.

I do beat the ambulance back, and when I get home I check in with the nurse and let everyone know that Barry is on his way and that he's not totally coherent.

When the ambulance seems to be taking longer than it should, I get impatient. *Bring my husband home! What the hell?* I thought ambulances were supposed to be fast.

My head and my heart are in competition for my attention, but neither is winning in my blur of thoughts. I take a bottle of wine out of the fridge, set it on the counter, and pour myself a generous glass. I'm taking a big gulp when the phone rings.

"Is this Mrs. Keevil?"

"Yes."

"Yes, I'm calling from the North Shore Ambulance. We're heading to your house with your husband here, and we're uncertain whether you want a no-code resuscitation order. Normally, we would be taking a person in this condition *to* the hospital."

"What? No! He's coming home. What is a no-code resuscitation order?"

"We need official direction. We need to know if it is a no-code resuscitation order. Are we to revive him if he has a heart attack?"

"Well, no, no, I don't think so, but I need to check on that." I can't think straight or make any more decisions. If Barry dies in the ambulance, then the ambulance will be delivering his dead body. Holy fuck. I have no idea what to do. I think I can probably get ahold of Bradley. "Can I check with the doctor and call right back? I'll call you right back. He's coming home. Don't turn around. Give me your number, please." I write it down on the steno pad that I keep with me at all times. Bradley's number is on the pad as well. Thank God, I reach him right away. He informs me that this *is* a "no-code resuscitation order" situation. The paramedics will not revive Barry if he has a heart attack. "He'll make it home, Rosemary," he reassures me.

As I'm fumbling to dial the ambulance, I can't get my fingers to do what I'm telling them to do, and I start to cry.

"Mommy, Mommy." Dixie comes up to me and hits my thigh. "Gramma is making me to go bed. I don't wanna go to bed. I wanna wait for Daddy."

"Dixie, I'm busy. You need to go to bed. I'll—"

"Mommy, Mommy . . ."

Thankfully, my mom appears and shuttles Dixie off.

I reach the ambulance and confirm a no-code resuscitation order.

Within the half hour, the paramedics arrive and transfer Barry to his bed. Although he's delirious and unable to talk, I have a strong sense he knows he's home. The nurse straightens the sheets around him and sets his head straight on the pillow, making him comfortable. Willow comes to his bedside, and he shows some recognition that she is there, touching his face and kissing him on the cheek, even though he says nothing and his eyes are closed.

The nurse has a thermometer in her hand, about to tend to Barry, so I say to Willow, "Let's get you ready for bed."

We go down the hall, and my mom has actually gotten Dixie into bed, despite her protestations. Leaving the girls with their grandma, I go into the kitchen and get my glass of wine from the fridge, where I put it before I ran back to the hospital. Leaving the fridge door open, I take a long, cool gulp and feel it dancing down my throat so gracefully, I need more. I fill up the glass and take it with me back to the bedroom, where the nurse is checking Barry's temperature. It's just risen from 101 to 102 degrees. I set my wineglass on the bedside table and lie beside Barry on the bed.

He has apnea spells and doesn't breathe for twenty-five to thirty seconds at a time, after which point he gasps, startling me. This is followed by rapid breaths. I'm lying at his right side with my right arm on his chest, my right hand on his left shoulder. He cannot communicate, but I know he knows he's home and I am beside him. He keeps moving his left arm toward me. It flops on his stomach, and I take it and massage it. It slides back down to his side again, but he flops it back up again. He stops breathing. He struggles to breathe. He flops his hand toward me. It falls back.

"I love you so much, hawney. I love you," I say, as I feel our hearts melding together.

I know he hears me. And he's communicating with me, too. We are one.

Practical thoughts float in and out, like, *When will I call Barry's family members?* They need to be here soon, but not now. I need him to myself. I am greedy for him. He will wait for them. There is time. Somehow, I just know there is time.

The next morning, Sunday, September 22, I call Barry's mom and his older siblings—Nathan, Janey, Samantha, and Henry—and let them know they should come to the house. They've all been to see Barry over the length of his illness and have wanted to help, but Barry said he was uncomfortable with too much visiting. He also has five younger half-siblings from a different mother (Grandfather was busy), who have also been very caring and supportive.

It becomes quite a busy home with some dozen people, including my mom and the girls, mingling about. But what can you say when you know the only reason you're gathered is that your loved one is about to die? We make tea. We make coffee. We drink tea. We drink coffee. Silences are awkward, as is small talk, but at least the kids provide consistent distraction. They love having so many family members around.

We all congregate in the kitchen, the family room, and the living room, but mainly in the living room, as it's a strategic location. It faces the hallway that runs from the master bedroom to the kitchen, which means that when someone who has just been in to see Barry leaves the master bedroom, they have to walk into the hall. Anyone in the living room can see them, so it's a cue for another person to go and say their goodbyes.

Everyone graciously defers to my need for Barry, subtly careful not to visit when I may want to and not to intrude when I'm visiting. But even when I'm not in the bedroom, I'm attached to Barry. Our relationship has become symbiotic; it's like the one a pregnant mother has with her unborn child. It's a profound connection.

The nurse tells me Barry's temperature has reached 107 degrees. I call Dr. Bradley and tell him.

"I'll be there soon," he says, in a tone that means he is not going to try to revive Barry. I'm unsure why he is even coming, but I trust him. I set the receiver on its cradle and go stand at the kitchen counter with my mom and Nana. I fill my cup with freshly brewed tea.

"Wow, fresh tea. If in doubt, drink tea, I always say," I exclaim, trying to be light. But then I add, "Barry's temperature is getting really high. Dr. Bradley is on his way. Why would—"

"Mommy, Mommy," Dixie interrupts me. She's standing in front of the fridge, holding the door open and staring inside. I ignore her.

"Why would Dr. Bradley be coming? And—"

"Mommy, Mommy," Dixie says again.

"Yes, sweetheart." I go over to the fridge, kneel down, and look in it with her at the grapes, the dill pickles, the eggs, the cheddar cheese, the vegetables, the milk, the orange juice, and wonder what looks enticing to her. "Do you want something?"

She turns her eyes away from the food and looks right at me. "Grandfather's here," she declares.

I stare at her incredulously.

She was nine months old when Barry's dad died. That was two years ago.

I look up at Nana and my mom. All of us are wide-eyed with shock.

"I just got the shivers," my mom says.

"Yes, dear," I look back at Dixie and hold her arm. "Grandfather's here."

I immediately go and lie beside Barry, set my hand on his chest, and tell him what Dixie just said. His chest lifts up ever so slightly. I know he's telling me, *I know, my hawney, I'm ready. I know Grandfather is here to help me pass over.* Then he drifts off into sleep—but seconds later, an apnea spell comes on and he's fighting for air again.

Uncle Henry brings a speaker into the bedroom and puts on Van Morrison's CD *Avalon Sunset*, then leaves the room. I'm left alone with Barry. I lie beside him, close my eyes, and savor this moment, the last minutes of his life. The words of the love songs permeate our united hearts.

I whisper in his ear, "I love you so much, my darling."

He stops breathing for shorter periods of time now, and when he catches his breath and breathes again, it is much more restful. He's not struggling for air.

"You've been through so much, you're brave, you're wonderful, you've had such a struggle, I love you, I love you." I start sobbing and can't talk, can't tell him how much I love him. I'm crying too hard.

My tears finally stop, and I enter that collected and gentle zone I feel after the physical purging of emotions that have become irrepressible. I know I need to allow Barry's family to share these last moments with him, so I slowly move myself away from him, keeping my eye on him for as long as possible. I go into the bathroom and make a feeble attempt at touching up my makeup, then walk down the hall to the living room, where some family members are—the signal that they can visit Barry now—and make my way to the kitchen to drink some more tea.

As soon as I get the kettle on, Samantha comes in and says, "The nurse says his heart rate and pulse are slowing down."

I follow her back to the bedroom, where the nurse is beside Barry with two fingers on his left wrist. She steps back, gently shaking her head, and whispers, "I can barely find a pulse."

Everyone gathers around Barry, who is lying on the far side of the king bed, and I kneel on the bed to his right, between family members.

Both of his eyes are now open but blank. I take his right hand and guide him into death with words from my living soul to his departing soul. "Go find peace," I say. "You've fought such a tough battle. Take our love with you. You're so special. You're so wonderful."

Willow comes into the bedroom, and my gut tells me this is too traumatic for a five-year-old to witness. I hear myself telling her she should not be here, and Barry's brother Henry leads her out. Dr. Bradley appears and walks over to Barry's left side. He moves the pillows out from under Barry's head and lays him flat. Barry starts making gasping noises—groaning, wheezing, croaking noises. He gets quieter and quieter and struggles less and less.

Then . . . nothing. He's gone.

Dr. Bradley closes Barry's eyelids and stands up and out of the way. Someone puts *Avalon Sunset* on again. I lie with Barry and cling to him. Slowly, the family members all leave the bedroom and I'm alone with him again. He's no longer with us, but he's still warm. His body is making gurgling noises, seeming to settle. I straddle his body and then lie on top of him and squeeze him tightly, like I haven't been able to for seven months. I cannot be too close to him. I cannot hug him too tightly. I squeeze and squeeze as Van Morrison sings a line about squeezing me and not leaving me.

"You have some peace now, my hawney. It's been a horrid, horrid battle. You've been very brave. It's been horrible seeing you be so sick and knowing you have to leave your three girls. We miss you so. I love you so. Please have some peace. Know I love you forever." Van continues singing, "Have I Told You Lately."

12

"You Are My Sunshine"
Ray Charles

Sunday, September 22, 1991

B arry lies there in our bed.

What do we do now? I wonder.

Janey knows, from when their dad (Grandfather) died of cancer two years ago in his home in Vancouver. She knows not to call the undertaker right away.

"Wait," she suggests. "Wait until we all have some time with Barry. Call when we're ready to say goodbye."

I had the foresight to have Barry's will delivered to the house over the weekend, but I still haven't opened it. But now I need to know whether Barry gave specific instructions for his body. I walk into my office and see the brown, eight-by-eleven-inch envelope sitting there. Plain, nothing written on the outside, but what is inside is anything but plain.

I pause, my upper teeth biting my lower lip with such pressure that it begins to hurt, then walk in slow motion to my desk, my right hand stretched out toward it. My eyes close as I lower my hand to the document—but then I freeze. Opening this envelope will make Barry's death too real. It has been surreal up to this point.

I force myself to open the envelope, pull out the papers inside, and lay them down. The top page is entitled "Memorandum." Below that, on the left-hand side of the page, is the word "cremation"—exactly what I was looking for.

Thank you, Barry, for making this part as easy as possible.

"It is my wish that I be cremated and that Rosemary choose some quiet evening at sunset in Seratami to paddle around our islands, scattering the ashes on our usual swimming run. You might consider saving a teaspoon for deposit in the front lip (northeast corner) of the sand trap at the front right of the ninth green at the Whistler Golf Club. (Dave and Heather may recall this is where I sunk a birdie chip in 1990.)"

I know instinctively that before the undertaker comes, we need to change Barry's clothes and dress him as if he were going to the cottage on a holiday. I have Willow and Dixie help me decide what he should wear. We choose his faded orange-and-pink Mauna Kea Beach Hotel golf hat, his green khaki shorts, and one of his favorite T-shirts, which has pictures of the girls on it, along with the words "Blame It on the Rain," printed across the front. Willow and Dixie used to sing that Milli Vanilli song so often that Meredith had the shirt custom-made.

Barry also needs something on his feet. We choose his beige socks with blue trim and his blue runners. He'll also need his sunglasses, seeing as he's going to be on Lake Seratami at sunset.

Janey and I dress Barry, but his body is getting hard and discolored as rigor mortis sets in. There are large, dark patches on his back and side, just under the skin, as if maybe blood is gathering in splotches near the surface of his body. But his facial skin looks creamy and smooth. He wears this wry little grin—a better smile than he's had in months of facial paralysis. A lone candle flickers at his bedside, highlighting the side of his face and his expression—his so very untroubled expression. I cry; my sweetheart has finally found some peace.

Willow brings Barry some wilted yellow roses and a school note-book with "I Heart U" written all over it. She places them on his stomach. Then Dixie adds a gold-colored paper crown, like the ones that snap out of Christmas cracker toys—a tradition at our Christmas dinners. She also brings him a fluffy black-and-white panda puppet that he gave her from the hospital gift shop—but then she takes it back. Then she puts her hands on Barry's cheeks and squishes his face so his lips are all puckered up—like she might do if she were pretending he was a fish.

"Don't, Dixie," Willow cautions. "He's dead."

"Uh," I say, entirely uncertain about what to think of what Dixie is doing. I have no idea what is appropriate.

Oh, fuck it, I say to myself. "It's probably okay."

Barry lies on the bed for two hours as family members say their goodbyes. Finally, Janey and I decide it's time to call the undertaker—but then he doesn't arrive right away and I become concerned about Barry's body stiffening even more from rigor mortis.

It's five thirty—a good three hours after Barry died—when the undertaker rings the doorbell. Barry's sister Samantha leads him into the bedroom. His large, rotund frame fills up most of the doorway. Willow and Dixie and I are at Barry's side, and this time it's Willow who is squishing Barry's cheeks with both her hands. Somewhat embarrassed that she's doing this in front of the undertaker, I say, "Maybe you shouldn't do that."

"That's okay. I'm Irish," the undertaker says, with a gap-toothed, jovial grin.

I assume he's making a reference to Irish wakes, which I know are traditionally merry. I smile.

The undertaker and an assistant put a stretcher beside Barry and lower it to the height of the bed. Barry is still wearing the outfit the girls and I chose for him. They transfer him onto the stretcher, cover him with a sheet, and push him out of the bedroom.

Daddy is taken away, never to return.

It is Sunday, September 22, 1991. Barry dies at two thirty in the afternoon. He is forty-one years old. I just turned thirty-seven. Willow is five, and Dixie is two and a half. Barry and I were married six years, eleven months, and two days.

Later that week, the autopsy reveals that Barry's body was infested with lymphoma—in the sac around the heart, the abdomen, and the spinal cord at the base of the brain. This non-Hodgkins lymphoma—insidious, sinister, cruel, and tenacious—hid itself from the doctors for seven months, ever since the first chemo treatment on Monday, February 11, 1991.

A couple of months after Barry passes away, I take Willow away for the weekend, just the two of us. I'm hoping that if she has me all to herself, she might be able to tap into how she's feeling and talk to me about her father's death. Then I'll try to do the same thing with Dixie.

I choose to take Willow to Victoria, the capital of British Columbia. The trip is not too long and is a bit of an adventure in itself—a two-hour ferry ride over the Georgia Strait to Vancouver Island, then a half-hour drive from the ferry terminal to Victoria.

We stay in the legendary Empress Hotel, which has graced Victoria's inner harbor since 1908. The Empress is known for its grand, château-esque architecture and its traditional afternoon high tea, enjoyed by royalty and dignitaries alike—and me, of course. We also order room service, watch movies, and shop. Willow is so clingy it makes me claustrophobic, but this time together seems necessary to draw her out about this profound loss in her life, the death of her beloved daddy. Over dinner, I ask her what she remembers about the day he died. "I remember when he came home and I asked Aunt Samantha if Daddy was going to die today, because he didn't look good. He looked like this." She reclines in her chair, eyes closed, arms and hands flopped out. "And I said to Aunt Samantha, 'I hope Daddy doesn't die today.' Then Dianne and Dixie and I were watching TV and we heard the nurse in the hallway, saying, 'Barry Keevil is dead.' Dixie and I ran down the hall and looked in the bedroom, and everyone was crying. Uncle Henry wouldn't let me see my daddy and took me away, and I ran into my room and slammed the door and hid behind the blue chair to cry. I had dinner there—beans, potatoes, carrots, macaroni, and brussels sprouts. Dixie ate with me. I wanted to cry. I love Daddy. He was my best friend. Now you are my best friend."

I keep running and swimming to deal with my stress, and visiting the wine cellar, as every day has become a Bâtard kind of day, as Barry and I dubbed challenging days what seems like so long ago. Sometimes I don't even take the time to find the Bâtard-Montrachet, however—I just grab the bottle closest to the wine-cellar door and end up having to suffer through a Corton-Charlemagne or an Australian Rosemount.

I read voraciously about how to grieve, especially how to help my children grieve. I buy so many books at Duthie bookstore about death and dying that the saleslady asks me, "Do you work on a palliative-care unit?"

Everything I read says it's imperative that I help the girls do something with their sadness, confusion, and anger; otherwise, they'll develop serious issues at school, with alcohol and/or drugs, and with forming loving relationships. Although this seems a far too formidable and onerous task, I do try to apply some of the suggestions I read in these books as I navigate my way through these turbulent days.

I learn that I should tell the girls' teachers and caregivers what they are going through, as they need as much support as they can get, and that I have to encourage them to talk about their feelings. I also need to be aware of their level of development when it comes to processing grief. Dixie, as a preschooler, will not understand death as a permanent condition; it's possible she'll think Barry has just gone away for a while. But elementary school children, like Willow, who is in kindergarten, can comprehend the finality.

The books also tell me not to push Willow and Dixie into "normal activities" before they're ready. Grieving takes time and is exhausting. They warn that grieving children can develop "maladaptive behaviors." This certainly rings true for my girls. In the months following Barry's death, Willow and Dixie tell the nanny, Lainey, they hate her. They tell Nana they hate her. Dixie says she doesn't love anybody. She tells everyone, including her teacher and classmates, including shoppers in the supermarket, "My daddy's dead, dead, dead." Once, she tells a stranger, "It's my birthday, and my daddy's dead." Willow is somewhat more subdued about this information, but she does tell random people her daddy has died, though I think many don't believe her.

"Who do I tell about Daddy dying?" Willow asks me one day.

I explain that she can tell her teachers and friends and friends' parents, but that if she tells someone, she should probably explain that Daddy was fine last Christmas and then he got sick with cancer and died in September. She reminisces about our last, cozy Christmas with Barry, when he was healthy and we all went skating on Alta Lake at Whistler.

Willow understands that her grandfather and Daddy are together in heaven now. At night she sobs in bed, sobs from deep in her heart, from her very core. Heart crying. She is having nightmares. She dreams I die in a car accident. She continues to have the dreams where the yellow eyes at her window haunt her.

It often happens that Willow and Dixie have screaming outbursts simultaneously, in stereo. This can happen at any time, day or night, and it sure as hell seems like a "maladaptive behavior," but what the fuck am I supposed to do about it? On Thanksgiving, we're driving through heavy traffic to Aunt Janey's for dinner, and Dixie starts screaming—and then Willow starts screaming that she can't hear the music we're playing because Dixie is screaming.

But bedtime is when the "maladaptive behaviors" become diabolical.

One night, when I'm trying to tuck Dixie in, I hear a banging coming from the kitchen, so I tell Dixie I'll be right back. When I leave her room, she starts to scream from her bed, "Mommy, Mommy, Mommy, I wanna sleep with you. I wanna sleep with you. I wanna go into your bed and sleep with you." As relentless as she is, I head to the kitchen, worried about what Willow might be doing. There are two doors to the kitchen. Both are shut. I open one of them to see Willow lying on her back on the floor in front of the other door, which is closed. She is banging the door with both her bare feet.

"Ahhhhhhhhhhhhhhhhhhhhhhhhhhhhhhhhhhh . . ." When she sees me, she begins shrieking as loudly as she can. This has become a regular occurrence—screeching like a never-ending train on a very tight curve. She'll break into this ear-shattering squeal when she gets a tiny cut, when she doesn't get the exact treat she wants when she wants it, or for what seems like no reason whatsoever.

I'm so distraught myself, I'm afraid I might hurt one of them, so I run down the hall, through my bedroom, to my office, shut the door, sit at the desk, put my hands on my face, and bawl. I tell myself I need to get it together. I'm the adult around here. I need to get some control. I need to allow myself a mini-breakdown. I go to the bathroom and grab myself a box of ammunition—Kleenex—and return to my desk and my breakdown position. Five minutes and half a box of Kleenex later, my bawling has been reduced to a whimper. I am rehabilitated enough to face the parasites.

I walk back out and down the hall. There is still screaming going on, but the decibel level has decreased somewhat. When I walk into Dixie's room, her wailing stops and I tell her I will be right back, which seems to be enough to keep her on standby. In the kitchen, Willow has stopped shrieking but is still banging the door with her feet. I get myself a large goblet of wine and sit down beside her on the floor.

"Willow, pleeeeeeeease stop it," I say calmly, whereupon she slows down the tempo of her banging. I set my glass down on the floor, well away from her, and then hold both her feet, at which point she actually stops kicking. I say, "Thank you. That's better. Let's go to bed, sweetheart. Please go to your room, and I'll tuck Dixie in and be right there."

"But that always takes so long. Dixie is such a brat," she complains as she gets up.

I get up with her, put my glass of wine on the counter, and take her hand, leading her into her room. "Just get into bed, and I'll be there as soon as possible, pleeeeease."

"Will you lie with me after you tuck Dixie in?"

"Yes, I will," I say, thinking I'll do anything to get through this.

I go back to Dixie and tell her she can't sleep with me tonight but maybe tomorrow.

"Promise?" she asks.

"Yes," I promise, not really thinking about how I will handle that when tomorrow night comes. I'm in survival mode, just trying to get through tonight.

"Can I have a glass of water?"

"Yes, sweetheart." I get her a glass of water. She sits up in bed and takes two sips and gives it back to me.

"I want Daddy Bear," she demands, wanting a stuffed animal that is not there.

Oh, shit, I think. *Where* is *Daddy Bear?*

"Just a sec," I say, as I head to the family room, where I think I saw it last, and, thank God, there, lying on his back on the sofa, is Daddy Bear—a fluffy, light blue, big-eyed, innocent-looking teddy bear. I take it to Dixie, and when I promise she can sleep with me tomorrow night, she seems calmed enough to let me leave the room.

Next, I go into Willow's room. She is sitting on the side of the bed, waiting for me.

As I walk in, she lies down. I say, "Roll over." I get in bed beside her and spoon her. Her soft hair smells like baby shampoo, and her little five-year-old body feels so fragile. My anger is fighting with my heartache. I'm impatient and just wanting to get my wine and go to my own bed. I keep checking my watch, and after twelve minutes of silence, I roll away from her and sit on the side of the bed.

Willow immediately demands, "Mommy, I want you to lie with me."

"But I just did—for twelve minutes."

"But I want to you lie with me some more."

"I don't care what the fuck you want," I hear myself say, and I spank her bum through the sheets. I have never, ever done this before—never sworn at the kids *or* spanked them. I break down crying.

"I'm so sorry, sweetie," I say, "so very sorry," and I lie beside her, hugging her precious little head against my bosom, against my pounding heart.

I feel like I'm gasping for air and think that this must be what waterboarding is like. Maybe I'm having a panic attack. But this position with her head against my heart is comforting for both of us. I've come to the surface for air, my heart rate is calming, and relief gradually infiltrates my pores. . . . Eventually, we slip into horizontal mode and sleep graces both of us with her peace.

—

We have smatterings of normalcy and tenderness, like the time when I'm tucking Dixie in and we're talking about Barry. She hugs Daddy Bear, and I hug a bear we call Barry Bear, and Dixie says, "Because he's your husband and my daddy." Then she pounces on her bear. "I'm jumping on him like I did before he got sick."

One Sunday, we spend the day at the Chateau, the signature Whistler Fairmont hotel. We toboggan on the kiddie hill in front of the hotel, enjoy the buffet brunch at the Wildflower restaurant, and swim in the pool, and there's not one scream all day.

In more reflective moments, I feel honored to have them both. They're so different and so special in their own ways. And I can see that they truly love each other. They are genuinely happy to see each other after they have been apart.

One sunny day, Willow and I visit Granville Island Market together. We eat lunch on a wooden bench by the water, watching the boats sail by and enjoying the music of the island buskers. I tap my feet and occasionally break out into dance. I tell Willow I'm planning a one-on-one visit with Dixie to Granville Island as well, and she says, "And do all the same things with her that we're doing today."

Without these oases of remission from the tumult, I might act on my desire to drive our red Jeep Cherokee, with the kids in it, right off the highway into the Tantalus Canyon on the ride down from Whistler. Fortunately, this remains a fantasy.

Rob is declining rapidly. On November 20, two months after Barry died, Rob is admitted to St. Paul's after falling and hitting his head. In fact, he has fallen a number of times in the previous two weeks, as his balance is completely off. His body seems to be rejecting him on all fronts. He had a temperature of 104 degrees when he arrived at St.

Paul's and had so much trouble breathing that he was put on oxygen, mouth sores so bad that he was put on a feeding tube, seriously low blood pressure, scarlet eyes, and a widespread skin rash. The doctors suspect an infection in the bloodstream and/or pneumonia. Dr. Katses, the saint of a doctor who has been looking after my brother, tells me he might die very soon.

Although Rob does rally somewhat, he never leaves the hospital. There are repeat scenarios of what happened with Barry. The doctors x-ray Rob's chest, looking for pneumonia, just as they x-rayed Barry's chest, looking for cancerous lumps. Eventually, they conclude there is nothing more they can do for Rob but make him comfortable in his dying days—again, much like what happened with Barry. Rob is assigned to the palliative-care ward of St. Paul's Hospital. His blood transfusions perk him up, just as Barry's transfusions did for him.

Willow worries I am going to be going to the hospital every day to see Rob, just like I did every day to see Barry. I don't go daily, but I do visit regularly, though I stay only an hour or so.

Rob is unable to talk now, and his expression is mostly flat. At first he responded to questions with a shake or nod of the head, but now he's become unresponsive. However, I'm certain that, on at least two occasions, I've seen emotions penetrating through his eyes. Once, he seemed very angry that I did not stay longer—or at least that's how I interpreted it, probably because of the guilt I was feeling. Another time, his eyes emanated abject sadness. I felt ashamed for feeling like I needed to get on with *my* life and not *his* dying.

Rob is off his feeding tube now but cannot feed himself, so the nurses have to feed him. When Mom was in town, she took the time to feed him his puréed mush. I never have, though.

By the end of February 1992, Rob is extremely weak, pale, and gaunt; he looks exactly like what you'd think an AIDS patient would look like. He has tumors in his mouth, and his lips have a permanent crusty layer on them. He is congested and coughing; his eyes are watery and bloodshot; and he is incontinent, noncommunicative, and confused. When I walk into his room on March 12, the nurse is holding his hand and he will not let go. He appears very frightened and weeps continuously.

On March 18, 1992, six months after Barry dies, I receive a phone call from Dr. Katses at 6:45 a.m.

Rob died at 6:28 this morning. He was forty-two years old.

PART TWO:
TEN YEARS LATER

13

"You May Be Right"
Billy Joel

Saturday, April 13, 2002

I roll over in bed, open an eye, and try to focus on the clock radio. It's 8:03 a.m. What day is it? Saturday.

Slowly and blurrily, my brain starts to register where I am and what happened—or didn't happen—last night. *Fuck, what happened last night? More blackouts? Shit, I can't keep doing this. I have to stop. Are the kids okay? Am I okay?*

I sit up, put my left hand to my heart, grab my cell phone with my right hand, and check for messages. Nothing. A good sign, I guess. I head to the bathroom. *Jesus Christ, who is that psycho in the mirror?*

Then I remember. I drove the girls to Timbuktu last night, didn't I? Panic. Are they okay? I check on them: both sound asleep. Thank God. They're here. They're safe.

I drove Willow to her youth group in Coquitlam, right? Right. And Angel. Angel came with us. Angel? Angel? Did I lose Angel? I race out my room and down the stairs. Angel is sitting on the landing.

"Angel." I crouch down and pet her head. She looks up at me with her innocent, bulgy eyes, smushed-in Shih Tzu Chin nose, and protruding lower jaw exposing two crooked teeth. "You're an angel! An ugly angel, but an angel. Well, so ugly, you're cute. Thank God you can't talk. I love you."

I take a shower to clear the confusion out of my head, but it doesn't help. Do I dare call Melba? I feel I must.

"Ah, good morning, Melba. Um, I'm just wondering about last night. You know, um, could you please . . . well, did you take Dixie to . . ." I stop myself, not wanting to reveal how much I don't remember. I need Melba to fill in the blanks.

"Well, um, Rosemree," she stutters, in her strong Filipino accent, "you were late to pick the girls up from school. And, Dixie, well she was crying. She was crying so. You came home and went to bed. I took Dixie to Surrey. You took Willow to Coquitlam. Oh, and, um, Angel."

"Oh," I respond, and I feel my tear ducts bulging. "Well?" I clear my throat. I want her to continue without my having to ask.

"Uh, you came home and went to bed?" She says it like a question—like she's uncertain whether she should actually tell me the truth.

"Did I pick them up?"

"Oh, no, no, no, Rosemary," she says.

I raise my eyebrows in anticipation of the rest of the story.

"I did," she says.

Feeling incredibly grateful that I got through yet another potential catastrophe without injuring myself or one of the girls, I promise myself and God that I will never drink again. I'm feeling fragile but need to scheme about how I can make it up to the girls. I will not drink today. I won't. I'll plan a little Saturday evening at home with their favorite meal. We can rent a movie.

When I hear Willow up and in the bathroom, I go to say good

morning, hoping her reaction to last night will not be too drastic. But she's completely aloof. She has no reaction. Her reaction is an absence of reaction. That's how she's dealing with it.

"I'm so sorry about last night," I say again and again, not knowing exactly what I'm apologizing for.

As Willow and I are talking, Dixie starts yelling at me from her room, "Mooom, c'mere, c'mere!"

As I turn to tend to Dixie, Willow rolls her eyes, as if to say, *Why and how do I put up with you two?*

I go to Dixie and sit on the bed, and she continues to say, "Mooom, c'mere, c'mere."

"Dixie, Dixie," I say. I put my index finger on her lips and continue, "I'm here, and I'm so sorry about last night. I'm so sorry. Here." I move over and pat the bed beside me to indicate for her to sit up. I say, "You c'mere. You c'mere," in a soft tone.

She looks at me, her eyes watering, "You were really scary last night, Mom." Her brown hair is all a muss from sleeping, and I comb it gently back off her face with my fingers.

"Dixie, I'm so, so sorry. It will never happen again." I hug her thirteen-year-old body. She feels so vulnerable.

"Did you mix Ativan and wine again?" She pushes me away and looks at me.

"I may have—but it will never happen again." I cup her cheek.

"Mom, you were screaming and driving and screaming. Melba had to take me to Lisa's."

"Yes, I know, sweetheart. I'm so terribly sorry. I would like to make it up to you. How about a movie tonight in the media room? Just the Keevil girls. I'll make our favorite: Rosie's Greasy Spoon drumsticks and cheesy noodles." Rosie's Greasy Spoon is the nickname we use for our kitchen.

"And cookie dough ice cream," she says, and bounces up and down.

"I scream, you scream, we all scream for ice cream," we say in loud unison.

"Willow?" I yell out. "Did you hear that? Drumsticks and cheese noodles and cookie dough ice cream?"

She comes to Dixie's bedroom door in her jeans and Whistler sweatshirt, her canvas book bag hung around her shoulder.

"I'm going to Robby's to work on our French project," she announces in a serious tone. "Will you drive me? I think you seem capable of it this morning."

"Yes, dear," I say, feeling the punch of her disdain. "Then join us for dinner, okay?"

"I guess so."

"Thank you. It'll be fun, just the three of us." I get up and hug her. She wants to be unreceptive, but I feel her body unstiffen a bit as I hold her. "I'll take you to Robby's now," I say. I turn to Dixie. "Get dressed and come with us, and you and I will go shopping on the way back."

"I don't want to wait for her to get dressed!" exclaims Willow.

"Yes," goes Dixie.

"No," says Willow.

"Now, just a sec. Please, let's work this out without a fight," I plead. "We haven't eaten breakfast. Let's go have some cereal."

"I gotta get to Robby's," says Willow.

"Can you call him?" I hold both her arms at the elbows with my hands and look right at her. "Pleeeeeeeeaaase, Willow. You *do* have to have breakfast."

"Me, too," repeats Dixie.

"Oh, all right," Willow concedes. "Hurry, Dixie!"

I turn to Dixie. "Just get dressed quickly and come to the kitchen."

Somehow we get through breakfast and the ride to Robby's in relative peace. Every moment feels like a gift—as if all I deserve is bad behavior.

Dixie and I go to the store to buy the food for dinner. In an attempt to atone for my sins, I let her choose whatever food she wants. I let her have vanilla cupcakes from the bakery, Froot Loops cereal, a handful of Double Bubble gum, and, of course, Häagen-Dazs Cookie Dough Dynamo ice cream. That makes us think of the chocolate chip cookies we often make together, so we buy the ingredients for that.

Later that evening, after we get home, we make the cookies and I prepare dinner: barbecued chicken drumsticks, broccoli with cheese sauce, stir-fried carrots with mustard and brown sugar, and very cheesy broad egg noodles. The movie we have chosen is *28 Days*, because Sandra Bullock is in it and we loved her in *Miss Congeniality*. But in *28 Days* she plays an alcoholic journalist who fucks up so badly she has to go to rehab. I can relate a little too much to the protagonist in the movie—a journalist who drinks too much, sounds familiar— but I certainly don't need rehab. I'm not that bad.

The following Tuesday, April 16, a letter arrives in the mail from the West Vancouver police: "You were seen driving erratically on the Upper Levels Highway on Friday, April 12, at about 4:00 p.m."

Apparently, a citizen called and reported me.

I call my lawyer and confess, "I have a problem with alcohol. I received a letter in the mail from the police about my driving." I tell her what it says.

"Just ignore it," Eileen says. "Call me if they come to your door."

This advice reminds me of an inquest I covered for CFTO TV News about the mysterious baby deaths at the Hospital for Sick Children in Toronto in the 1980s. Forty-three infants died under suspicious circumstances. Investigators suspected nurse Susan Nelles. When the police arrived at the door to arrest her, she was carrying a piece of paper in her housecoat pocket with the name of her lawyer on it. This very act implied guilt.

—

I manage to stay sober until the kids get to sleep, and then I gulp down a couple large goblets of white wine—so large that one glass takes a half a bottle of wine—and smoke a number of Camel Lights out on the balcony off the bedroom. I pass out until seven o'clock in the morning, when it's time to get Willow and Dixie ready for school. I'm feeling shaky and would love some of that California Sterling chardonnay beckoning me from behind the milk in the fridge. But I resist, prepare breakfast and lunch, and take the kids to school.

I have a lunch date with my girlfriend Monicka to celebrate her forty-seventh birthday. We're meeting in the trendy South Granville area of Vancouver, which means I have to travel from West Vancouver—over the Lions Gate Bridge—through downtown and over the Granville Street Bridge.

I've known Monicka since 1972, when we both attended Neuchâtel Junior College, a Canadian school in Switzerland. She's stunning, with high, model-like cheekbones and wavy, shoulder-length blond hair. When she speaks, she twirls a curl of blond hair in her forefinger and holds her chin up somewhat higher than normal, which accentuates her refined manner.

Getting to the restaurant requires driving past Christ Church Cathedral, where Archbishop Michael Ingham will confirm Willow at the end of April. Eleven years ago, when he was the minister at St. Francis-in-the-Wood church in Tiddly Cove, in West Vancouver, he christened her. Since he became the bishop of the diocese of New Westminster, he has boldly supported same-sex unions, igniting controversy within the Anglican Church. He's a man I admire, and I am proud that Willow is experiencing these rites of passage with him. I'm aware she may or may not choose to follow any religious path, but I figure I'm giving her the option.

I decide I have time to go into Christ Church and pray. I park near it and walk into the empty, dimly lit nave. Rows and rows of empty pews face the massive stained glass window at the front of the church, under which stands a large golden cross framed by ornate, shiny gold posts. Beneath all this opulence is the altar, donned with a cloth that has orange and gold swirls on it, reminding me of the altar cloth that Barry and I had at our wedding—orange and yellow flames, which complemented the minister's bright robes.

Not wanting to disturb the sacrosanctity, I practically tiptoe halfway down the center aisle toward the altar. The cross seems to cast its disapproval upon me as I step into a wooden pew in the middle of the church, put the prayer bench down, kneel, clasp my hands, and rest my elbows on the prie-dieu.

The tears gush out.

Oh, dear God, please be in me.

Oh, dear God, please get me through this one, and I promise I will behave from here on out.

Oh, dear God, please be in me.

Be in me.

Be in me.

During this ten minutes in the cathedral, all the emotions that have been accumulating in me—shame, guilt, fear, anger, anguish, and sorrow—twist together into a tight gnarl that globs onto my stomach like barnacles on beach rocks.

As I get up from the pew and make my way out of the church, I experience the occasional zephyr of strength, enough to propel me forward, into the car, and to drive. I feel safe, like I have a divine chaperone benevolent enough to forgive me yet one more time. I make my way to the restaurant where Monicka and I are meeting, Ouisi Bistro. Monicka usually chooses places I have never tried. I find a parking spot close by, and before I get out of the car, I pull her birthday card out of my purse. I haven't signed it yet. I place it on the consul between the two front seats—to have a hard surface to write on, but I'm battling a hangover and my hands are almost too shaky to write. Out of necessity, I make my written birthday greeting short, though it feels inadequate. I sign it simply, "With love, Rosemary."

I arrive at the restaurant early, maybe to compensate for my lack of mental clarity. Monicka arrives a few minutes late.

"I'm so sorry I'm late," she says. She touches her face. "My makeup is all smudgy because I've been crying with my spiritual counselor in her office." She wipes under her eyes with her napkin. "It's in the basement of Christ Church Cathedral."

"Oh, I've been crying at Christ Church, too," I tell her, "but in the nave."

This launches us into an intimate discussion about why both of us are crying on a Wednesday at noon in a church. I'm intrigued by the fact that she actually sees a spiritual counselor. I didn't realize there was such a thing.

"What kinds of things do you talk about?" I ask. "Is she taking more clients? Maybe I need a spiritual counselor."

Her name is Sheena. She talks gently, her words emerging slowly from her like thick cream, the kind you get at high tea with crumpets and strawberry preserves. She has a reassuring half smile that does not expose her teeth. She's older than my forty-seven years, but ageless, really. She wears flat, round-toed, sensible black shoes, and a single string of white pearls. Her hair—brown, with hints of gray—is pulled back from her face in a bun. She has luminous blue eyes that seem to peer right into my soul. I feel exposed but protected at the same time.

On the wall behind Sheena is a three-dimensional wall hanging of Jesus on the cross. The bookshelf is lined with titles like *The Book of Common Prayer*, *The Book of Blessings*, and *Choose Love*.

"I drank a lot of wine, took a couple of sleeping pills, and drove the kids. My kids, my girls, they're only thirteen and fifteen. I did $4,000 worth of damage to the clutch on my car." I pause and shake my head and let the tears gush out as I finish my confession. "I almost lost the family dog, and I blacked out at the wheel. It's a miracle I didn't have an accident. Then I got a letter from the police that I was seen driving erratically. I'm wondering . . . well . . ." I pause and wonder exactly what I *am* wondering. I get up my nerve and finish my thought: "Do you think I need a spiritual retreat?"

Keeping her eyes on mine, Sheena rolls her chair closer, so she's about three feet from me. I have squeezed myself into the corner of what feels like the proverbial psychiatrist's couch.

"What about rehab?" she asks.

"Rehab?" I say, incredulous.

With her hands still folded on her lap, she nods twice, ever so gently.

"Does that mean I can never have a couple of glasses of wine on a Friday night to relax ever again?" I ask.

"Rosemary, is it just sleeping pills and wine you're worried about, or . . ." She pauses like she is searching for the right word. "Or are there other substances that concern you?"

Fuck, I say to myself. *Does she know? Does she have a direct line to God or something?* I search through my scrambled thoughts for exactly what I want to reveal to her. I really should tell her about *that*. But I'm so ashamed. I'm afraid even to mention the word.

"I have had a problem with . . . well, I don't anymore, but . . . I did use, um, well, ah, cocaine, but, but . . . I don't now." I rush on. "I just feel that, since I'm here, well . . . You know, I thought maybe I should say it, but it really isn't relevant now, is it? I mean, you know, it's over and done with."

"Maybe it's not quite over and that's why you feel you need to mention it." Mercifully, she leaves it at that. "A colleague of mine just started as the head therapist at a new center on Barefoot Island, The Meadow."

"What about something like Betty Ford?" I mutter in protest.

"Why, Rosemary? Does that seem more dignified?"

I study my hands, which are clutching my knees, and try to breathe as deeply as I can, but the breath stops at my heart—a too-familiar feeling. I look back up at her.

"How long is rehab?"

"Perhaps a month."

My first thought is the girls. "I don't think I could leave my daughters for that long. We have a trip planned to Toronto, and—"

Sheena stops me with her eyes. "I'll get Graham's number for you, Rosemary."

She stands up and walks effortlessly over to her desk, as if she's floating. She picks up a personal notebook, thumbs through a few pages, and stops. She writes on a yellow sticky note and returns to her chair. Sitting down, she hands me the piece of paper. "Graham Fitzpatrick, the Meadow," it says, with a phone number that I can't read through my tears.

I turn my head slightly to the side and look up at the ceiling with a slight shake of my head. I've been snared like a wild animal that has ventured out of the woods and straight into a trap. No matter how much I struggle, I can't escape the truth. This is it. The jig is up. Guilty as charged. Sheena has caught me; she's caught me out.

I stand up and go to shake Sheena's hand but stop myself. Too formal. I hug her instead, thank her, and get the hell out of there.

I head toward home, aware of a gnawing knowing deep inside me, a pocket of clarity submerged beneath all my emotional pandemonium. I'm able to access a distinct decision. God has arrived; he has answered my plea and delivered his dictum. I am going to rehab. I am an alcoholic who is going to rehab, rehab, rehab. I am going to rehab.

But I need to process. How am I going to get from this state I'm in to wherever I need to go? How am I going to tell the kids? I need to figure out what else needs to be done.

I'm going to call Betty Ford. "More dignified." Huh. Well, fuck, maybe she's right. I'll call The Meadow, and other places, too, and research until I find the right one. But how will I tell the girls? How will I leave them for a month? Maybe I can go for a shorter time. I have to start making a list of questions. Is there availability? Whom should I tell first? How will I tell the girls?

I need a drink. Maybe I can have some Bâtard-Montrachet just to help me through this. Oh—what about a big, fat line of cocaine? Oh, what bliss—yes, bliss. But short-lived—so sweet but so shameful. How could I have done that? A mother snorting cocaine in her bathroom with the door locked to hide it from her kids. I remember the time Willow was knocking at the locked bathroom door and I was in there, doing lines. Oh, the fucking shame.

I need to talk to my mom. What will I say? I'll phone her now. No, I'll wait until I'm not driving. I'll drive through Stanley Park.

I quickly change lanes to enter the park—and immediately regret this decision, as it reminds me of another drunk-and-pilled-up driving performance from a few weeks ago. Dixie and I had just been at her friend's bar mitzvah, and I was resentful that she had insisted I attend. In the car on the way home from the service, Dixie told me that I embarrassed her—something about chatting really loudly in the synagogue—and I had no idea what she was talking about and got mad.

"What do you mean, I embarrassed you?" I yelled. "Why did I have to go to Peter's bar mitzvah anyway? He's not *my* friend."

She cried.

My mind switches from that ghastly memory back to my current clusterfuck—committing myself to rehab and all that decision entails. Telling people. Getting from here to there. As I follow Stanley Park Drive, which circles the one-thousand-acre park, I try to calm myself, take in the sights: downtown Vancouver, the floating Esso gas station, the underbelly of Lions Gate Bridge, the North Shore Mountains, the big yellow piles of sulfur which, as I always tell the kids, really *are* made of plastic.

I'd better call Mom. What will I say? I'll wing it. No, I'd better have a line ready.

Oh, just bloody well call.

It seems as if the car guides itself to the pullout viewing area at Brockton Point, the port industry with its huge cranes and jutting piers staring back at me through the April drizzle. I park and call Mom.

"Hello, darling," she says, all enthusiasm. "It's sooooooo good to hear from you. Henry and I were just talking about you. How are those daaaaarling girls? Henry, come quick. Rose is on the phone."

"Wait, Mom," I say quickly. "I can't speak to Dad now. I have a problem."

"What is it, dear?"

I scratch the front of my neck.

"Rose, darling? What is it?"

"I'm going . . . I have . . . I think . . . I have a problem with alcohol. I drink too much. I think I might be going to rehab." *There, I said it,* I say to myself, feeling as if I've just landed on the tarmac in a plane that was taking forever to touch down.

"Oh, sweetheart, Rose. You don't drink too much. You just drink a little too much white wine sometimes."

I try to breathe, but the breath stops, again, at the top of my ribs. I'm permanently short of breath.

"I drove the kids, I drove them . . . drunk." I start to sob but try to reveal more through the tears. "I almost . . . I could have . . . I blacked out when I was driving."

"You what, dear?" I hear her asking, but I just continue.

"It's a miracle I didn't have an accident." I catch my breath and quickly add, "But I'm going to rehab."

"You mean, like Betty Ford?"

"Yes, or something like that. Apparently, there's a place on Barefoot Island, which is near West Vancouver. But, Mom, how can I leave the kids—it's for a month or something. Could you come out?"

"Of course, dear. Are you all right? Are the girls all right?"

"Yes, Mom, we're all physically fine. I need to go. I just wanted to tell you. You're the first person I've called. I'll call you later, 'kay?"

"Okay, my darling. I love you. I'll do whatever I can."

I press END on the phone, put it in my purse on the passenger seat, and am surprised that I feel somewhat relieved. Huh! I guess that Jesus guy wasn't too far off when he said, "And the truth will set you free."

I stall for a couple of days and then start making some phone calls. Betty Ford has an opening on Monday, April 29. It's now Friday, April 19. Twenty thousand US dollars. *Wow.* Twenty-eight days. How could I possibly leave the kids for twenty-eight days? I can't do it. It's so far away.

The Meadow is much closer, a short ferry ride away, and the ferry terminal is just down the road at Horseshoe Bay. And it's much cheaper. But, oh, God, I would probably see people I know on the ferry. What would I say?

What am I going to do? What am I going to do?

Shaking, yet again unable to breathe, I try to think how to calm myself. Glass of wine? No! Ativan? No! Tylenol? Yes! I study the piece of paper with Graham Fitzpatrick's name on it.

Finally, I pick up the goddamn phone and call. A very friendly receptionist answers and puts me right through.

"Graham? I was given your number by my spiritual counselor, Sheena."

"Ah, yes," he says. "She's wonderful, isn't she?"

"Yes, yes. Well, uh, she suggested I go there. Can you tell me a bit about it?"

"Yes. We've just opened up. It's a converted bed-and-breakfast here on Barefoot Island—so peaceful. A good place to sober up. Is that what you need?" Graham has an encouraging tone, and I detect a slight rounding of his vowels—a hint of an American accent.

"Um, uh, ummmm . . ." I gulp. "Well, I guess, yes, maybe?"

"How much do you drink?" Graham is frank but not intimating— no judgment in his tone.

"Um . . ." I decide to underplay it. "About half a bottle of wine or so a day."

"Do you do anything else?"

"Well, uh, I guess some pills, like, you know, sleeping pills and Ativan and stuff."

"How much?"

"And I did do"—oh, I feel sick saying this—"cocaine."

"How much?"

"Well, I was able to stop that about five months ago—at Christmastime."

"Do you want help?" he asks.

"Well, I didn't think it was that bad. I jog every morning."

"Yes, I'm a jogger, too," he says. "It's a perfect way to deal with a hangover, isn't it?"

"I have two daughters," I blurt out. "They're thirteen and fifteen. I drove them drunk . . . but they need me here. I couldn't possibly leave them for twenty-eight days. Can I come for a shorter time?"

Graham explains that there is a ten-day program but that most people need at least twenty-eight. "You'll love the spot," he assures me. "It's beautiful, by a meadow, cozy main house, lovely rooms, all shared with someone. No isolating around here. About your children: you're no good to them unwell."

"I just don't know if I could leave them for that long. We're going to Toronto to look at a school for Dixie."

During a recent holiday to Australia, we met a woman who attended Bishop Strachan School, my alma mater, in Toronto. Dixie became convinced she wanted to go there in September for ninth grade. I was surprised she wanted to go away for school, but I've gone along with it, secretly and ashamedly thinking it might be easier with her at boarding school. She and her sister each have an inheritance from their father, and hers will cover it.

"What's your availability?" I ask halfheartedly.

"Things change all the time," he says. "We have only twelve spots. There's space now, but who knows two weeks from now?"

"Could I think about it and call you back?"

"Certainly. Remember, you've got nothin' if you don't have your health. Check out our website."

"Thank you."

"Bye for now. Oh, and Rosemary, stay safe."

I do check out the website. It looks bucolic. They treat alcoholics and addicts. Families can visit. Therapy groups. I hate group therapy. Psychiatrist on staff. Oh, dear God, I certainly need that. Swimming pool. Yoga. Those will be good for me.

The kids, the kids, the kids. I'll call a family meeting after I pick them up from school. I'll ask them what they think about my going to treatment for a while. I'll tell them I've been drinking a little too much, that we'll still go to Toronto. But what if there is no spot at the Meadow when we get back?

I call Graham back, and he tells me I should come as soon as possible.

"You need to stay safe," he says. "You need to tell your kids you're not well, and you need to address your drinking."

It costs $10,000 for one month, and a percentage of that for ten days—the absolute minimum length of time one can stay. If I taper off my drinking now, I may not need to detoxify, though if I do, I can do it there. Saturday is family visiting day, but not the first Saturday. I can jog in the driveway and around the Meadow, but I can't leave the grounds. No single rooms. No personal cars allowed. He'll pick me up at the ferry.

"Can someone close to them come stay with them?" he asks.

"I have a full-time nanny. Melba is reliable."

"Is there a family member who could help out, Rosemary?"

"I could ask my mom to come out from Toronto, but Dad doesn't like her to leave him alone at the farm."

"Can he come, too?"

"He hates flying. He hates change."

"Tell your dad you really need this. It's a matter of life and death."

"How will I tell the children? What will I say? What should I say?"

"Tell them you're not well, that you need to go away to get well. That's why it's important to have a loved one stay with them."

"Well, hmm, well, Graham . . . I guess . . . I guess I'd better book it?"

"That would be a wise decision, Rosemary."

As it turns out, Dad is very supportive of Mom's coming out to help for a few weeks. I book a check-in date at the Meadow for Friday, May 3; it's now Tuesday, April 23. We can still go to Toronto.

I'm going through the jumble of plans in my head as I prepare the girls' breakfasts, obsessing over how I will break it to them that I'm going away. I'm so sad that I have to leave them.

Dixie is upstairs, yelling for something.

"Why don't you just come down for breakfast?" I yell up to her. "Just get ready for school!"

She comes down the stairs and whines, "I have a stomachache, Mom."

"Oh dear, sweetheart," I say, as I set the Cheerios down on the table, trying to hide my shakes from her. I turn to her and kneel down. "Where does it hurt?"

"Just all over here." She pouts and rubs her entire front torso.

Fuck, I say to myself. *She's lobbying to stay home, and I can't be bothered to fight it.*

I set her in front of the TV and take Willow to school. She complains the whole way there, "Why do I have to go to school and Dixie gets to stay home?"

When I get back to the house, Dixie says, "I'm hungry. Can I have toast soldiers and eggs?"

"Whaaaat? I thought you had a stomachache," I say, hiding behind the open fridge door so I can pour myself a glass of Pouilly-Fuissé to battle my jitters without her seeing me. Ahhhh . . . I feel such relief as I gulp down a glass of the nice, light French chardonnay. It's a perfect breakfast wine.

I still have an emotional headache, so I take another Tylenol with codeine, using the wine to wash it down. That straightens me out enough to go join Dixie on the couch.

"Can we go to Granville Island, Mom?"

Something about this idea doesn't seem right, but it sounds like fun, and that way I won't have to tell her now about rehab. I can tell her over lunch.

"Okay," I say, "let's go."

On the way to Granville Island, I realize I'm quite drunk. I probably shouldn't have had all that wine before driving, but it took the shakes away and I won't be doing this anymore as of May 3. Besides, this is a good way to pass the day with Dixie, and we need to have some togetherness.

Once at Granville Island, I'm hoping some food will help sober me up. We buy french fries and sit on the benches near the water. We share the fries with the seagulls just like Rob and I used to do. There are a lot of them. They're really close. They're really big close-up like this. Dixie is laughing gaily. Are they dirty birds? Their beaks are so long and pointy. There are so many around us, making such a racket. Why are they so hungry? Maybe when they stop eating, if they stop eating, I can tell Dixie I'm going away to treatment. Yes, tell her here, beside the water, with the birds around. I'll ask her if that's okay—that I go away. She's laughing so hard right beside me, but it feels like I'm watching her on TV.

We leave Granville Island without my having said a fucking thing about my pending misadventure. We are on the Upper Levels, heading west toward our exit, and I see the sign coming up, with an arrow—WESTRIDGE—and I still have not said anything. Finally, I swallow, try to stop my shakes. I need more wine. I have to stop the shakes. I have to get up the nerve to tell her. *Goddammit!*

"Dixie, I have something to say." I try to talk above the song that she has put on in the car. It's Prozzäk singing "Tsunami."

"What?" She turns the music up louder.

I turn it off in a huff. "Dixie, I have something to say!"

She immediately turns it back on and laughs.

"Yeah? But you love 'Tsunami,' right? Do the dance, Mom," she shouts above the music, as she plugs her nose with her left hand and motions in a vertical wave in front of her face and down to her chest with her right hand—like we always do when we play this song.

I lunge toward the power button and stab it off.

"Dixie." I try to sound in control. "What would you say if I went away for a bit, to, uh, get some help with, uh . . . um, well, I'm drinking a little too much wine."

She turns the music back on and continues her drowning dance.

I punch the button off again. "Dixie! I mean this. The other day when I picked you up from school, I did take an Ativan, and I had mixed it with wine."

"I thought you just had some Ativan and that's why you were so crazy." She goes to turn the music back on.

I grab her hand. "No! Don't turn the music on. Listen to me. I mixed the Ativan with too much wine. The doctor says I need some help with . . . with, well, my wine. I'm drinking too much of it. I won't go very far away. It's just on Barefoot Island, and you could visit me in a week."

"Who will stay with us, Mom?" she asks. "I don't want you to go away. Are you going to a hospital?"

"Well, it's a treatment center. It's called The Meadow, and I'm going for treatment." I put my turn signal on and take our exit, aware that we are only a short drive away from home and my opportunity to finish this agonizing conversation. "Melba will be here, and Gramma."

"Graaaaamma? Oh, Mom, she's so crazy. You can't leave us with her."

"I thought you loved her."

"I do, but she's kinda crazy. Why do you have to go away?"

"I just have to," I say. "I can't seem to stop the wine myself. I really need your help. You'll be okay. Barefoot isn't far, and you can visit me."

"Oh, don't go, Mom."

I grip the steering wheel harder. "Dixie, please don't make this so difficult. I'm really struggling with leaving you guys. I'm really struggling."

I turn into our driveway, and Dixie opens her door, forcing me to stop the car before I enter the garage. She jumps out and storms off into the house.

I realize I'm still shaking. I need some wine to settle me. I park the car, and, instead of going to say hello to Melba in the kitchen, I head straight to my bathroom, where I have a bottle of wine and a goblet hidden under the sink. I fill the goblet and down the wine, not caring that it's not cold. *Ahhhh, that does the trick.* I refill the glass.

Locking the door to my bedroom, I sit in the armchair with my wine and stare at the trees and the creek that runs behind the house. I notice the creek's soothing gurgling and laugh at myself—as if one gurgling brook could tame the commotion bombarding my brain, my heart, my soul.

Oh, God, please help me. I don't know if I can do this. Can I leave the kids like this? I can't even tell them I'm leaving—let alone leave!

Dixie's reaction was upsetting. I'm lost, so lost. I've been set adrift, like the astronauts in the movies who are suddenly untethered from their ship and waft away into the deep abyss of space.

Half an hour later, I'm still staring at the trees and the creek and drinking my wine. It's time to pick Willow up from school, where she has been tutoring a third-grader in math. Willow works really hard and wants to excel. She's pursuing her school's "four strands"—academics, arts, athletics, and service. The tutoring goes under "service."

I'm grateful I have never had to badger either of my girls to do their homework. They both just seem to do whatever homework they have, and they do very well at school. Although I'm no dummy, I figure their smarts come from their father, who was a brilliant academic—first in his law class.

It's late when I pick up Willow, and she wants to go to Earl's Tin Palace for dinner. She and I often have "dates" at Earl's. It's darker and fancier than the White Spot, the family restaurant that we like. Earl's caters to a youngish, hip crowd. It has an excellent menu without being too elaborate or overpriced—foods like good-quality steaks, Thai carrot soup, seared albacore tuna, hand-smashed burgers, and key lime pie. We always share the shrimp rolls.

When we enter the restaurant, the hostess, who is young, slim, and dressed in a black, cleavage-baring dress—just like all the other female servers at the restaurant—gives us a big smile and tells us there is a fifteen-minute wait for a table but there's room at the bar.

The hockey game is playing on the TV above the bar. I watch

long enough to determine that the Detroit Red Wings are trouncing the Vancouver Canucks. Curiosity satisfied, I turn my attention away from it. Fortunately, it's not too loud. We order our usual, and I ask for the wine list. Although Earl's doesn't have a fine-wine list, it's decent. I choose a California Stag's Leap chardonnay—not fantastic but acceptable.

"This is my last glass of wine," I tell Willow, as I hold up the glass. "I'm going away for treatment because I . . . well, I drink a little too much wine. Gramma is coming to take care of you, and, of course, Melba will be around," I say. I take a sip and keep holding the glass in the air. "I'm just going to Barefoot Island, so I won't be far. I'll go after the Toronto trip, and you can visit me."

I deliver this information as quickly as possible, and have two more gulps of wine before I set the glass back on the table.

"Where're the appetizers?" Willow asks. "I'm hungry."

"Willow, did you hear what I said? I have to go away for a bit."

"Why?"

"Because I drink a little too much."

"Oh . . . here are the shrimp rolls. They look awesome," she says with wide eyes as the bartender delivers our food.

I press on. "I need your help with Dixie. She seems upset."

"What else is new?"

"Gramma's coming, and I won't be far, and you can come to see me. You can visit me on Barefoot Island."

"Freddy White lives on Barefoot. He takes the ferry every day to school. Isn't that cool?"

Willow remains distracted throughout dinner and on the ride home, refusing to talk about my treatment plans. Once home, I say goodbye to Melba, open a cold Louis Latour Beaune, down a glass, fill it up again, and then put the glass in the fridge on the top shelf behind the milk so the kids can't see it. I fantasize about topping this off with a little mountain of cocaine—about five lines' worth. But I know I'm just not going to do that—the shame, the contempt I have for myself, about that fucking cocaine.

At bedtime, I go to Dixie to tuck her in. She's on her top bunk, so I climb up the ladder and lie beside her. I've had an Ativan and the wine, so I'm loose enough to deal with any requests she may have. *Read me a story. Give me a back rub. I need some water. I want an applesauce back tickle.*

She asks for a back rub and a back tickle. I say, "I'll give you an applesauce back tickle and a brief massage."

She lies on her stomach and pulls up her pajama top so her back is bare. I sit beside her and tickle her back with both hands while reciting, "Tick-tock, applesauce, spiders crawling up your back. Tight squeeze . . ." I squeeze her ribs, and she giggles. "Cool breeze . . ." I blow on her back, and she quivers. "Now you have the shiverees."

I massage her shoulders and back for a couple of minutes. Then I kiss her back and say, "I've got to go to bed now." I crawl down the ladder, hoping she lets me go without protest. I turn off the light and say, "Good night."

As I'm going through the door, she says, "Mom?"

"Yes, sweetheart."

"How long are you going away for?"

"Twenty-eight days."

"That's not treatment. That's rehab."

14

"Out of Bounds"
Amanda Marshall
Friday, May 3, 2002

My mom drives me along windy, seaside Marine Drive to the Horseshoe Bay ferry terminal, about five miles from home. She pulls over so I can get out and buy my ticket.

"Wait here for now, 'kay?" I say to Mom as I get out and walk to the ticket booth. I lean toward the window. "A ticket for the three thirty to Barefoot Island, please."

"Vehicle or walk-on?" the attendant asks.

"Walk-on."

"One way or two?"

"Uh, hmm, one way for now, I guess?"

"That'll be $20."

I pay her. She issues the ticket and points toward a walkway. "Over there."

"Thank you."

It's far away enough that Mom will have to drive me with my heavy bags and drop me off. Getting back into the car, I motion to her where to take me.

"Over there, please, James," I say, trying for a moment of levity.

The cars are all waiting for the ferry in rows under the high cement Upper Levels overpass, casting a dark shadow on all the ferry hustle and bustle below. Mom drives to the designated drop-off area, where I get out and fetch my two large suitcases from the trunk.

Turning toward her open window, I kiss my hand and blow her a kiss.

"Thanks so much, Mom. I love you."

"Love you, too. Knock 'em dead, baby," Mom says, in her usual, "everything is normal" voice, which I appreciate because it's much better than acting the opposite and treating me like the horrific mother that I am.

"Yeah, okay, whatever you say, Ma. I don't think I can make phone calls for a week, so be sure to remind the kids. I'll be in touch as soon as possible. Meanwhile, if you really have to reach me for some reason, all the contact information is in the kitchen by the phone."

"Okay, dear. They're great. Don't worry."

"Thank you, Mom. Love you. Bye."

"Love you, dear. Goodbye." She drives away as I turn around and see the ferryboat arriving. It stops and lowers its gargantuan door, which hits the ground with a loud, jarring bang. The door becomes a plankway for cars to drive onto the ferry. Vehicles race out as I struggle with my bags—one in each hand, both on roller wheels, plus a handbag slung firmly over my left shoulder. I follow the other pedestrians to the elevator, go up to the main level, and walk outside to the bow of the boat, where I grab a seat.

We're traveling west toward Barefoot Island. The sun is beaming on the vast, deep, choppy, moody ocean. The snow-topped mountains to the north are crystal clear.

Leaving my bags at my seat—I trust that they're way too heavy for anybody to be interested in stealing them—I attend to my first orders of business: a tea and a pee. Then, armed with a very strong cup of tea, I head back to my bags and plunk myself down on the cold metal bench. Now I have no more distractions, no more reasons not to think, not to reflect on what the fuck I'm doing.

What have I done?

What does this mean?

What will happen?

Will Willow and Dixie be okay?

What if I see someone I know on the ferry? What will I say? Shit, that I drove my kids drunk and high and blacked out and have booked myself into an insane asylum? 'Cause that's what it feels like.

Stuck as I am in my mucky thoughts, I don't realize that we're already about to dock. The twenty-minute boat ride is almost over. *Oh, shit. I'm not ready. No, I need more time. What's happening? Can I turn back now?* People are standing up and heading to the stairs. I'll wait until the very end. Oh, that's stupid. Graham is waiting. That's rude. He'll think I changed my mind. Well, maybe I have. I could do that. I could stay on the ferry and turn right around and go back.

No. I really, really need to stop drinking. I really, really need to get out of this bleak torture chamber I'm living in.

I take a deep breath of cool salt air and stand up. Onshore, a row of cars waits to board. Pedestrians stare at the arriving ferry as it gets closer and closer to land and begin to pick up their bags. Then a thud and a jolt, and with a clamor the gargantuan door cum plankway is released.

It's time. *Fuck!*

I throw my purse over my shoulder, put the handle of each bag in each hand, and join the lineup of walk-ons exiting the ferry. I'm having trouble thinking straight. *This cannot be happening*, I think. *Please, may I awaken from this nightmare?* But I know I can't avoid my reality anymore. I walk off the ferry.

A fellow in chinos, an open-collared shirt, and a leather jacket notices me immediately. This must be Graham. He walks right up to me and says with a smile, "Hi, Rosemary. I see you brought some baggage."

"Yes, well"—I look at my bulging suitcases and laugh—"I threw in decades of diaries. I figure I've some sorting-out to do."

"Yes, perhaps."

Graham is about my age, forty-seven, with a good head of graying hair and a friendly smile. He looks a bit like Harry Hamlin from *L.A. Law*. He is the head counselor at The Meadow. He drives me in his Toyota Tercel through quaint Sugar Cove, up around the bend on a country road with forest on either side.

Graham makes a hairpin left turn into a driveway and stops at the gate beside a subtle wooden sign on the left that reads THE MEADOW. We are buzzed in.

We wind our way through an orchard, and then Graham pulls up beside a sizable old wooden house, attached by a short second-floor walkway to a two-floor, inn-type building.

"This was once a bed-and-breakfast. Your room's up there." He points to the far end of the inn part of the structure. "You've two roommates, a balcony, and a large bathroom, complete with tub. You'll like it." He's smiling again and motioning for me to get out. "C'mon, I'll help you with your baggage and introduce you."

I barely have time to set my bags in the room, as dinner is at five. I sit apart from the other mental patients—there are only about eight of them—during the meal. What will they think of me? I talk to no one and cry, feeling very self-conscious. When dinner is over, I bolt to my room, collapse on my bed, and sob.

What the hell have I done? My thoughts immediately gravitate toward Barry. *I'm so, so sorry, Barry. I'm sorry.* What have I done to the kids? What will become of them? I have to get out of this dark, dark, dark hole. I'm at the bottom of a deep, dank well. I'm so petrified, I'm shaking. *God, help me out of here. How can I do this? I can't be without my girls. Will they be okay? God, be in me. God, take away the torture. God, release me. I can't breathe. I need a sip of wine. Huh! How about a bottle? I need Ativan. God, no. Release me from this hell.*

I ignore my roommates when they come in. I pretend to be asleep. One plays *Forrest Gump* on the TV in the room. Good songs—I should get that soundtrack. "Break on Through," by the Doors; "Everybody's Talking"—dunno who sings that; Bob Seger's "Against the Wind." Yes, I should remind myself to do that when I get out of this place.

I start my first morning in rehab with a jog on the green grass on the hill in front of The Meadow which, I am told, leads down to an orchard of trees. My feet pound against the earth while my mind spins. Then it strikes me: I'm not hungover. I am not fucking hungover! Distracted from my distress, I open my eyes wide to take in the verdant scene around me and realize I'm not running in an orchard of trees. I'm running through grapevines. I thought this was an orchard. This is a has-been vineyard! This ain't no orchard; this was a fucking vineyard. *God, you really are twisted.*

I manage to stop crying for the thirty-minute run, but it does not give me the pick-me-up it normally does. I'm just so distraught and unhappy to be here. I can't speak at breakfast, and I barely eat, as my throat is swollen with emotion. My eyes are red and swollen, too.

After breakfast, we get into a group and I can't stop thinking about how much I hate group therapy. I'm so not a group-therapy person. *Get me the hell out of here.* What time is it? I check my watch. Only 10:05. Shit, this thing goes till noon. We do this every day, Monday to Friday? I won't survive.

All nine inmates are here. There's Brad—a big dude, about

thirty-five, with short, straight, prematurely gray hair and one of those permanently boyish-looking faces. He's from Vancouver Island, where he works in construction when he's not high on crack. There's Stetson, a cute guy, also about thirty-five, who lives in Vancouver's trendy Kitsilano district with his wife and two little children. Not sure what his poison is, but he sure looks innocent, with this thick curl of brown hair that keeps flopping onto his forehead, Hugh Grant–style. Rodrigo is also a young father and is from Colombia, replete with cocaine and beautiful women. There's Henderson, a businessman who smokes crack in the shower in the morning before work so his family won't smell it. I wonder if that actually works. Jason is about twenty-four, with a disfigured face—not sure what the fuck happened to him. I think he's strictly an alcoholic. There's Fred, who is American and closer to my age—also a crack addict; not sure what his occupation is. Then there are my two roommates: Celia, a garden-variety alcoholic housewife from Toronto, and Nicole, a grandmother who lives right here on Barefoot Island and is addicted to pharmaceuticals. Apparently, there's a fourth woman coming soon.

All I can think about is how fucking depressing it is that I'm stuck with all these losers. I cry more, right through lunch. I stop the waterworks long enough to listen to a psycho-ed session after lunch. It's a like a mini-lecture on drugs and their effect on the human body. Heroin is the most addictive and the most difficult to quit. Crack cocaine is the next-most addictive, then nicotine. Most people here smoke cigarettes. Although I smoke when I'm high or drunk, I don't smoke when I'm straight and I'm not about to start. This makes me a bit of a social outcast, as everyone gathers in the smoking corner outside to puff and gab and laugh.

After the top three drugs, the next-most-addictive and toughest-to-quit drugs are methadone, crystal meth, alcohol, and cocaine, in that order. Most of today's lecture is about cocaine—the seventh-most-difficult drug to give up. It creates euphoria and energy, as well as potentially dangerous physical side effects, like rising heart rate and blood pressure. (Man, I've experienced that!) In its powder form, cocaine is either inhaled through the nose or dissolved in water and injected. Crack is cocaine that has been made into a rock crystal, which is smoked. Injecting or smoking cocaine gives you a drastically fast high, but after about five minutes, a drastically low low sets in. Snorting cocaine has a less dramatic effect but lasts longer—about fifteen to twenty minutes. I wonder if, when I smoked a hunk of cocaine on the end of a cigarette, I was actually smoking crack.

After the psycho-ed class, I have an appointment with the in-house psychiatrist. He's an affable fellow whose name is so difficult to pronounce, everybody calls him Dutchy. He's about fifty-five and balding and has an appealing je-ne-sais-quoi quality. It must be the pink shirt and bright yellow tie he's wearing. I like him and trust him immediately.

Dutchy asks me about my history of drug and alcohol abuse.

Where do I start? How much time does this guy have? Even though I do trust him, I don't know if I can own up to all my shameful behavior. I don't know if I can tell the whole truth.

As if he's reading my mind, Dutchy says, "Relax, Rosemary. This isn't a test. It's your recent history of drug and alcohol use that's most important right now. This is a time to be truthful. Otherwise, we can't help you. You want help, don't you?"

"Yes, Dutchy," I say with resignation. "That's why I'm here. Well, it started . . . hmm." I think back to when Matthew delivered a stash of cocaine, and I tried to find a razor blade to cut it into lines. I hadn't done that much cocaine, and it was way back in my twenties—some twenty years ago. Matthew promptly got out a credit card from his wallet and handed it to me, as if to say, *Here, use this.*

"It started in October 1996, about five years after my husband died. Matthew, a colleague turned bad-choice lover." I shake my head and continue. "Anyway, I now call him Mr. Wrong. He brought over this cocaine, which I had given him the money for, and I was really excited. We snorted a couple of lines each, and, oh my God, it was like the answer to all my problems. I wanted more of this uncluttered brain I was all of a sudden experiencing. I wanted more coke. I wanted more of this, this, this . . ." I look around the room for the right words. "This scarcity of negativity! Shit. It was heaven!"

I know I'm kidding myself blaming this on Matthew, as if the fact that he supplied the cocaine absolves me of all my crimes. But I decide to spew out the history of my cocaine abuse, because there is a defined beginning and end and I am not currently addicted to it, so I can't be that bad, can I?

"I did coke daily for a year, then off and on for four more years, mixing it with copious amounts of white wine. I cut down on the cocaine after that and had it about every weekend for a while then once a month for about a year, and in January of this year, 2002, was able to quit it for good. So that was six years of cocaine use off and on."

I'm able to deliver this information to Dutchy without falling apart—like I'm reporting facts versus feelings. He's looking at me and saying nothing, as if to encourage me to go on, which I do.

"When I finally quit it, I was able to consume even more wine at a time, like somehow the cocaine had increased my tolerance for booze. My alcoholism progressed to the point where I was drinking as soon as I got up in the morning." My voice starts to break, as I'm starting to live in the gravity of my words, not just report the facts. "I became . . . uh, um, well, desperate and depressed and anxious, which made me drink, which made me more depressed and anxious, so I popped pills to counteract everything."

At this point, my waterworks start again and I'm crying too hard to continue. Putting my head in my hands, I start to bawl, haunted with guilt. I feel nauseated when I think about the abominable shit

I've done—shit I can't tell Dutchy, like when I whipped into the bathroom at the 7-Eleven on the way to Whistler with the girls and snorted some cocaine to get myself through the rest of the trip, but then realized when we arrived at the Whistler house that I was without my wallet. We had stopped at a restaurant, and I had left my wallet there. A police officer dropped it off at the house. I was so incredibly paranoid when he showed up. What an acting job I did with him, as if everything were perfectly normal.

I also couldn't tell Dutchy the truth about how I was using cocaine during the years when I had an early-morning shift at CFAX radio, hosting my own live interview show and producing my colleague's. My 4:30–9:00 a.m. shift gave me plenty of time to work, nap, snort, pick the kids up from school, snort, research my next day's programs, have enough wine to kill the cocaine high, go to bed, and then wake up and do it all again.

I'm finally able to stop my crying fit, lift my head out of my hands, and look at Dutchy. Unmoved by my hysterics, he talks as if we are having a normal conversation.

"It's not unusual for cocaine to increase a person's capacity for alcohol," he says. "How much were you drinking and what kinds of pills were you taking, Rosemary?"

"About a bottle of wine a day. Though I guess it could have been more than that, considering I started in the morning and basically did not stop all day. And the pills, well . . . some little blue ones for sleeping, and Ativan for anxiety."

"You mixed them with wine?"

"Yes," I say hesitantly. "Oh, and extra-strength Tylenol with codeine. And I'd take one or two zoplicone—is that what it's called? Zoplicone, for insomnia?"

"*Zopiclone*," he corrects me.

"I took them nightly to sleep," I say, leaving out the fact that I also took them in the daytime. "I took two or three Ativans every few days," I lie. "And a few Tylenol every couple of days, too. Always with wine."

"When was the last time you drank?" he asks. "Do you need to detox?"

"I'm not sure. I tried to stop entirely two weeks ago, when I spoke with Graham, but I couldn't. But I did cut back significantly. I haven't been drinking when I get up in the morning, which I started to do a few months ago."

Dutchy concludes that I am an alcoholic and not currently a drug addict because I quit the cocaine months ago and the pharmaceuticals I've been taking have the same effect as alcohol.

"I'll treat you as an alcoholic," he says. "And I'll give you some Valium to help you sleep at night."

Valium? Yippee! The thought of getting drugs to help quit my pills and alcohol seems ironic—and appealing.

Dinner that night is a succulent roast beef, and this time I can actually eat something without it getting caught in my throat. I guess Dutchy has loosened me up, because I'm also feeling more sociable. I'm sitting across from Jason—the kid with the disfigured face. Brad asks what his poison is, and he says, "Plain ol' scotch. Can't seem to stop it. I work in a mine on the island, and I bring a mickey of scotch in my lunchbox every day. That's not enough, though. I barely make it through the afternoon. My buddies are real worried; so're my parents."

Jason shovels a huge bite of potato salad into his mouth and continues talking. "Tried to end it," he says, pointing to his face—his nose half missing and his left cheek sunken in. "A Colt pistol. Just turned twenty-three, and I tried to end it." He swallows, puts his fork down, and picks up his water glass. "Next time might work."

Betsy, the woman who did my intake session, comes to the dinner table and sits down, leaning toward us. "After dinner, we're heading out to the AA meeting at the church here on Barefoot," she tells us.

Ugh! I have been to two of these in the last two weeks. They're boring; all people do is sit there and whine. I don't want to go to a fucking AA meeting.

"Is this mandatory?" I whine.

"Rosemary," Betsy says in her soft British accent, "you never know who's going to gain something from what *you* say."

As if I could offer anyone any wisdom at all.

We all pile into The Meadow's white van, which the other inmates have nicknamed the Druggy Buggy, and head to the meeting.

When it's my turn to speak, I almost say, "I pass," but stop myself. My eyes dart about the small room. About a dozen of us are jammed in here.

"My name is Rosemary, and"—I press the first three fingers of my left hand in the crease between my eyebrows and slouch—"I'm an alcoholic." This is the first time I have said that out loud, and I feel relieved. I continue, "A couple of weeks ago, I drank a lot of wine, took some Ativan, and drove my kids. I blacked out. By some miracle, I did not do physical damage to myself or the kids. However, I did do $4,000 worth of damage to the transmission of my car." People laugh. Wow, there can be laughter in the midst of misery.

There, I admitted it. I am astounded I actually admitted it, said it out loud. Telling Sheena was different—she's my spiritual counselor. Admitting my shameful, reprehensible, scandalous behavior to *these* people—well, something has shifted. It's intangible, but it feels like there's a new hue on everything. I sit up straighter in my chair. The heavy stones and rocks that have been burdening my upper back and shoulders are tumbling off me.

At the end of the meeting, we all stand and hold hands, and everyone else recites, "God, grant me the serenity to accept the things I cannot change, courage to change the things I can, and wisdom to know the difference." I try to listen to what they are saying and think I can remember for next time.

Feeling so much better than I did before the meeting, I start to walk out the door, but Stetson comes up to me and sets his hand on my forearm.

"Rosemary, Rosemary," he says, with a glazed look in his eyes. He sets his hand on my forearm. "Your share just reminded me of something, something I did, something I had actually forgotten about."

"Really? What?"

"I have two tiny children, one and two. Your share jogged a terrifying memory. You know what I did? I actually tucked them in and left them there. My wife was away. I left them at home at midnight, and I went downtown to score some cocaine. What if something had happened to them? You know?" He looks at me with horror in his eyes.

What can I say? How is that different from what I did? I believe that what I did was actually worse.

I'm so exhausted when we return to The Meadow that I can hardly stay awake for the nighttime check-in. Once again, we all sit in a group and say how we're feeling, just a brief few sentences about how our day has been. It's actually quite comfortable in the center's living room—cozy couches, dim lighting, and a stone fireplace. At one end is a dining room table, which is big but not too big, long enough to fit about a dozen people. At the other end of the room is an exit to the outside patio and swimming pool. Stetson and I have challenged each other to a swim-off—we're going to see who can swim forty minutes nonstop. I know I can.

I can't wait to go bed, which I do as soon as we are dismissed. When I lay my head down on the pillow, I detect a scent of a smile on my face. I touch my lips and then my cheeks. No tears. Holy shit!

—

The next day, I have another jog through The Meadow, enjoy the meals, and am not so put off by the group therapy. I'm starting to get to know my roommates and relate to them. I'm missing Willow and Dixie terribly and feel sick at the thought of being away from them, but I know I'm doing the right thing. When I go to bed, I'm proud to have made it through day two in rehab.

The next morning, my third day at The Meadow, the manager, Galveston, wants to talk to me after breakfast. What could this be about? I go downstairs to his office and knock gingerly on the door.

"Hi, Rosemary," he says, and then continues, without any pleasantries, "Darlene has just arrived and is in a double room alone, and that's against the rules. We need for you to move in with her."

"What?" I recoil. "Uh, I really don't want to move. I was finally feeling like I was starting to like it here. I like the room I'm in, and Celia and Nicole. I think I can relate to them. It's the nicest bedroom here, and I'm all settled in. Why can't one of them move?"

"You're the newest. You gotta move."

"That's the shits, Galveston. I may just leave. I miss my kids so much. Can I at least phone them?"

"Another rule—not until the end of the week."

Rattled, I complain about this change of circumstance during the morning check-in, but it seems nobody is going to do anything about it.

At the group session, Fred tells us how his father sexually abused him from about age ten to about age sixteen. He is American and fought in the Vietnam War. He trained to become an addictions counselor but can't keep off the crack, even when he goes years at a time being clean. His dad just died, and he has written him a letter forgiving him, something he never, ever thought he could do.

"Oh, Fred, what did it feel like to have to forgive him?" I ask. "I can't—"

"No cross-talk on someone's share, Rosemary," Graham interjects.

Huh? I thought I was being compassionate.

It's Brad's turn to share. "I need to get something off my chest," he says. "I can't stop the crack. I work with Dad, and we do construction together, and I go a couple of weeks without it, but then I gotta score again, ya know? Shit. I turn around and go on a bender for a weekend. Oh, God." He rubs his eyes. "Oh, God, ya know, at the end of one of these benders, I got into a fight with my wife, and, well . . . I . . . I hauled off and slugged her one. That's it. That's it. I'm done. I actually told someone. I told you. It's outta me."

It's such a heavy session that there's no place for small talk at lunch afterward. All I hear is the clanging of knives and forks and spoons as we eat our Sante Fe chicken salad and homemade bread.

"Another tough day at the office," Henderson pipes up at one point, but it does little to break the tension.

After lunch, I go upstairs and dutifully lug my shit from my lovely corner bedroom with a balcony and a view to the middle bedroom on the lower level, which is dark and dreary. If this were a hotel, it'd be like moving from the presidential suite to the room beside the kitchen.

When I enter the room, I don't see anyone, but I hear someone in the bathroom. I put my suitcase on the bed and hope she comes out soon.

The toilet flushes, and she emerges.

"Hi, I'm Rosemary," I say, holding out my hand to shake hers.

She is about forty, with shoulder-length blond hair that's parted in the middle and tucked back behind both ears. She's about my height—five foot five—and plain-looking, but it's the kind of plain-looking where you can tell she could be very striking if she did herself up a little, sort of like the schoolmarm-librarian who morphs into a sexy tigress in the movies.

She has a pack of cigarettes in her hand and takes one out. "I really need one of these," she says, ignoring my handshake and not introducing herself. I drop my hand.

"The smoking area is out by the pool," I tell her. "What's your name?"

"I'm Darlene, and I don't know what I'm doing here," she says. "I mean, I've been on methadone for a while, so my heroin addiction is at bay. It got bad, I tell ya. Real bad." Darlene talks slowly, in a lazy manner that makes it seem like she doesn't give a shit about anything. She's wearing a loose-fitting denim shirt untucked from her jeans, which are clearly too big for her skinny frame.

Uncomfortable with too much information too soon, I respond by trying to make lighter conversation. "Do you have any children?"

"I have a daughter," she says. "Adopted her as a baby. When she was ready to be picked up from the hospital, my husband and I were supposed to go for her, but I stayed at home in bed." Darlene pauses, pushes up her left sleeve, and does a shooting-up-heroin motion, pretending her cigarette is a needle. "I shot up instead. I keep the needle and junk between the mattress and the box spring."

Darlene is talking like she's proud of this behavior, but I'm sickened—so sickened I can't spend another moment with her. I excuse myself and barge into Galveston's office.

"I refuse to stay with Darlene. I'm moving back upstairs," I inform him, shocked by my own audacity, at the same time irate about the audacity he had to order me to change rooms.

Galveston looks up at me, drops his pen down on the desk, and says nothing, just squints at me.

"I'll just walk right out of here and see my daughters if you insist I stay with Darlene." I resist the urge to say, *Go fuck yourself,* but that is certainly how I feel.

"Well, Rosemary, this is not wise," says Galveston, drawing out the word: *w-iiiiii-se.* "We move you around for a reason. Life is full of inconveniences."

"That's too bad," I retort, and turn around and leave, shutting the door behind me—careful not to slam it, suddenly concerned about my dramatic behavior and what it might mean.

I move myself back upstairs.

Fuck this bullshit.

15

"Lucy in the Sky with Diamonds"
the Beatles

Tuesday, May 7, 2002

Surprisingly, there are no repercussions at breakfast for my room rebellion. I'm hoping this means I get to stay in the lovely corner room with Nicole and Celia.

I'm four days into my sentence at The Meadow now, and I'm feeling myself getting into the groove of the center. I'm even beginning to understand the group-therapy process. But I'm a little nervous about what I need to do today. It's time for me to deliver on the assignment Graham gave me: "Rosemary's First Memories."

Graham wastes no time after group starts and says, "Rosemary, you're up."

"Well . . ." I look out the window and twirl a strand of hair around my index finger, trying to get into the mind-set to time travel to long, long ago. "You know, I was bullied when I was little. I had a lisp, and kids picked on me. I couldn't say my r's and my s's. Imagine that, with a name like Rosemary Parrett . . . *Wothemawwee Pawwett*. I was bucktoothed, which was the reason for the speech impediment. I got called Peeface, instead of Rosemary. I assumed it was *Pee*face, as in urine, not *Pea*face, as in pea, the vegetable, because I assumed the worst."

At that, some in the group giggle, which I expected, but Darlene's laugh is a little too emphatic—she's enjoying my self-deprecation a little too much.

"Anyway," I continue, "I was just not as good as everyone else. I remember a couple of incidents in particular. One day—I was about seven, I guess—I was walking home from school, and there was Susan Trathaw, standing out in front of her house as I passed by. She was a show-off and a smarty-pants, and she came over and slapped my face—because I was stupid or something, I guess." As I speak, I feel myself being catapulted to that time when I just did not fit in. I shift around in my seat, trying to get comfortable.

"I'm just feeling like I'm back in that little seven-year-old body." I look down at my lap and fold my hands in an effort to stop fidgeting. "Let's see, where was I? Oh yeah, Susan Trathaw. Well, it was the same with that meanie Thomas Nella. I'm talking like I'm seven years old, but I don't care. That is exactly what I called those two: Meanie and Smarty-Pants. So, I was sitting beside Thomas Nella in class—grade two. I remember the teacher. She had a ponytail like a Barbie doll—I never owned one of those Barbies. They were a luxury we couldn't afford. But anyway, there I was, minding my own business, sitting beside Thomas Nella, and he poked the top of my head with a very sharp pencil and made me cry. Who gets in trouble from Miss I Look Like a Barbie Doll teacher? Not Thomas Nella, but me." I put my hands on my hips in indignation.

"Oh, and later, by the way—much later, when we were teenagers and Thomas was at King George College, a boys' school—he was driving his buddies the night of the prom after drinking, and he hit a lamppost on Mount Pleasant Avenue and one of his buddies was killed! I thought it was so bad that Nella had been so irresponsible—drinking so much that he hit a lamppost and killed his friend—and here I am, decades later, and I almost killed my own children and could have killed others because of my drinking. I just wasn't as unlucky as Thomas Nella."

I see Celia and Nicole nod and Stetson scowl. I see that Henderson, Fred, and Jason are all staring at me, waiting for me to go on. Rodrigo is looking at his clasped hands, and Darlene is looking out the window.

I breathe in deeply and am about to continue, when Graham says, "Rosemary, do you see a theme here about how you think of yourself?"

"Yes, I guess so: stupid."

I see Nicole mouth *no* with a scowl, defending me against myself.

"But you aren't stupid," Graham says. "You know that. I'm just making the point that low self-esteem can be deep-rooted. Low self-esteem is a common theme among addicts and alcoholics."

"You mean I can blame Susan Trathaw and Thomas Nella for my deep psychological scars and my drinking and drug problems?"

I hear a few snickers.

"Yeah, right—if only it were that easy, Rosemary," Graham says. "What happened to the lisp?"

I shrug. "Mom sent me to speech lessons. I also had my buck-teeth fixed. Anyway, probably more relevant was my father's drinking. Dad hated the passage of time or anything that implied, by its very existence, the spending of money—like Christmas or birthdays. We didn't celebrate birthdays. And Christmas was not a celebratory occasion, either. I never really liked Christmas until I met my late husband, Barry. He died in 1991, when our kids were two and five. He showed me how warm Christmas can be, and he was so generous—not that it was all about the presents and all."

I force myself back to childhood again. "You know, Dad"—I shake my head—"he was always mad, particularly at my older brothers. There were four of us—boy, girl, boy, girl. The boys . . . well, in their twenties, things changed drastically for them. Rob came out as gay, and Gavin became schizophrenic. Dad rejected both of them—like, acted like they weren't his. Poor Rob—he died in 1992, of AIDS, and never had the opportunity to resolve his relationship with his father. I was going through that at the same time my husband was dying—another story. I'll get back to that.

"Dad liked Bacardi and Coke. He drank *a lot*. And there was a lot of yelling and screaming. But somehow never at me. I was the youngest, and a girl, and, well, you know, I guess I had a special spot in the family. But he would come home late at night and we'd hear him from our beds, throwing pots and pans around, and the next day we'd see them all bent. He'd yell for Mom in his drunken stupor, 'Audrey, where the hell are you?' When he found her, he'd yell at her about money, and all we could hear from Mom was a muffled murmur."

I stop and strain to hear what Mom is saying, as if I'm little again, lying in my bed. I just can't pick up one word. I've always thought their behavior was normal. It was *my* normal. Today is the first time I've let myself embrace the fact that this was incredibly *ab*normal.

I look at Graham and Stetson and Henderson, who are on either side of Graham. It looks like Stetson is clenching his teeth in anger and Henderson is fighting tears. Graham looks at me and nods, telling me with his eyes to continue.

"Sometimes when Dad came home, Mom hid in my bed with me to protect herself from him. She'd lock the door and crawl under the covers between me and the wall, and there'd be crashes and doors slamming downstairs, and Dad would be yelling Mom's name. He'd get to the locked door and rattle it and rattle it and rattle it . . ." I move my hand as if I'm grabbing a door handle, and I'm staring at my hand the same way, as a little girl, I stared at the shaking door. Then I realize I am actually shaking. Did I shake as a little girl? I can't remember. I can't remember what I felt. I'm confused. Why can't I remember any feelings?

"Once, when he couldn't get in, he got a ladder and went up the side of the house to our bedroom. He stood on the copper awning—the ones that turn aquamarine with age—and banged at the window. But he couldn't get in, so he went back to the bedroom door and pounded on it again. I remember him breaking the lock to the bedroom door one time and getting in and standing there in the doorway, just standing there, this screaming, gesticulating silhouette. He couldn't see Mom, though, so he turned and stomped back down the hall." I cringe at the memory.

"Actually, come to think of it, he always stomped down the long hall from his and Mom's bedroom to our room, screaming for Mom. You know, God, you know, I . . . I just had a very painful revelation. It's history repeating itself in a horrifying way. *I've* done that. Oh my God. I've stomped down the hallway from my bedroom to the girls' rooms, screaming. I don't know what I was screaming about, but I remember I had a hangover and it was a Sunday morning and I was really tired and upset. I'm sure I did that more than once. I did exactly to them what my father did to us."

I stop talking and hang my head and put my thumbs and my middle fingers on either side of my temples, waiting for the tears and then embracing them. It's a purging; I can feel that I need to be crying right now.

"Rosemary, what did you feel when your father was acting like this?" Graham asks.

I'm silent. Nicole grabs a box of Kleenex from the windowsill and hands it to me. I wipe tears from my cheek as I try to unearth emotions from my little-girl self. I can see Celia and Fred and Brad, all looking very serious and concerned and anticipating my next answer. I just realized that these events in my life were momentous times. I've never spoken about this. It's always been one of those foul secrets that all the family members are aware of but pretend don't exist—like if we don't acknowledge it, maybe it will go away. But it's right here.

Now I am collecting it; I'm sweeping up the debris of the past. But what am I going to do with it?

"You must have been terrified, Rosemary," Graham says gently.

"But the thing is, I don't remember feeling *anything*," I admit.

"What would you say to your father if you had the chance, then?" he asks.

"Um . . . 'You shouldn't be talking to Mom like that with Sally and me here like this. And, Mom, you shouldn't be seeking protection from that bully in my bed—me, your baby girl.'" I choke on my words. I close my eyes and relive the terror. My father is getting closer and closer to the bedroom. He is stomping down the hallway, louder and louder and louder. He's at the door. *Crack.* It breaks. He barges in and . . . *Please, please, please, don't, Daddy. Please stop, Daddy.*

Then I think about my own little girls and the fear they must have felt when I clomped down the hallway in a rage.

"You can stop now, Rosemary," Graham says. "You need a break. You need to process. This wasn't easy, and you did really well. The only way to take the energy out of this is to do exactly what you're doing: shining a light on the skeletons in the closet."

Graham's comments are reassuring, and they answer my question about what I'm going to do about the debris I collect. Collecting it and acknowledging it for exactly what it is—that is what will start to dissolve the power it has over me.

"Yes," I say. "I'm really, really exhausted."

After the session, some of my fellow inmates gather around me to offer their support.

Brad gives me a hug, and I almost get lost in his big, burly body.

"You *are* big," I say, as I smile and separate from him.

"That was incredible, Rosemary," he says.

"It really was," Celia agrees, and she gives me a warm, lingering hug.

"You smell good," I tell her.

"Thanks," she says, smiling. "It must be my vanilla shampoo. I'll let you use it if you want. You did a really good job there, Rosemary. How do you feel?"

I look at her and check in on my feelings. How do I feel? "I feel lighter."

Stetson butts in. "That looked really difficult, Rosemary."

"Well, I was just telling Celia that somehow I feel lighter—like it was some kind of purging. Something about it feels right."

"Well, do you think that a swim-off would be the right change of pace, or is that insensitive of me?"

"Oh, man, that would be the perfect thing to do right now." I break into a smile. "You're on!" We high-five, and I say, "Meet you at the pool in ten."

Nicole joins us at the pool to serve as the referee.

"One, two, three, go!" she cries, and Stetson and I both dive in.

As I hit the water and my body goes under, my consciousness enters slow motion. The water is gushing through my hair, over my face, over my entire body. My mind becomes a cool clearing in a deep, thick, dark forest. I am immediately transformed. For a moment, my mind and heart are luminous, relieved of their cumbersome load of emotions.

Then I suddenly remember I'm racing Stetson. I pop up from my dive and break into a robust breaststroke. I can't do the crawl very well. Stetson's ahead of me, but I feel strong and steady. He may be thirty-seven to my forty-seven, but I'm in great shape and am used to swimming a mile nonstop.

As I plow through the water, length after length, I slowly start creeping up beside him, narrowing the gap between us—but then I can't gain. He's increased his pace, and I'm losing my breath. I don't know if I can keep going.

Yes, you can, Rosemary. I harden my resolve. I may not be gaining on him, but I'm not going to lag behind. I think he's slowing down, but I just can't push myself any faster.

Finally, we're on the last lap and I've kept the pace, but so has he. Maybe I can pass him on the home stretch. I hate and love this part of any race—swimming, running, skiing—the final stretch, when you've already given everything you possibly can, pushed your very hardest, yet you need one last gust of gas, though you still don't know if that will be enough to beat your opponent.

I can't catch up. I touch the end of the pool about three strokes behind Stetson.

Stetson holds on to the end of the pool, faces me, and says, between gasps of air, "Holy shit, Rosemary, you're in great shape." Then he shakes his head so water flies everywhere.

"I think I put on a respectable showing," I concur.

We get out of the pool, shake hands, and say simultaneously, "Let's eat."

We laugh, as does Nicole, and the three of us walk out of the pool area together.

That night I am completely spent—zapped of all my energy, emotional and physical. Now that the day's activities are over, there is space inside me for more feelings to emerge. I guess this is what they call processing.

As I lie there, I ache for my girls. I feel it all over my body. My stomach is churned up. This is a familiar feeling. This is what it feels like to grieve. It's exactly the feeling I had when Barry died—raw, unforgiving grief clenching my heart. I'm grieving for my girls. I'm desperate to see them. *Barry, what have I done? What have I done? Barry, help me. I can't bear it any longer.*

I'm frantic. They need me. How will they get along without me? They're not okay. I haven't been able to call them, and even if I could, I need more than speaking to them on the phone. It's Mother's Day this Sunday. I have to be with them for that. I have to leave. I'll tell Graham in the morning, I need to go. I can't stay. I need to be with my girls.

I manage to drift off to sleep.

I'm in a swimming pool, looking up at Willow and Dixie. They're standing beside the pool, looking down at me, their little faces all distorted by the water. I'm reaching for them, but I can't swim up. I'm stuck in one spot, unable to breathe, my hands reaching up to my precious daughters. It looks like they're crying. I can't scream because I'm underwater. Then I awaken from my nightmare with a feeble little whimper.

Fuck, that was a dream. What a fucking relief. I can't stay here at The Meadow. I need to be with my daughters. I'm leaving tomorrow.

When I wake the next morning, I am laden, dizzy, blurry, hazy. I have a hangover. How can this be? This isn't fair. I haven't been drinking or using, and I have a hangover. I've heard about emotional hangovers; I guess this is what they're talking about.

I sleep through breakfast, despite my roommates' urging to join them, but I make myself get up and ready for group. As I dress, I practice in my head exactly what I'm going to say about leaving.

When it comes to my turn to share in group, I don't hesitate; I blurt out, "I've been thinking about Willow and Dixie. I woke feeling really ill this morning. I think they need me. I'm not sure they can get along without me. I don't know how much emotional support they're getting. Melba, the nanny, is good but not much of a support in that way. And their grandma . . . well, she's a little out there. You know, not crazy—she's fun—but she has some different ideas. I think I have to leave. I have a pain in my gut, right here." I hold my stomach right below my rib cage. "It's paralyzing. I know it's emotional pain. Emotional hurt. I used to take Tylenol with codeine for this, but now I'm not allowed to. I need to see my girls. And Sunday's Mother's Day. They'll really feel my not being home for Mother's Day. I'm going to pack up after group."

I stop talking and wait for Graham's response.

Nothing. Silence.

My heart palpitates. My stomach screams. My mind chatters.

Graham finally says, "Well, what does the group think?"

Celia responds first. "It seems like a mistake, Rosemary."

Then Brad: "I thought you were making good progress."

Then Nicole: "Sounds like serious separation anxiety. What are your kids—fourteen, fifteen?"

I nod and mumble, "Thirteen and fifteen."

"I've had this," she says. "They'll be okay. Like I was told, 'What good are you to them sick?'"

Stetson repeats what Celia said: "It seems like a mistake, Rosemary."

"Anyone else?" Graham asks.

"I don't want to sound too harsh, Rosemary," Henderson says, his voice soft and affectionate, "but are you completely nuts?"

Silence.

"Nicole's right, Rosemary," Graham says. "This is genuine separation anxiety. But I can tell you this"—he looks directly into my eyes, though his body is still facing the group—"if you leave, you *will* drink. I repeat, you *will* drink."

Knowing I will do anything to never, ever drink again, those words, "you *will* drink," land at the very base of my stomach, heavy. They stick there as I try to grasp my new reality. I won't be going home until twenty-four days from now.

"Tell you what, Rosemary," Graham says. "We'll break the rules and let you speak to your kids during the first week. You can call them later today, during phone time. And they can visit on family day this Saturday. It's not Mother's Day, but it's at least Mother's Day weekend." He leans back in his chair and folds his hands in his lap like it's all decided—a plan for Rosemary. "Phone 'em and plan it. You'll get to be with them on Mother's Day weekend, Rosemary."

"Graham, Graham, Graham. Thank you so much. I feel like a peacock who had broken feathers, and finally they're fixed and I'm in full bloom. I'm so happy." I get out of my seat and go give Graham a hug—well, as much as one can hug someone who's sitting down while you're standing up.

"I guess this isn't exactly group protocol, is it?" I ask.

"No," he says good-naturedly, standing up and ending the hug. "Group's done for this morning anyway. Let's end in the usual manner: the Serenity Prayer."

We all stand and recite, "God, grant me the serenity to accept the things I cannot change, courage to change the things I can, and wisdom to know the difference."

I'm excited and nervous to talk to Willow and Dixie as I head toward the phone, which is at the bottom of the stairs, tucked in a nook beside the TV-movie room. But when I get to the top of the stairs, I hear a voice. Shit, is someone on the phone?

I go down the stairs far enough to see that it's Darlene. There is nowhere to loiter down there, as the door to the TV room is shut. I go back up to the top of the stairs and lean on the banister. Why is there just one phone? And why does it have to be Darlene, the one person I feel uncomfortable with here, on it? And she just arrived here at The Meadow! She's not even allowed to be on the phone in her first week.

I'm thinking I should go and tell someone, when Brad comes along.

"Hi," I say. "I'm waiting for the phone. Darlene's down there."

"Oh, she's on the phone again," he says. "I thought we weren't allowed the phone in the first week."

"We're not. You heard Graham giving me special permission, right? Well, I didn't hear him giving *her* special permission. I haven't spoken with my kids yet. Should I go tell a staff member she's on the phone?" I'm careful not to say this too loudly; I don't want Darlene to hear me.

"I was finally getting the nerve up to call my wife," Brad says. "There's not much time before dinner. But never mind telling anyone. We don't want to be tattletales." He cups his hands over his mouth and yells down the stairs, "Daaaaaaaaaaaarleeeeeeeeene, There's a lineup up here."

"You're brave," I say. "She can be a little snarky."

"I'm big, remember?" Brad walks away. "I'll call later. See ya at dinner."

A few minutes later, Darlene gets off the phone and walks non-chalantly up the stairs. When she walks by me, she says, almost inaudibly, and without looking at me, "It's all yours."

I go down to the phone and dial my number. Mom answers.

"Hi, Mom, it's me."

"Daaaaaaaaarling, how are you? The kids are just *great*."

"Really? Are they okay? Do they miss me?"

"They're great," she says. "That Dixie's so smart and fun. She had a friend over, and they watched a movie and laughed and laughed. And that Willow—wow, what a winner she is. You got a couple of winners here, honey. Oh, okay, just a sec. Willow's right here. Say hi to your mom. I'll go get Dixie."

Mom always says everything is okay. I need to talk to the girls and find out what's really going on.

Willow gets on the phone. "Mom, are you okay? What's it like there? Are you getting better?" She sounds so sweet and caring and mature.

"Oh, sweetie, it's so good to hear your voice. It's really pretty here, and the people are really nice, and I really, really miss you. Are you okay? How are you doing without me? How's school?"

"School's good. I got 96 percent on my math test. Melba took me and Robby to kickboxing last night, and I'm going to test for my brown belt soon."

"That's fantastic, sweetheart. I'm so proud of you. When is the kickboxing test? I don't want to miss seeing that."

"I don't know, but, Mom"—Willow lowers her voice to a whisper—"Gramma's insane."

"Why? What's she doing?"

"Oh, just everything, like dumb rules. Like, we can't have chocolate because she says we're allergic."

I make a mental note to tell Mom that the kids can eat chocolate.

"It's stupid rules and stuff. Dixie and I are both mad. We're fighting a bit. But I'm okay, and I'm proud of you, Mom."

I'm a little taken aback at Willow's telling me she's proud of me. It's like role reversal. I'm supposed to be the mama, the proud mama bear; she's supposed to be the cub in need of protection. Surprised but also deeply moved, I say in earnest, "Thank you. Thank you so much, sweetie." I pause and change the subject. "What are you and Dixie fighting about?"

"Oh, like, she stole my school tie and said it was hers because she lost hers, so we kinda argued, but it's okay."

I make another mental note to talk to Melba about the ties, but then I realize I'm micromanaging and I need to be managing myself right now. I need to let go. It is just so tough—so, so, so hard—to let go of my little babies. *Let go, Rosemary, let go.*

I hear Dixie in the background, "I'd like to talk to Mom. I'd like to talk to Mom. And that was actually *my* tie, Willow."

Oh, this is just what I was dreading. They're fighting, and I sense Dixie's having a tougher time than Willow is about my leaving. She is younger and more vulnerable. My departure has really dislodged her. Oh, the pain is eating away at me. I feel a wrenching toward my girls deep in the core of my heart.

"Just a second," Willow says, irritated. "I'm talking to her."

"Gimme the phone, Willow," Dixie insists.

"No," Willow says.

I'm crying now. They're fighting and I'm here, totally unable to do anything. How can I let go of them?

I hear my mom say, "C'mere, c'mere." I don't know who she's talking to, but the next thing I know, Dixie is on the phone.

"Hi, Mom. I love you. I miss you. When are you coming home? Gramma won't let me keep my window open at night, and Willow stole my school tie."

"Oh, Dixie, I miss you guys so much, too. Gramma won't let you open your window? And aren't there a few school ties around? Ask Melba. I'll speak to Melba about it."

"Rosemary, dinnertime!" a staff member yells down to me from the top of the stairs. Oh, shit—now I have to say goodbye. This has been horrible. Now I see why we're not allowed phone calls in the first week. I feel like I need to leave again. But Graham says I'll drink if I leave now. How does he know?

"Dixie, Gramma is going to bring you here on Saturday to see me. Isn't that fantastic? But right now I have to go to dinner. You guys can come and see me this Saturday, and we can celebrate Mother's Day a day early. What a great present. I can't wait to see you. I miss you so, so much. I love you, my baby Dixie. Can I talk to Gramma now?"

"Wait, Mom, don't go," Dixie pleads.

Her words land on my heart with a thud and get heavier and heavier. There's an almighty magnet from my heart to theirs. It's almost impossible to fight it. I pause, close my eyes, and force myself to say, "I have to. I'm sorry. I'm so sorry, Dixie. I'll see you Saturday. Give the phone to Gramma, please. I love you and really miss you so, so much."

"Oh, all right. Here's Gramma." She surrenders, and then Mom is on the phone.

"They've been good as gold till now," she says. "They're really okay. They're really good kids."

"Will you bring Willow and Dixie to see me on Saturday?" I ask. "There's a noon ferry. The schedule is there by the kitchen phone. I can't wait. But I need some things. Will you bring me a sweater or two and some sweatpants, a large purse—"

"Wait," Mom says, "a what? A purchase? Is that what you said? Spell that, please."

I start to repeat myself. "Two sweaters—"

"Wait, wait, I'm writing it down," Mom says. "Spell that, please."

Man oh man, I'm going berserk here.

"Mom. Mom! I have to go. Can you pleeeease give the phone to Willow? Thanks for everything. I can't wait to see you Saturday. I'll call again the next chance I get. I love you."

"Hi, Mom." Willow is back. "Gramma says you need some things."

"Yes, I need some sweatpants and sweaters and some kind of bag for all my papers. You can look in the bottom drawers in my room for the tops and pants, and maybe check the top of the cupboard for some large purses or something. I have this binder I carry around with me all day—like a workbook—and I need, like, a book bag or something, and some pens. Oh, and I need another pair of glasses. They'd be in my top office drawer with the pens. Thanks so much, sweetie. You're wonderful."

"Okay, Mom." My little Willow is taking on the motherly role, so capable—and with better hearing than Gramma. Meanwhile, poor Dixie is really struggling with my being away. She's regressing, and Willow is fast-forwarding far too quickly into adulthood—all in my absence. It's so hard not to just leave right now and go straight to their arms. But Graham's words keep echoing in my head: *If you leave, you will drink.* I can't ever, ever drink again. I need to do whatever it takes.

"Thank you," I say. "I love you so much. Maybe I'll try to come home sooner than three and a half weeks from now. Maybe you can help comfort Dixie."

"Okay, but do what you need to do, Mom. I love you."

"Thanks, sweetie. I love you, too."

That night when I finish eating dinner, I pick up as many dishes as I can carry and head to the kitchen, where Brad has already started cleanup. We're both on dish duty tonight.

"How about I clear and you wash?" he suggests. "I hate washing."

"But isn't there a dishwasher?"

"Yes, but a lot of stuff doesn't go in it. Look at all those big dishes and pots!" he exclaims, pointing to a stack of stuff waiting to be cleaned.

"Ugh," I say, "but I actually like washing." I start filling up the sink with water and dumping some dishes in.

"And I like this song," Brad says, turning up the volume on the boom box in the kitchen. It's Tina Turner.

"'Proud Mary'!" I turn to face Brad, bend my knees, lean back, and put both hands out so my thumbs are up, dripping water down my arms and on the floor in the process. "Let's get down!"

Brad grooves out to the dining room on dish-pickup duty, and I dry my hands and turn up the volume a little more.

While Tina croons and I wash the dishes, I'm taken back to my twenties, when my boyfriend Jimmy and I used to blare this song in the sauna at the home I grew up in. Once he and I and our other university friends were in the sauna, we got into the alcoholic punch and the joints.

My mind stays back in the '70s as I continue to scrub the dishes. I'm feeling nostalgic but also experiencing a reality check. I have always assumed my drug use in my twenties was just "playful," but in hindsight I can see the budding alcoholic and drug addict that I was. I could never say no to one more toke, one more line. Until recently, I had forgotten about having tried cocaine back then. I also did MDMA, amphetamine, Quaaludes—horse tranquilizers!—LSD, and whatever else I could get my hands on to get wired.

"Hey, Rosemary, sing along," Brad yells over Tina's voice.

I take the dish scrubber, put it to my mouth like a microphone, turn around, and sing. Brad harmonizes with his broom-guitar.

We finish the dishes just in time for an in-house AA meeting. I make myself a strong tea and bring a bowl of Jujubes—my favorite candy—into the living room. Jason puts on a fire, and a staff member introduces three guest speakers as we all get comfy on the sofas around the coffee table.

One guest—a bald guy, about thirty-five, cute and hip—is one year clean and sober. The second visitor is a funky girl with blond dreadlocks and a tattoo of what looks like a dream-catcher on the inside of her right forearm. She's about twenty-five and is two years sober. And a third guest, a businessman type, is three years clean and sober. Holy shit! How do they do it? How are they able stay sober that long? I need to be able to do that, too. I listen intently as each one shares their story, all different but with a central theme: these three sober guests could not stay clean and sober on their own; they needed the fellowship of AA's twelve-step program, which is the basis of the program at The Meadow.

It reminds me of the resolve I need to have to stay here. I so desperately want to go and be with my girls; the phone call made me miss them and worry about them even more. But I need to do whatever I possibly can to never drink again, and I clearly need to stay

16

"Visiting Day"
Widespread Panic

Saturday, May 11, 2002

The alarm interrupts my sleep at 6:00 a.m.

My eyes open and try to adjust to the bright morning light, as I focus on the day ahead. I know it holds something pressing. My scrambling thoughts finally converge. It's visiting day. My girls are coming today.

I check in with my feelings, as I have been learning to do here at The Meadow. Hmm. I am vacillating between fear and excitement. Yes, I'm excited but definitely also anxious. I'm uncertain of what will happen. It could be a complete disaster; they may be so clingy that they won't leave—or won't leave without me.

I go for a quick jog in the vineyard-orchard, take a shower, and carefully choose what I'm going to wear. I want to be cool for the kids so they don't say I'm, in their words, "lame." They are my fashion cops. I pick my low-waisted jeans and American Eagle belt. I'm pretty sure that will pass muster.

I'm just not hungry at breakfast. I notice that Stetson and Brad are not at the table. Then I see Stetson coming into the dining room with Graham.

Graham sits down at the table and says, "Morning, everyone."

We mumble "Morning" back.

He leans in toward us. "I regret to say I have some bad news. I'm sure you've noticed Brad is not here. He left last night." Graham looks around and puts his arms out on either side of him. "We believe he went to Main and Hastings to score. He did contact his folks, but now they've lost track of him." Main and Hastings is the skid row of Vancouver.

"He seemed downright jolly when we hit the sack last night," Stetson says. "He's my roommate. He's my friend. How could he do this? And could I have done—"

Fred interrupts, looking equally disturbed. "He was saying the other day he didn't have one more binge in him, that it would take him out. Where'd he get the cash to score? And how—"

"Hold on a sec," I interrupt. "I just don't believe it. I feel close to Brad, too. Just last night we were groovin' to 'Proud Mary' in the kitchen. I feel some responsibility for him. Could I have done something? Should I have asked how he was doing—like, really *doing*—instead of dancing? And how do you know he's gone to Main and Hastings?"

"Yeah, you can't really *know* he's gone to score," Fred says. "Where'd he get the cash?"

"He had some contact with his folks, who said he mentioned scoring down on Skid Row, and Main and Hastings is where he has normally gone to score in the past," Graham said. "We don't know much else. This is the sad truth of the disease. Right now, crack is making the decisions for Brad. It has hijacked his brain. We'll keep you posted if we hear anything. In the meantime, you need to deal with your own sobriety. Don't let this jeopardize that. Let's pray for Brad. Let's have a moment of silence for him."

We set down our knives and forks and close our eyes. I can picture Brad's face, distorted among the prostitutes, pimps, used-needle-ridden back alleys, cockroach-infested rooming houses, alcoholics, derelicts, and ruffians of Main and Hastings, looking for a fix. Then I think, *My God, what makes me any different than those alcoholics down at Main and Hastings, my "high bottom"?* Just because I didn't total my car and lose custody of my children doesn't make me any better. I am exactly like those people. Alcoholism and addiction—the great equalizers.

We open our eyes, and Nicole, the grandmother, is crying. I'm so absorbed by Brad's disappearance that I've forgotten Willow and Dixie's impending visit. I try to comfort Nicole, who is now sobbing.

"Can I help?" I ask. "Nicole, do you want a glass of water? Coffee? Tea? I make a mean cuppa."

Nicole manages a polite giggle, then blows her nose and wipes her eyes with a Kleenex. "No, thank you. It's not all about Brad. It's just that something got triggered. I'm thinking about Kelly." Kelly is her daughter, who is still out on the streets and using heroin. Nicole and her husband split up because of the stress over their daughter. Nicole later got remarried, to a man who drinks. She has been self-medicating for years, mainly with Percocet.

As I attempt to comfort Nicole, I look up and am shocked to see Sheena, my spiritual counselor. I completely forgot she was coming today. She wants to help prepare me for the girls' visit. I stand up, put my hand on Nicole's shoulder, and tell her I need to go see Sheena but can make all of us a cup of tea if she wants one.

"No, that's all right," she says. "Thanks anyway. I'll be okay."

I leave Nicole with a final squeeze and greet Sheena with a quick hug.

"It's great to see you," I say. "I'm quite nervous."

"It's good to see you, too, Rosemary," she says. "You'll be fine." She speaks slowly and methodically, completely grounded, especially compared with my worked-up state. Her twinkling blue eyes look into my soul, just as I remember them doing during our first meeting. This quality of hers—her ability to penetrate my veneer—is both reassuring and disturbing.

"You're looking well," she says.

"Thanks." I smile. "Would you like a tea or coffee?"

"No, thank you," she says. "Let's talk."

"Yes," I say. "I don't think the group-meeting room is being used today, so let's go there." I lead her across the walkway that separates the main building from the meeting rooms and the bedrooms, and we sit down in the group meeting room for an impromptu therapy session. She says to remember to stay calm, that I'm a good mother, I'm getting well, my children really love me, they will be fine without me for three more weeks, I'm not good to them sick, and she will stay here at The Meadow today if I need her to help with them.

I check my watch. It's 12:40. The ferry arrived at 12:20. They'll be here any second. I thank Sheena and go into the bathroom for one last pee and a check in the mirror. I'm reminded of the mirror assignment from Graham: "Who do you see when you look in the mirror? What do you see coming from the inside?"

When I'm not using, I see someone I like in the mirror. I'm intelligent, talented, and fortunate. When I'm using or suffering the after-effects of being high or drunk, or both, I look in the mirror and swear I'm going insane. I don't know who the hell I am.

I snap myself out of my mental soliloquy and head back across the bridge to the main building. A set of steps leads down to the driveway. I stand at the top, and I see my white Land Rover arriving. It's my mother, with the kids in the car. She parks, and the three of them get out.

Mom catches sight of me and gives me a big smile and wave. She turns around to the girls. "Over here, over here, darlings," she says, pointing up at me, shuffling them along.

I melt at the sight of my girls.

They start walking up the stairs to me. "Hi, hi, hi, hi, hi, hi," I say. Willow reaches me first. I hug her tender frame and savor our melding into one. Then Dixie bumps into us with a devilish laugh.

"Dixie, I was hugging Mom," Willow protests. Fearing a fight over me, I say, "Family hug, family hug," and that appeases them—we fall into a three-way embrace.

"I've missed you so much," I tell them. Pulling away, I see that Dixie's eyes are red. "What's wrong, Dixie? It looks like you've been crying."

Before she can answer, my mom arrives at the top of the stairs. "Hi, Gramma," I say. I hug her and whisper in her ear, "Has Dixie been crying?"

"Yes!" says Dixie, who overheard.

"Oh, they're just squabbling over some gum. It's nothing. We had a lovely ferry ride over. Gosh, it's beautiful here. We've been having so much fun. We had vanilla pudding and peppermint tea onboard—it was so sweet."

"Mom, Mom." Dixie tugs at my hand.

"Mom," Willow says simultaneously.

Then my mom says to me, "You look terrific, dear. You're doing somethin' right, baby."

I'm still grappling with how I'm going to deal with both girls at once, when I notice Dixie looking dejected. I bend down slightly to her height, hold her hands, and look into her eyes. "You mad I'm here, honey?"

"It's kinda awful without you." Dixie lowers her voice as Mom swoons over the view from the Meadow. "Gramma's a retard. She won't let me keep my window open and makes us lock the side door all the time. Are we allergic to chocolate, Mom—" Dixie has no idea that the term "retard" is ableist but, at this point, I need to choose my battles.

"Mom, Mom," Willow interrupts.

I stand straight up and turn to her. "Willow, be kind to your sister. She's younger than you and needs your support."

"I made a Mother's Day present for you," Willow says. "And I have your clothes and things."

"I made you a present, too, Mom," Dixie says, handing me a package the size of a large book, wrapped in colorful paper.

As I take it, I realize I can't focus while both daughters are competing for my attention. My mind and heart are being bombarded. Shit! Maybe I should have had them come separately.

"Thanks so much, Dixie," I tell her. "I want to save it to open until later, when we're sitting down. Let me give you a tour of the joint first."

Devoid of emotion, Dixie stares at me and says, "I'd rather not right now." She turns around and heads back down the stairs, toward the car.

A wave of defeat consumes me as I murmur to myself, "Poor thing. It's her way of dealing with me wrenching myself away from her for four weeks. I totally understand her dismay."

Willow and Mom and I stand at the top of the staircase and watch Dixie heading to the car. I really don't know what to do. Mom looks at me, shakes her head a little, gives a shrug, and puts her hands up, as if to say, *What can you do?*

I'm not sure how to handle anything, and I feel my anxiety increasing. I guess I should tell Mom to lay off all these rules. But really, I don't know what the hell to do next. I am so fucking lost.

Then Sheena suddenly appears, intercepts Dixie, and says something to her that makes Dixie turn around and walk back toward us.

I almost collapse with relief. "Thank you so much, Sheena. I'm going to give them a tour."

We enter the main house from the top of the stairs so I can show them the eating area, the kitchen, the cozy living room with the fireplace, the basement phone area, and the TV/movie room.

"We watch some pretty good movies and eat popcorn," I say.

"That sounds like fun," Willow says.

Dixie and Willow are lagging behind in the TV room, out of ear-shot, and I figure this is a good time to address some issues. "Mom, why are you locking all the doors and windows? West Vancouver is very safe, you know. And I don't think they're allergic to chocolate. Do you think it makes them hyper?"

"What?" Mom says, unable to hear me.

Shit. My cluttered mind is telling me that I need to let go and stop micromanaging. Both Sheena and Graham have told me I can't sweat the small stuff. It just doesn't matter.

I lead my little family through the dining room and living room and outside to the pool. "And this is the pièce de résistance. Stetson, that young guy over there with the little kids"—I point to Stetson and his family, who are on the other side of the pool—"and I had a race, and I almost won."

Willow sees Stetson with his two young daughters and says, "They're so cute, Mom. Can I go and see them?"

"Yes, they're adorable. But let's not visit with them right now. Let's give them time alone."

Sheena appears again, almost magically, as if poised to trou-bleshoot at any time. I suggest we all sit in the sunshine by the pool, on the side opposite Stetson and his family. Between us are Darlene, her husband, and her daughter, Mimi, who is seven. She has curly Shirley Temple locks, only jet black, and deep blue eyes, big cheeks, and dimples. Mimi is on the pool deck, drawing; Darlene and her husband are chatting with other family visitors. I hear Darlene saying, a little too loudly, "Yeah, I kept my heroin with me at all times. Always in my purse—when I went grocery shopping, when I went to pick Mimi up from school. I could shoot up anywhere, really."

The fucking gall! It's like she's bragging. And she obviously knows we can hear her. Willow looks horrified. Thankfully, Gramma can't hear. *What a bitch that Darlene is.*

As I'm wondering what to say to Willow, Mimi walks up to her and asks, "Do you like my picture?" She holds out her sketch to Willow. "That's my mommy, that's my daddy, and that's me," she says, pointing to the corresponding figures. She has Darlene holding a glass of wine, and the glass of wine, which is three times as big as any of the people, is front and center in the picture. The three people are tiny figures in the background.

As I stare at Mimi's drawing, it strikes me that either of my daughters could very well have drawn the same picture. The face of the little girl in the picture morphs into Dixie, and the mommy morphs into me, but the wineglass still dominates the scene. I think about my own drinking and how often I've had a glass of wine in my hand while raising the girls. I kept glasses of wine everywhere so I wouldn't ever be without. I've sometimes had two or three going at once—under the counter in the bathroom, behind the milk in the fridge, in the cupboard in my office. In the evenings, I left notes for myself about where the glasses were so I would not forget about them the next day. I had so many empty chardonnay bottles, I didn't know what to do with them. I couldn't put them in the recycling bin, because everyone would see them. And Melba would certainly notice if I threw them out. So I'd collect them in a tote bag and get rid of them somewhere else—sometimes in the garbage can outside Shopper's Drug Mart, in Ambleside—an area where I got my prescription drugs—sometimes in a dumpster in an alleyway in the little village of Dundarave. I could see the headlines every time I drove down the alley, looked around surreptitiously as I got out of the car, and then emptied the tote bag into a bin: "West Vancouver Media Personality Caught Heaving Empty Wine Bottles into Dumpster in High-End Dundarave."

I watch Willow chatting with Mimi and notice how much she

looks like her father. I've always thought Willow looks more like my side of the family, but now I can see the Keevil in her. And Dixie looks like Barry in pictures of him when he was a kid. She really resembles Barry's mom, Nana.

"That's really good," Willow says of Mimi's drawing. "What's your name?"

"Mimi, and I'm seven years old," Mimi says with pride.

"Hi, Mimi," I say. "This is Willow, and I'm Rosemary." Willow holds the drawing out for me to see. "Look how talented Mimi is. Isn't she adorable?"

Willow looks at me, then at the picture, and then back at me, telling me with her eyes that she knows this is no ordinary drawing. I look at her and acknowledge this with a little nod of my head.

"Yes, it's a lovely picture, Mimi."

Mimi walks away with her Rembrandt, showing it to another family sitting by the pool.

"Mom, open my present," Dixie insists.

I notice Sheena and Mom engaged in conversation and think this might be a good time to try to talk to the girls together.

"Dixie, I'll open your present in a moment. I just want to talk to you both." I pull a chair around for Dixie so we're in a little semicircle.

"I miss you both so, so much. Here, give me your hands." They each reach out both hands, and I take all four of them in my own two. "I miss you so much that I almost left this week, but—"

"But, Mom," Willow says, her brow furrowed.

"Just wait," I say. "I was told, in no uncertain terms, that I would not get better if I left early. I really love you both, and it's very difficult for me to be apart from you. But I need your cooperation. It's only for three more weeks. I'm sorry Gramma is a little crazy. Doesn't she give you lots of love?"

Dixie ignores this. "Mom, open my present, please."

"Okay, okay."

"But why are you opening hers first?" Willow complains.

"Sorry, dear," I say. "I'll do yours right after."

"She always goes first."

"But then I'll have time to savor yours, sweetie. Please be patient."

Luckily, Sheena and Mom, who are sitting at a nearby table, notice the friction between the girls.

"Come join us, Willow," my mom says, patting the chair next to her.

"Oookay," Willow reluctantly agrees.

"Thanks, sweetie," I say. "We'll open your present together later, just the two of us."

I turn back to Dixie and open her card, which reads:

How can a mother not be loved by everyone around her, but you are loved by far the most and of that I am sure.

When you are driving you always break the law, but what amazes me the most is that the policeman never saw.

You take us up to Whistler a lot and we always have a lot of fun, and skiing down the mountain with you is the best thing I've ever done.

None of the other moms are weird or dumb, but the reason I love you by far the most is because you are MY mom.

"What an incredible poem!" I say. "Thank you. It's so sweet. I can't believe you wrote this for me. I'm honored." I hug her tightly, let her go, and read the poem aloud again.

"Thank you so much, Dixie. It's fabulous, and so are you." Meanwhile, the line about breaking the law when I'm driving is jumping out at me.

I unwrap Dixie's present and discover a homemade, stained-glass-like windowpane made of colored plastic.

"You put it in the window, and the sun shines through it, and it's like real glass," she said.

I smile widely. "Dixie, it's absolutely beautiful. Did you make it?" "Yeah, we made them at school. Do you like it?" I hold it up so the sun shines through it. "Yes! Look at that! Isn't it pretty? I'm going to put it up in my room right away. You really are very talented. I'm so proud of you. Thank you, thank you, for the very, very special card and gift. I can't wait to show you my room." I hold her cheeks in both my hands and give her a big kiss. "You look very beautiful, Dixie. I'm sorry that you are sad I'm here, but I need to stay. I need to get better."

I want to say how sorry I am for driving like a madwoman and likely terrifying her. I can't get out of my head the image of my driving on the wrong side of the road to Whistler, whizzing past cars at unsafe speeds. But Dixie interrupts my bad trip down memory lane.

"Mom, it's hard without you," she says, looking down at her feet.

I try to give her a hug, but she resists. I thought she was coming around, but clearly she is not. I feel like giving up. It's all I can do not to offer, *Okay, sweetheart, let's forget this rehab thing and all go home.* I'm sucked right into her suffering little soul.

Willow returns to the table and admonishes her sister, "Dixie, Dixie."

"That's not helping," I scold Willow.

Dixie's face drains of emotion again, and she turns and walks away, toward the main building. Sheena notices the discord and stops Dixie by grabbing her shoulder gently. "Dixie, your mother's trying to make healthy changes in her life," she says, and gestures at me, as if to say, *It's okay—I have a handle on this.* Dixie keeps on walking away, and Sheena follows her.

I turn to my mom. "I'm so sorry."

"Oh, I'm mainly concerned about how upset she must be to act like this," Mom says. "But she's in good hands with Sheena, who's really wonderful, isn't she?" She looks at Willow, then back to me. "I think you two could use some quiet time. I'm going to the bathroom."

I close my eyes and try to digest what's going on. As painful as it is to see Dixie taking this poorly, I need to shift gears—from the shock of my younger daughter's understandably having trouble dealing with my taking off on her to giving attention to my older daughter, who is sitting right here with me.

I stroke Willow's soft cheek. But in my mind I'm looking back on the countless times I've seen her innocent face tortured with fear and concern while I'm drunk or high or hungover. There is one time in particular that haunts my headspace right now—the time a few years ago when she came into my room one morning and my nose was all goopy from snorting cocaine the night before. She later told me that she kept asking me if she could go visit her camp counselor in Seattle, and all I did was yell nonsensical responses. She called her friend Robby and told him how scared she was. He stayed on the phone with her so she had someone to talk to.

I jolt myself back to the current moment. Willow's looking at me with great care and love. I believe Willow is now connecting the dots—that Mom's previous, terrifying behavior was directly related to her alcohol abuse. I've purposely said nothing about the cocaine. I have another entire level of shame and guilt built up around that.

"C'mon." I stand up and take Willow's hand. "I want to show you my room. We can open your present there." We walk into the main building, through the living room and dining room, and onto the connecting walkway to my bedroom.

She says all the right things. The view is aaaaawesome. The big bathroom with the old-fashioned tub is aaaaawesome.

"What are your two roommates like?" she asks. "I hope one of them isn't Mimi's mom."

"They're great. And no, Darlene is not one of my roommates. I was supposed to room with her, but I refused. And somehow I got away with it," I say, almost to myself. "I'm sorry you had to hear her talking like that. I think she likes the attention she gets when she speaks with such shock value."

Willow nods. "Daddy would like this room, wouldn't he, Mom? He loved rooms with views, right?"

Willow's words hit me in the heart. What *would* her father think of this place? Of my being here? I feel my body heating up all over as the familiar wave of shame envelops me.

"Well, he liked views, all right," I say, "but I don't think he would like seeing me here." This subject is just too tough, so I look at the gym bag in Willow's hand and ask, "What did you bring me?"

Willow starts pulling stuff out. "Look, I brought these comfy pants for you and the other stuff you asked for." She dumps the bag out on my bed and says, "It feels like I'm visiting you at camp."

She's right. What a role reversal.

On the bed are my gray sweatpants and sweatshirt, some pens from my office drawer, my heavy black cardigan, a large cloth bag for books and things, and a blue-and-red pullover fleece with the words WHISTLER BLACKCOMB on it. I lift it up with a quizzical look.

"Yeah, Mom, that's mine," she explains. "I want to give it to you."

I pull it over my head and put it on. "It fits beautifully. I love it," I say, as I walk to the mirror in the bathroom, where I admire it. "It's soooo cute. Thank you."

I walk back into the bedroom.

"I want you to get better, Mom," Willow says. "Here's your Mother's Day present." She hands me a large, thick scrapbook stuffed with notes and photos. She is glowing with anticipation.

I clutch the binder to my heart and beam with pride. "I'm so proud of you, Willow. You're acting so grown-up. Be sure to be good to your sister. Remember the pain she's going through, and that she's younger than you. She's less equipped to handle this turmoil. And I have caused such turmoil. . . ." I pause, then continue, "Let's go out to the balcony and look at this book together."

I put two chairs together facing the view, ceremoniously place the treasure Willow has given me on the table in front of us, and open it to the first page.

This is to the best mother in the entire world. It may be messy and scattered, but I hope you enjoy it anyways. It has two titles:
A Glass of Wine for Mom
Chicken Soup for Rosemary Keevil's Soul

My throat swells, and I squeeze Willow's hand. I look into her eyes and hope she can sense the deep gratitude rising inside me. I look down at the book and turn the page with great reverence.

Love
Thank you for bringing us up with this much love.
Just look ahead if you don't believe me.

The first photo is of Willow and Dixie with their sick daddy. Willow is five and wearing a pink party dress and a pink headband that pulls her messy, long blond hair off her face. Dixie is two and a half years old and nude, her hair in ringlets. Barry is bald, having lost his hair in chemotherapy, and he's lying on our bed in our West Vancouver home. Willow and Dixie are sitting on either side of him, and they're all looking, greatly intrigued, at two photos Barry is holding in his hand. I think about how Dixie missed out on memories of her dad. At that age, she wasn't quite old enough to establish them. I feel so sad for her.

"That is such a sweet picture. Do you remember what the photos are of?" I ask. "I'd love to know."

"I think they're of Hawaii. He was telling us he wanted to go back there," Willow says.

"Hmm," I say, thinking about all the trips Barry wanted to do. "Yes, that's one of the things he wanted to do before he died—go back to Hawaii and that lovely hotel on the big island—but that never happened. He did get to Seratami, but that was less than ideal—too far away from the doctors to be able to relax."

My eyes shift to the next photo, taken about three months later. Willow and Dixie are sitting down on a grassy field in Hawaii. Willow is beside Dixie, looking at her. Willow has her arms around Dixie's tummy. Dixie is wearing a Seratami T-shirt and looking with wonder at the camera. You can tell by their hair that they've been swimming. Beside them is a trademark Mauna Kea Beach Hotel towel. It's a time I remember very clearly. We were in Hawaii at the end of November, two months after Barry died. I can feel and smell the warm air, fragrant with Hawaiian plumeria—bittersweet, as I could not share the moment with my hawney, Barry. I took the girls back to one of our favorite holiday destinations in a desperate attempt to . . . well, to what? Good question. I don't know what I was trying to do. Survive? I didn't know what the hell I was doing without Barry—how to be a widow at age thirty-seven.

There is a section called "Beauty" in the scrapbook that includes highlights of our trip to Australia, which we went on in March and April of this year—just six weeks ago.

Beauty

Thank you for capturing all of this beauty for us to remember. You are an amazing photographer and should honestly send some of your pictures to National Geographic.

I am so overwhelmed by Willow's support that I'm confused. How can she understand so well what I'm going through and what

I need? It feels like evidence that I am not a complete failure as a mother.

I feel nauseated as I flash to mental snapshots of the excessive drinking I did during that holiday. Every time we arrived at a hotel, I would go directly to the minibar. When I was finished drinking the white wine in the fridge, I would immediately order more from room service. I even filled my water bottle full of white wine to take with us on our snorkeling excursion.

I remember sitting in front of the mirror in the Hayman Island Hotel and knowing full well that I was getting loaded even though the kids were in the hotel restaurant, waiting for me to come to dinner. I never showed up. I passed out on the bed. When I awoke and looked at myself in the mirror again, blurry eyes staring back at me, I knew that my drinking was out of control and vowed to make a dramatic change when we returned to Canada. What that looked like, I had no idea, but I knew I could not continue the way I was.

Then we got home, and I just kept on drinking.

The last page of the book reads:

Love, fun, beauty, memories, and relaxation. You realize the importance of these things and have let your daughters experience all of them. You are an amazing mother! (Please note that drinking is NOT one of these things, and you should turn to this instead of a glass of wine to see how much I love you and need you to be sober.) I LOVE YOU SOOOOOOO MUCH!!!

I am left with a mélange of emotions. I am astounded by Willow's maturity and compassion. My resolve to stay sober is fortified. My guilt and shame are reinforced, because I know I'm drunk in some of the pictures. I feel like I don't deserve such a remarkable pearl of love as this. Willow has reminded me that I have not always been a bad mother, that I've done a lot of things right. I need to hold on to this encouragement in order to move forward.

I wrap my arm around her as I admire the photos. "Sorry we don't have more time to go through every one of these pictures, as they all have a story. Thank you, sweetheart. This is the most special gift I've ever received. You have worked really hard to help me, and I can't tell you how much this means to me. You're being incredibly mature and responsible—like a little parent."

Willow smiles and puts her head on my shoulder, and we both look out at the view of the garden and Sugar Cove, where the ferry lands. After a minute, she and I separate and I turn toward her and hold her shoulders.

"I promise you I will get better," I say. "It's not that easy being here, but I know it's the right thing."

"Stay as long as you need to, Mom."

There's a knock on the door.

"Come in!" I holler from the balcony.

It's a staff member; she sticks her head in the door to inform us that visiting time is almost up.

"Thank you!" I yell back. I look to make sure the door is shut and then say to Willow, "I'm sorry Dixie is so sad I'm here and Gramma is acting a little crazy."

"Dixie and I are having some fun, Mom. And Gramma isn't all that bad," she says. "I'm glad you like the present. I really like it here. When can I come back?"

"Next weekend," I say, smiling. "I already can't wait. I'll be looking forward to it all week." I stand. "I guess we'd best meet up with Gramma and Dixie now." As we stand up to leave my room, I open the drawer in my bedside table and place the book in it. "Hey, look, it just fits. Perfect."

"Hey, you have a TV," says Willow. "I didn't notice that. That's cool, Mom. This place is awesome."

"Wanna stay?" I smile.

"It's not *that* awesome."

"Let's go." I head to the door.

We're not sure where Gramma and Dixie are, but we decide to check the car first. We make our way to the parking lot, and as we walk toward the Land Rover, my mom hops out of the driver's seat. She greets us with her reliable smile.

"Hi," I say. "Everything okay? Where's Dixie?"

"Oh, she's in the backseat. We're having a little quiet time."

I check out the backseat of the car and see Dixie solemnly planted on the passenger side, refusing to acknowledge our arrival.

I open the back door on the driver's side and get in the car beside Dixie. I hate the thought of her leaving while we're on bad terms.

"How are you, sweetie? I'm so sorry this is so upsetting for you," I say. "Remember, I love you." I give her ribs a gentle tickle. Her lips move ever so slightly in the direction of a grin.

All the other visitors are gone now, and I know it's really time to say goodbye to my family. I open my window and say to Gramma, who is standing outside the car, "I'll ride up the driveway to the gate with you, then hop out and walk back. It's only about five hundred yards or so."

She gets back in the car. Willow sits in the front passenger seat, and we start up the driveway.

I stroke Dixie's head and whisper, "I need to get better, dear. I'll be home soon. I'm so sorry this is so difficult for you. I miss you. I love you. I miss you. I love you."

I pull back a little and look at her, still holding her hand. I feel like giving in to her and staying in the car and going back to West Vancouver with my family. I think about it. I try on the feeling. It feels really good, but that feeling doesn't last—sort of like one more line of coke or that fourth glass of wine. Once I play out the tape, it's clear I will be very sorry if I choose to leave The Meadow.

I try again. "Dixie, Dixie, Dixie, please, please talk to me."

She turns her head slowly toward me. I look into her exotic eyes and melt. She's so fragile, and I have been such a monster.

She whispers, "I love you."

Oh, God, thank you.

Then she adds, "I'm sorry," to which I respond, "You don't need to be sorry. I'm so sorry for what I have put you through. I don't blame you for being upset. Thank you so much for coming. Will you come back next week?"

Right then, Willow says excitedly, "There's Sheena. Gramma, stop the car." I swear at Willow in my head for interrupting my special time with Dixie.

Sheena is at the side of the driveway, waving. Mom stops and rolls down her window.

Sheena peeks in and blesses us with her benevolent smile. "How are we all?"

"Super," says Gramma.

"Thank you very much for your help, Sheena," I chime in. "I think I'll get out of the car now and come back to the house with you." Sheena has special visiting privileges because of her connection with Graham.

I embrace Dixie, and she gives me a heavenly hug in return. I lean in to the front seat and kiss Mom on the cheek. "Thank you. I'm going to get out and hug Willow from the other side."

When I get to Willow's side of the car, she has gotten out and we share a warm hug. I whisper in her ear, "Thank you for coming. Thank you for the incredible gift. I love you. See you next week."

She gets back in the car. I look through the back window at Dixie, who has a little smile on her face. I blow her a kiss. "Bye, Dixie. I love you. Thank you for the precious card and gift." I stand back and say, "Thanks, Gramma. I'll call soon."

"Bye, darling. You're terrific," she says, and starts moving the car forward slowly.

Sheena and I turn to walk down the drive to the house, but then I hesitate and turn to look at the Land Rover as it makes its way toward the gate. I can't see inside it. The glare of the back window reflects only leaves and sky.

17

"My Own Worst Enemy"
Lit

Wednesday, May 15, 2002

As I make my way to my session with Graham on this pleasant May afternoon, I detect a hint of confidence brewing inside me—a most foreign feeling indeed, but it's enough to make me stand a bit taller and see a bit more of what's in front of me. I stop and smell the cool red bark on the arbutus tree before me. I pick off a loose piece of it and recall that this tree, in the First Nations Salish culture, has medicinal qualities. I think, *What an appropriate place to have a medicinal tree—at a treatment center designed to heal people.*

With a piece of delicate arbutus bark still in my hand, I head to Graham's office. The door is ajar, so I knock lightly and peek my head in.

"Hi," Graham greets me. "Have a seat."

He gestures to the beige three-seater couch across from him. I plunk myself down in the corner of the sofa, as I have done a few times now, and set my homework bag beside me.

Graham rolls his chair around from the back of the desk so he is facing me, with nothing between us. This must be a therapist's trick. Sheena does it, too. I feel more exposed and challenged when they do this than when they are tucked neatly behind their desk. Even so, a slight sense of safety is sifting into my psyche, making me less scared of revealing the details of my gnarled web of self-destruction.

Once he's settled a few feet away from me, I joke, "Oh, you again!" We both have a snicker.

I take a breath and say, "I was just thinking how, well, it's been ten days now here at The Meadow, and, hmm, I've become a bit more comfortable in the spot on this couch, your office, and this joint in general." I pause and am able to home in on exactly what the change in me is: "I'm less raw."

"I told you you would like it here. I've been thinking, too, Rosemary. . . . This is probably a good time to address this." He leans forward with both elbows on both knees, his hands folded. "I want to make sure you're working on your grieving. You seem to skim over it or ignore it. I wonder if you've really addressed it. I think it's crucial for you to dissect the year your brother and husband were dying."

I shift in my seat and stare at the painting of tulips on the wall beside Graham, realizing that they are blue. How odd—*blue* tulips. I hear Graham continuing, almost as if in the background.

"Now, this won't happen all at once. It's a process. It's just that it, well, it appears you've never given yourself a chance to digest it, to really grieve. What do you think?"

I take a deep breath and blow the air out. "Weeeeellll," I say in a nasally tone, like Samantha Stevens on the old TV program *Bewitched*, "yeah, I just don't want to sound like a self-pitying victim wallowing in misery."

"There's a difference between being a self-pitying victim wallowing in misery and healthy grieving. It must have been horrific. You can acknowledge how hard it was for you, you know," Graham says.

His words filter into a virgin area of my psyche. He has given me permission to acknowledge how ghastly that year was. I never even considered that as an option.

"It was awful, Graham. Both my brother and my husband were dying at the same time. And poor little Willow and Dixie, they were just two and four. There wasn't really any time for me."

I pause and think about the swirl of emotions that congregate when I relive that year. I decide to allow myself to go into details for Graham—the endless visits to the hospitals, the kids fighting, the nanny problems, the inability to make any plans, Barry's perpetual side effects, Rob's demanding smoking breaks, his suicide attempt, the abject sadness of it all. As I talk, I become more comfortable sharing what I thought would be just a burden for someone else to hear. I'm starting to understand why it's important to talk about this.

My eyes begin to water as I am thrust back to the horror I lived eleven years ago. I grab some Kleenex from the box conveniently placed on the table beside the sofa. "I feel like I might be coming up for air just now. What a fucking nightmare. It's just so goddamn fucking sad. I'm sick of being sad."

I look back at the sad thirty-seven-year-old I was then and cry for her. I'm looking back at my former self as if she were a separate person, and I feel deep compassion for her.

"Rosemary, you've been traumatized," Graham says.

"I've never looked at it as being traumatized, but I guess that is what it was," I say. "It's a good thing I didn't know how fucking tough it was going to be—grieving myself and handling grieving little girls at the same time. When Barry and Rob first died, I was living on anxiety. Despite everything, I was haunted by ambition and really wanted to return to work."

I explain to Graham how important my jobs have been in my life—TV news reporting, radio-show hosting, a couple of contracts with the Vancouver International Film Festival. I wonder aloud about my wisdom, or lack thereof, in hindsight. I was so ambitious that I wanted to continue my career. I didn't have to—we were set financially—but I needed an outlet for my creative and professional selves.

I needed the creative, professional buzz that accompanies working with like-minded, productive adults. I feed off that; it energizes me in a way that being a mom never could.

I recall a fill-in-the-blank assignment that Willow wrote when she was six years old, and recite it to Graham: "My mom's name is *Rosemary*. My mom is *99 meters* tall. She weighs *100* kilograms. My mom likes to *read books*. To relax, my mom likes to *go to work*."

I laugh. "Somewhere in her little six-year-old mind, she knew I got a lot out of going to work."

Graham chuckles and smiles.

"I remember having panic attacks," I continue. "About a year after Barry died, when I was running a video production company, I'd be sitting at my desk at the office and be overwhelmed with debilitating anxiety."

"Is that when you started drinking and drugging?" he asks.

"No, not right away," I say. "At first I was put on Prozac, which helped—but then I did start drinking more and more and smoking dope, and then Mr. Wrong brought over cocaine one night—that was six years after Rob and Barry died—and I thought it was the answer to all my problems."

"Mr. Wrong?" he asks.

"Matthew, a colleague at work," I tell Graham that Matthew's acute sense of humor seduced me and we got romantically involved. The tangling together of Matthew and me and alcohol and cocaine was like mixing up a bunch of live electrical wires: at some point, they will ignite in a fiery cacophony of popping sparks and then fizzle out.

Graham says, "Rosemary, you have successfully managed to skirt around your grieving by talking about work, about Mr. Wrong, about anything but your sadness. But you have to face it. As I said, the only way past it is through it."

The only way past it is through it. The only way past it is through it. Fuck. All this time, I've been driving around it, down every detour I can find, driving anywhere that will take me away from the shit in the middle of the road. I haven't allowed myself to grieve.

Graham proceeds to tell me what type of work I really have to do: therapy and twelve-step work, including making amends to my children. "And it all starts right here at The Meadow," he says. "That includes, of course, the set of assignments. It's all part of the healing process." Graham pauses and looks over at the little clock on his desk. "I'm mindful of the time," he tells me. "Stetson will be coming for his session."

"Okay." I set my hand on my purse, poised to stand up. "Any word on Brad?"

"Not yet, I'm sorry to say. We're keeping in touch with his dad. We're all praying." He pauses respectfully, takes another gulp of his coffee, and looks at the calendar on the wall. "Our next session is Monday at the same time. You're doing well. How's the homework going?"

"Uh, well, I'm getting there." I point to my book bag, indicating that I have it with me. "I've finished the Wall of Defenses and started the Amnesia Checklist. All that shameful behavior, like the stuff I mentioned earlier, it's hard to dredge up. It makes me feel sick to my stomach."

He nods, and I know he understands. I stand up, bag in hand, and head to the door—and as I leave, I feel an eagerness to get well replacing my former intransigence. I've shed that cloak of dread.

On the way to my room, I walk by the pool and see Darlene standing still and holding a large maple leaf up to the sunlight. She is right by the door to the main building—directly in my path. I notice she has a bit of makeup on and has washed and blow-dried her hair. Along with tears, I seem to have shed some hostility in Graham's office. Maybe I'm feeling more secure, less threatened. I think of something

Graham said in group: "Try to do the next right thing." Right now, the next right thing would be to say hi.

"Hi, Darlene. You look nice," I say, acknowledging to myself that my behavior is actually changing. It feels right.

"Hi," she says. "I'm looking at the beauty of this leaf." She holds it up again so the sun shines through it. I stop and turn so I am beside her and can look up at it.

"Oh, yeah, it's almost transparent with the sun gleaming through it," I say, awkwardly aware of my physical closeness to her.

"I'm suddenly enjoying the beauty in everything. Everything has color I haven't noticed for ages." She speaks like a child looking in awe at something she's never experienced before.

"I know what you mean," I concur. "When I saw the arbutus tree outside Graham's office today, it was like the first time I'd ever noticed an arbutus tree. It's like life is focusing more in 3-D than two dimensions."

"Yeah, exactly. Well put," Darlene says. She set down the leaf and looks at me.

"Hey, Mimi is adorable," I say. "How did your family visit go?"

"Well, you know, my husband can be a jerk sometimes," she says. "But it was good to see him, I guess. And wonderful to see Mimi. Your girls were really great with her."

"Yeah, Dixie struggled a bit being here."

"I think George is struggling seeing me, too. He says he misses sex. Honestly? I don't miss sex with him. I just lie there and look at the wall and count the tiles."

"Hmm," I say, thinking that Darlene hasn't lost her penchant for oversharing. I decide to pull out a trump card and be equally frank. "That's too bad. I love sex. Sounds like you need to work on that area."

"Gee, thanks, Mrs. Therapist."

"Anytime, *dahh-link*. See you in group," I say, and I start to walk away.

"Yeah, see you soon," she says.

As I walk on, I feel that seed of confidence I detected earlier blossoming, and along with it a smidgeon of security. I realize the camaraderie with my fellow "inmates," as we call each other, is an important part of treatment—and treatment ain't so bad after all. I even look forward to our group therapy sessions now.

"Good morning, group." Graham starts the session with his usual salutation. Then he walks over to the whiteboard and writes:

> *The problem is not the problem.*
> *The problem is the coping with the problem.*

He reads his words aloud and continues, "Today we are going into our Wall of Defenses—those behaviors that keep you from being intimate and genuine. Rosemary, why don't you give it a go? You said you finished this assignment, right?" Graham nods for me to come to the board and holds out the marker.

"Okay." I get up and take the marker from him, then look at the group. "This exercise was kind of interesting."

I write *Wall of Defenses* on the whiteboard, and underneath it I write *Anger*.

"I realize," I said, "when I get angry I can be masking fear or sadness or hurt and frustration or disappointment, even in myself—like when I'm stomping down the hall, mad as hell at the kids, it's because I'm sad the kids aren't behaving, and I'm probably disappointed in myself for getting myself into this situation, and, well, there's a whole slew of emotions. Come to think of it, the hangover I'm experiencing when I'm doing that yelling is also a barrier to feeling my true emotion."

I hear a couple of *mm-hmms* from the group. Nicole nods, and

Darlene closes her eyes and smiles like she relates and can imagine herself doing exactly the same thing. It feels good to be striking a chord in people. Encouraged, I move on.

"I also realize that I tend to go silent, withdraw, like, give the kids the silent treatment—like that's really effective!" I write *Withdraw* on the board.

Then I write *Independent*, and under that, *Isolate*.

"I write these two together because something happened here at The Meadow that seemed to represent both these behaviors," I explain. "When I was lugging all my shit down to the room to be with Darlene, Brad and Fred both offered to help, but I refused. I could have used the help, but I wouldn't let them into my private torture—my anger that I was told to move rooms. I was being hardheaded, too independent and isolating. I always used to pride myself on my independence, but now I'm learning it can be a block to intimacy, not accepting or even asking for help when it would be appropriate, and that can encourage isolation."

"Excellent," Graham says. "You've all come a long way. Any comments?"

"Yes," I say. "I had no idea I used this type of behavior to hide how I was really feeling."

"I meant any comments from *others*," he says, grinning.

"Oh, okay, I'll shut up for a second," I say, flushing a little.

"We're always laughing, which can be great," Stetson says, "but maybe we use humor to mask what's really going on inside."

To which Nicole adds, "What about sarcasm, Rosemary?"

"You don't all have to be so enthusiastic about my Wall of Defenses. It's *my* Wall of Defenses, you know," I say, smiling. "But yes, seriously. I guess humor is a tool I use to defuse a situation that is too close for comfort. And sarcasm."

"What about jogging?" Graham suggested.

"Oh, so, running, physical exercise, can be a way of avoiding feelings?" I ask.

Graham nods. "In excess, that would be a way to, uh, *run away* from emotions. Pun intended."

"And swimming," Stetson pipes up.

"In excess, yes," Graham repeats. "Just something to watch for. Like, shopping is fine if you need a pair of runners, but when it turns into three, then that can be an activity you are using to distract yourself from your true emotions."

"Eeee," I say. "I could be guilty of that, too. 'I'll have three of those lovely polka-dot bikinis.' Guilty as charged!"

I write down *Humor, Sarcasm, Running, Swimming,* and *Shopping.*

"What else?" Graham asks. "Look at the list on the handout. What else stands out? Anyone can answer. We're past being shy about all this. Besides, I'm sure Rosemary is at a stage where she can handle it."

"Yeah, anyone speak up," I say. "I'm here to learn. But sometimes I can be too sensitive. That's another evasion tactic, right?"

"It certainly can be," Graham says. "It can get you stuck emotionally."

"Hmm." I add *Sensitivity* to the list, which seems to be getting rather lengthy.

As I look at my growing Wall of Defenses, I am shocked by how at ease I am with all these people—once complete strangers—exposing my dysfunctional coping mechanisms. It's like giving birth—all is so exposed, there's nothing else left to be apprehensive about.

"What about making yourself too busy to stop and think about anything, let alone feelings?" Celia asks. "I think I do—"

"Yes, guilty as charged," I interrupt her, thinking about all the stuff I cram into a day, blaming it on being bored easily. Maybe I just don't want any spare time because that would mean being in my own head. I've heard people in the AA program call the noise in their head the Committee of Assholes. "I'm getting a pretty fortified brick wall here," I say.

"Yes, this is the point," Graham says. "Anything else?"

"Sex?" Darlene asks.

"Sex?" I'm surprised. "I'm not addicted to sex."

"Yes, but do you use it to mask feelings?" Graham asks.

I think about this. "There was this one Greek fellow who I called up between relationships. That was a distraction, I guess, a way of coping with emotions I didn't want to deal with."

"That's exactly right."

I add *Too Busy* and *Sex* to the list.

"That looks like a pretty sturdy brick wall of defenses," Graham says, and gestures for me to take a seat.

I return to my chair and begin to process what has just happened. I've been living in a shell of dysfunction—but, to my surprise, this information does not depress me. Instead, my newfound self-awareness buoys me. But I do wonder: Where am I in all of this? Take away all these ineffective coping mechanisms, and what's left? How do I cope? I obviously have a lot of work to do, but I'm ready to roll up my sleeves and get this done.

When I walk into the main house for lunch, I see Brad sitting at the dining table.

"Braaaaaaaaaaaad!" I run to him and give him a big hug.

"Brad! Brad!" Everyone is calling out his name at the same time.

"Yeah, yeah. That's my name. Don't wear it out," he says, looking like he hasn't slept for the two days he's been gone.

"We were all so worried about you. Are you okay?" Nicole asks as she sits down, but everybody is talking at once. Stetson walks up to him and slaps him on the back, saying, "Good to see ya, buddy."

As it turns out, by the time Brad made it to Main and Hastings, he was really scared. He immediately got drunk and was desperate to score crack and get high. He ignores our question about where he got the money—which we're all wondering, because The Meadow took all of our cash and cards upon arrival—but says he somehow made it to his parents' place, and they were so worried, they couldn't be mad. His wife, however, won't talk to him.

"I don't blame her," he says to us. "I'm such a shit. I gotta prove myself. I really might not make it back if I do that again. If that's doing more research, I don't need any more of that. I'm gonna stay here on the lifeboat and not return to that sinking ship o' fools."

I sit on his left side, linking my right arm with his left one. "I was wondering who was going to be my musical accompaniment whilst on dish duty, Brad," I say.

"Well, I'll accompany you *while* on dish duty but not *whilst* on dish duty," Brad teases.

I smile and say, "It's so good to have you back. It just wasn't right without you. There was a hole in the group."

I didn't realize how much a persistent, gnawing concern about Brad was eating at me. Now that it's been expunged, it leaves more room in my head for the grace I'm striving for. Alcoholism and addiction can be fatal diseases, and any more "research" by any of us could kill us. They say the disease, unless aborted, ends in death, jail, or institutions.

I'm back in Graham's office and sitting on the couch, staring at my blank Amnesia Checklist.

"Ugh," I say to Graham. "I can't bring myself to dredge up all my shameful behavior. Why can't we just let it go? It's over. I'd rather forget about it."

"Give it time, Rosemary," he says. "As tough as it is to do the Amnesia Checklist, it's important. An alcoholic can easily forget how bad it gets, and suddenly they think it wasn't that bad. That's when you pull out the ol' Amnesia Checklist."

"I understand I need to face up to all my behavior, and, although

I can't change it, I can, as you've said, shine a light on the skeletons in the closet," I say. "But how will I ever make it up to the kids? How much do you think I've damaged them?"

"You're already making living amends to them by getting well, and that will continue as you are a sober mom to them," Graham says. "Children are resilient. It's hard to know how they will be affected, but you will be sober to deal with it. Let's christen you. Why don't you share some stories now, just to warm you up and maybe diminish some of the fear that seems to be paralyzing you?"

"Really? Now?"

Graham nods slowly, like he's not going to let me out of here until I give this a go.

I clear my throat, sigh, and am silent for a good minute, my mind swirling with myriad nightmarish behaviors I can't bear to own. One image that is for some reason screaming out above all the rest is something that happened six years ago, in 1996. Dixie was eight, and Matthew, good ol' Mr. Wrong, and I had been snorting cocaine. I was so high, I started hallucinating that the small stone statue in the master bedroom—a Buddha-type figure Barry had bought during his travels in Indonesia—was speaking to Matthew and me. I decided it was Barry returning from heaven to talk to me. I can't remember what the fuck we were talking about, but Dixie came in and we told her the statue was her daddy and to get it some cheese to eat.

"Imagine, an eight-year-old witnessing that! We've never talked about it since," I tell Graham.

He nods, nonplussed, and gestures for me to continue.

"I'm going to tell you about last Christmas and am going to try to get through it without crying," I announce.

"Sounds like a plan, Rosemary," says Graham, as he sits back and crosses his legs. I fold my hands in my lap in a poised manner, think about what I am about to say, and make sure I am prepared to share it. With a deep breath, I start.

"It was a complete shit show. I had Matthew and his seven-teen-year-old son, Harry, up to the house at Whistler for a few days, and one night Matthew and I were out for dinner and Harry called to say there was a large leak in the living room ceiling. It's a big, expensive house, so a leak in the living room onto the wood floor and leather furniture could be quite serious, but Matthew and I were drunk, and we took our time getting home. When we got there, Matthew put on music and started dancing in the water dripping from the ceiling. Meanwhile, I later discovered, Harry was downstairs trying to get fifteen-year-old Willow drunk on whiskey and high on weed.

"A couple of days later, Harry got thrown in the drunk tank. Thinking I was a big shot because I had dealt a lot with the police as a news reporter, I marched down to the station and ordered them to let him go. I don't know why the cops put up with me, but all they did was tell me I shouldn't be driving and to go park the car in the lot next to the cop shop and get a lift home. I said I would do that but promptly drove home drunk.

"Really, the nerve and bad judgment," I shake my head, thinking about all the things the girls have witnessed. "The kids have been in the car when I drove like a wild person many times. Graham, are they victims of neglect?" I ask, not expecting an answer.

He is silent, doesn't move, but maintains his compassionate expression. I'm suddenly aware of how quiet his office is, which seems to magnify the decibel level of my confessions.

"That Christmas holiday was the beginning of the end. Although I had said many times that I would never do cocaine again, after that Christmas, I actually did stop. That in itself was not that difficult, as I had already reduced my cocaine use to about once a month. But knowing I would never do cocaine again gave me a profound sense of insecurity. With this decision, I obliterated my option to detach in a way in which only cocaine can do for me—a jolt of tasty, numbing white powder up the nose and straight into the bloodstream.

Sheer bliss"—I lean back on the couch, flop my hands out, and smile momentarily—"for about fifteen minutes!" I sit back up and grimace.

"You know, the . . . knowing that I did not have that option for the ultimate, albeit brief, cocaine escape somehow had the effect of trapping me in a spiral of depression and anxiety and fear. I'd had these feelings before, but it was like now they had control of me. I wasn't locking myself in the bathroom or the laundry room to snort cocaine anymore, but I was locked in a straitjacket of self-disgust, remorse, and self-loathing."

I stop talking as my tears make headway. I'm compelled to finish what I'm saying, to get it all out. Graham uncrosses his legs and crosses them the opposite way. He folds his hands in his lap and gestures gently with his head to continue.

"I was able to drink more while snorting cocaine, but that did not change when I stopped the cocaine. I now had increased capacity for booze, or fine white wine, which, for some reason, didn't seem as bad as poor-quality whiskey out of a brown paper bag."

I think about that common denominator again—that inside I am no different than the rubbies on skid row—desperate. And if I continued on this path, I would end up just like them. By now, I'm crying huge, gushy tears that soak my face almost faster than I can keep it dry with Kleenex.

Graham offers me his glass of water, which he hasn't touched.

"Thanks," I say, as I take a sip. "It might replenish some of the water I'm losing through my eyes. There I go—humor as a defense against intimacy."

"Yes, a building block in the Wall of Defenses. You know, you're doing remarkably well, Rosemary. This is exhausting for you, and it's also important to look at your attributes. Did you do that section as well?"

"I did do that section. It wasn't that easy at first but then I got into it." I say, blowing my nose. "I like to think I'm intelligent. I've a great sense of fun and humor and a good spirit that comes through, no matter how tough things get. And, oh, yes, my brother's doctor told me, when Rob was dying of AIDS and Barry was dying of cancer, that I was 'good at crisis management.' But it seems like part of my problem is managing life when it is *not* in crisis." I pause and seem to have a revelation. "Maybe I've been living off the adrenaline of crises to avoid dealing with deeper feelings. Maybe I invite chaos?" I say, almost talking to myself. I gaze out the window into the garden.

Graham breaks into my trance by saying, "You're being brave and thorough, Rosemary, and insightful. That part about craving chaos—that is very much a familiar pattern for alcoholics and addicts, and it often begins in childhood. You are what you learn."

"I guess," I say, nodding. "Dad acted crazy when he was drunk, and so do I."

Graham repeats, "You are what you learn." He says nothing for a few moments and then says, "Rosemary, you're courageous. I know it's not easy revealing so much. This is like peeling away the layers of an onion. Each time, more layers will be removed. With more distance, sober distance, you will have better perspective and, more important, healing. Do you think you can continue with the assignment now?"

"Yes, thank you."

Having told Graham all this, I know I have released some of the energy around those events. These memories have been rattling around under the hood of my car, causing functioning problems, but now I've opened it up and am starting to see what the fuck all the commotion is about. I now understand the only way to beat your demons is to tackle them.

After this megasession with Graham, I go to the main living-dining room area, get a hot tea, sit down at one of the worktables, pull out my Amnesia Checklist, and stare at the first question: "Have you ever felt like giving up, wishing you would die? Describe."

I did think about it with Barry in the car. Then I remember when I thought if I could somehow drive off a cliff with the girls into Tantalus Canyon, that might be an answer.

I stare at my answer. Does this mean I was suicidal? Graham mentioned in group once that we can have suicidal ideations, like fantasies, without actually being suicidal. I know other clients here at The Meadow have been suicidal. Alcohol is so cunning, baffling, and powerful, it will drive you to that. That's why Jason's face is deformed, after all; he took a gun to his head.

Question 2: "What lines in the sand have you crossed? What things have you done that you said you would never do? Explain."

I think about this and realize I have done so much that I never thought I would be capable of. I mean, I'm a good person, aren't I? I write my answer: "I vowed I would never drive my kids or their friends drunk or high."

I think about all the times I've driven the kids drunk and high, and a fresh wave of remorse flushes through me. Hot tears gush down my cheeks. I could have killed the girls or myself, or maimed us, or killed one of their friends or someone else. Barely able to see the page through my tears, I continue writing frantically, trying to get all the wreckage of my past out onto the page. Remorse turns to outrage at myself, and I write with such fervor that the pen nib tears through the page.

I vowed I would never drink before noon.
I vowed I would never drink before breakfast.
I vowed I would never mix pills and alcohol.
I vowed I would never go to church on cocaine.
I vowed I would never go to work high.

By the time I have all this out on the page, I sit back, wipe my eyes, and breathe. I realize I've been holding my breath the entire time. I look at what I've written. It's difficult to read—the page is torn in places from how much pressure I was exerting on the pen, and my writing is larger than usual—but I know what's there. I don't need to read it.

I am suddenly calmer, like I've just expelled piranhas that have been gorging on my innards.

I add one more line in the sand I've crossed, something that seems less dramatic on the surface but gloms onto my heart like a barnacle: "I vowed I would never spend another Saturday with the kids high on cocaine, but I did it again and again."

I think of a number of times I took my personal corruption to an otherwise healthy family activity—the Saturday eleven-year-old Dixie and I hiked up Cypress Creek, which runs behind our house and then up the mountain and turns into a threatening gorge with seventy-foot cliffs on either side, water rushing through the valley. I was experiencing the flatness I always felt when I was coming down from cocaine and did not have the judgment a parent should have at that point. Was our hike even safe?

On another cocaine Saturday, my mother was visiting from Toronto and I was high and videotaping Willow and Robby's skit for their French project. They were being so silly, they kept having to retake and retake, and Gramma was impressed with my patience, but it was really my drug-induced lack of boundaries. I was floating on the cocaine high, and nothing could penetrate it.

I sit back, take the last gulp of my tea, and stare at what I have written. I never physically harmed the kids. But it's the harm you can't see that haunts me. I may have been present in body for these activities, but I was absent in heart and spirit. What damage have I done to my children?

Crestfallen, I put my head down, my elbows on the table, my

hands covering my face, and let myself sob and sob and sob. Still, as tortured as I feel in my abyss, I also have an inner sense of knowing that I need to be here in order to get out of here. I need to be here in these memories, and I also need to be here physically, at The Meadow. I reflect on my first day here—the shame and guilt and terror, the darkness. It was as if my eyes were glued shut and I was stuck inside my own misery. But now my eyelids have been pried open and there is something shiny dangling in front of me: hope.

18

"Cry Baby"
Janis Joplin

Saturday, June 1, 2002

When I return from rehab our home is in a state of anarchy. Twenty-eight days sober, I am trying to enforce rules that I never have before, and my thirteen- and fifteen-year-old daughters are rebelling.

I'm tidying the kitchen and planning to go to my daily twelve-fifteen women's AA meeting nearby, when Dixie comes rushing into the room.

"I'm going to Mandy's for a sleepover tonight and what's for lunch," she says.

"Whatever happened to *asking*? I need to talk to her mother first, make sure she's aware of the plans. Want to ask politely for a tuna sandwich?" I say, as I grab a bag of bread, trying to act as if it's natural for me to say no to my kids, when I have been a mother with no rules, nary a *no* in my vocabulary. I don't know how to do strict. It's not that I don't want her to go, but I want to have the option, as a mother, to say no. Right now, that's not an option.

I imagine myself morphing into one of those consummate TV

moms, like June Cleaver or Jane Wyatt. What would they do? First of all, no TV mom would ever have to go to rehab.

Dixie is wearing a Hello Kitty T-shirt and blue jeans, her wavy brown hair pulled off her face in a messy ponytail. I focus on her eyes, which appear much darker than their regular hazel-brown color, piercing and accusatory. I recognize this as one of those moments when I need to pause before acting. It's an AA thing: Beware of what your natural reaction to a given situation is—chances are, it's askew and needs some readjusting.

Uncertain what to do and alarmed at what Dixie might do, I stall. I open the can of tuna and drain the smelly fish water into the sink, my back toward her, knowing her eyes are fixated on me. *God, tell me what to do.*

I think about what I have been learning in AA—about identifying and acknowledging feelings. I scan my emotional landscape and home in on a familiar strangling sensation; something has me in its tenacious grip. I close my eyes and shudder at the realization that this vise is fear.

I am afraid. I am afraid of Dixie. I am afraid of Willow. I am afraid of my own children. I am disturbed by this revelation, but also relieved, because I'm able to identify the emotion—the first step toward dealing with it.

This sense of being disturbed and relieved at the same time reminds me of when Barry died. For so long, we lived in this unresolved zone of not knowing whether he would live or die—and, as devastated as I was when he died, there was a tinge of relief to my devastation, because at least the uncertainty was resolved.

I turn to put the tuna in a bowl and face Dixie, who is a few feet away from me, on the other side of the kitchen island. She eases up on her glare long enough to get a package of Double Stuf Oreos from the bottom drawer and grab a handful. As she kicks the drawer shut with one foot, she spouts, "I wish you'd just relapse. I liked you better when you were drinking. Ever since you got home, you just make up random rules!" She turns around in disgust, raising her voice. "You're so strict. You can't do this!"

"I can, too. And that's too many cookies!" I respond, my voice getting louder and louder the farther away she gets.

"What are you going to do?" she yells back at me, now rounding the corner from the kitchen to the hallway and heading up the stairs.

"I don't know, okay? I don't know!" I shriek.

And with that, the screeching contest is complete. She wins. I'm lost within my own futility—the futility of such a dysfunctional exchange—and my tacit condoning of the fanatical yelling by participating in it.

Practically catatonic, I methodically empty every dish from the dishwasher and carefully set it where it goes. I stare out the kitchen window at the rustling bamboo beside the creek that runs along our backyard.

Beckoned by the water's frameless flow, I go outside into the light drizzle, lie back on a chaise lounge, and let the elements embrace me. Maybe I'll just dissolve in the raindrops, as the Wicked Witch of the West did when she was drenched with water in *The Wizard of Oz*.

How can I let her talk to me like that? *Because I have set no boundaries for them.* I've never enforced consequences, and I've never been able to say no to any request, be it allowing more candies than I have allotted them at the 7-Eleven on the way to Whistler or buying a puppy on a whim from Noah's Pet Ark at the mall.

Oh, for a large goblet of chilled Bâtard-Montrachet, or a big fat line of cocaine, or a Tylenol with codeine, or an Ativan or a zopiclone. But I'm not going to have any of those mind-altering substances, as I have learned to play out the tape. If I have one, I'll have many. I can't have just one. One is too much, and a thousand is not enough. I will relapse if I take that first drink or line or pill. I also remember

HALT, which represents four situations one needs to be wary of in early recovery: hungry, angry, lonely, and tired. And I'm all four.

I get up and go inside to the fridge, where I pour myself a tall glass of cold skim milk and grab a spoon and the peanut butter and honey from the pantry. I stand there at the kitchen counter, crying, and eat by the spoonful until I realize it's almost time for my AA meeting. I've been told to do ninety meetings in ninety days, and I'm sticking to it. I'll do anything not to have another drink again.

I check the kitchen clock. Eleven thirty. I need to change out of my damp clothes and head to my meeting.

I finish making the tuna sandwich, cover it and set it on the kitchen table.

I go to find Dixie with no particular plan in mind. Turns out she's gone to her room at the top of the stairs after all; I can hear her on the phone. As I get closer, I can hear what she's saying.

"It's awful how she's trying to be so strict now." She pauses, and now, I suppose, Mandy, her closest friend, is speaking. Then I hear Dixie say, on the verge of tears, "Yes, Willow hates Mom's sudden rules, too."

Crippled with discouragement, I tell myself I need to get to my meeting. That usually helps dilute my agitation—temporarily, anyway.

On the last Friday of June, one month after leaving rehab, I attend my twenty-first meeting—the midday women's one at the Avalon Women's Center, where I first met Maureen, my sponsor. A sponsor's job is to guide you through the twelve steps and help keep you accountable and safe. If I'm struggling, lonely, desperate, or thinking about drinking, I'm supposed to call Maureen. It's one of the tools in the AA tool kit—the phone.

Maureen is in her mid sixties. She's a little rounded, as women in their midsixties can get, with short, straight gray hair and perpetu-ally rosy cheeks, as she is always warm and sweating a bit. I think this has to do with her diabetes. She knows her AA program—she's been around for some twenty-five years.

After the meeting, Maureen and I go for a walk in the hot late-June sunshine. We stop at the Starbucks at the Park Royal shopping mall in West Vancouver, two blocks away from the women's center where the meeting was held, and find a table that's a bit removed from the others.

When we sit down, Maureen pats the sweat from her brow with a folded brown napkin and gets settled to chat. She wants to go over the first three steps with me, which I completed at the Meadow, and then get me on to step four.

"For step one," she says, "we realized we were powerless over alco-hol and our lives had become unmanageable."

I take a big sip of tea. "Well, there are two distinct parts to the step—the powerlessness and the unmanageability. I had no problem admitting my powerlessness over alcohol. I tried a few times to drink grape juice, instead of wine, in a wineglass and all that did was waylay my wine drinking for an hour. I didn't try much harder than that." I shrug. "I knew after that that I could not quit, and that alcohol was much more powerful than my discipline."

Maureen nods her head in empathy.

"As for the 'unmanageable life' part—at first I thought my life was perfectly manageable," I say. "Roof over my head, car in the garage, two children doing well in school, an interesting career. I sincerely did not think my life had become unmanageable." I sip my tea again. "But at The Meadow, when I studied my day-to-day, minute-to-minute life while drinking and using, the unmanageability was glaringly obvious." I look down at the table, look outside at the people strolling by, and then continue quietly, my voice breaking with emotion. "I mean, having to drink half a bottle of wine before going to talk at the school's Career

Day, unable to sign a check for the babysitter because I was too jittery from cocaine, not to mention all the drinking and using and driving . . . How could I, for a moment, have thought that my life was manageable?" I put my head down and wipe my eyes with my napkin.

"It's all right, Rosemary," Maureen says. "You're doing an incredible job of working your steps."

Satisfied that I have mastered step one, we review steps two and three, which are about believing in some higher power that can help the drunk sober up, seeing as individual drunks don't seem to have the power to quit on their own. Some people in AA struggle with these two steps because of the believing-in-God part. But really, it's the belief in anything as more powerful than oneself that matters. Anyone can acknowledge the universe is more powerful than she is. Some people simply bow to the people in the AA rooms, who can be referred to as a Group of Drunks.

"I have an inherent belief that there is something going on beyond our physical bodies," I say. "I've experienced overwhelming emotion when at one with nature. Besides, when I was growing up, my mom had an unfailing devotion to a higher power, which she happened to call God. I think I adopted her faith through osmosis."

After I've gone into more specific detail about steps two and three, Maureen is satisfied with my understanding of them.

"Yes, Rosemary." She pats my hand. "Next is step four."

"Oh, Gawwwwwwwd, the 'searching and fearless moral inventory' of all the wreckage of my past and then figuring out all my defects of character. I have to admit, I feel completely overwhelmed and scared by this step," I say, making the sign of a cross with the forefingers of both hands. "I wish someone would just figure out all my defects for me, and I'll ask my higher power to remove them."

Maureen giggles, shoves her dirty napkin inside her coffee cup, and puts the lid back on. "We'll deal with that in our next session. Time to go."

I put my hand on her arm as she is about to stand up. "Thank you, Maureen, for being such a kind listener. I feel bad taking up all your time."

"Heavens! They say, 'You can't keep it if you can't give it away.' It helps me to help you, as I remember where I was when I first came to AA."

"I feel so close to you, like you're a good friend already, but we just met," I say.

She replies, "Me too, Rosemary. These things happen in AA—bonds form."

I'm seven months sober by Christmas, and the holiday is all about how much I can give the girls to make them happy. Video games, clothes, new cell phones . . . I provide an abundance of material possessions, as if this is going to make up for years of poor parenting.

Life in our household remains chaotic and disturbing, and I am still looking for work. On January 8, I pick up Dixie and her friend Mandy from school and take them back to our house, where they watch *Scary Movie*. Willow has gone to Robby's house. She turned sixteen this past summer and got her driver's license. She drives a lime-green Volkswagen Beetle now.

I settle into my desk with a hot cup of tea and handful of Jujube candies and start to apply for another job. This is not without a sense of guilt, as I don't really *have* to work for income. But I justify my pursuit of work by saying a happier, fulfilled mom is a better mom. I long to be an interesting career woman. Besides, a job might give me some semblance of normalcy.

I check the time: four thirty. Willow is at Robby's. I call her and tell her I want her home by five.

"Can I stay later than five, Mom?"

"No," I say, as I look at a photo of Willow and Dixie on my desk.

They are in the bathtub together, sitting facing each other. Willow is about four, Dixie two. Willow is spewing water out of her mouth like a fountain, and Dixie is looking up at her in awe.

"No?" Willow echoes me in disbelief. "Why do I have to be home at five? I put liquid dishwasher soap in Robby's dishwasher, instead of the powder, and now the kitchen is overflowing with suds. Please let me stay and help him, or he's going to be really mad at me," she pleads. "I've only been here for one hour. Why do I need to come home?"

"Because I said so. Now, come home immediately," I say, defiant in my need to be a stricter mother, even as I'm riddled with doubt about making such an arbitrary decision.

I can hear her crying as she hangs up without saying goodbye.

Now my own tears flow. What the hell am I doing? I feel the burden of being the only parent. I don't know how to do this. Will I ever run out of tears?

I am having difficulty breathing, and I notice that I'm shaking. All I can feel is impending doom. *It will be like this forever. My kids will never be okay. I will never be okay.* I make a mental note to talk to the psychiatrist about this. He has already upped the Wellbutrin I'm taking for anxiety and depression.

I check my phone to see if Dave has called, which he hasn't. *He never calls enough*, I lament.

I met Dave two months ago at an AA meeting. I introduced myself to him after he shared at the podium, because I thought he was cute. We went skiing together and have been "seeing" each other ever since, even though AA advises that newly sober people not date for at least a year. ("Your brains are still foggy, not capable of clear decisions.")

We have lots in common, including golfing and skiing—and AA, of course. He is twelve years younger than I—thirty-six to my forty-eight—and everything about him suctions me toward him: he's tall, with a bulky frame, a healthy head of wavy black hair, dark bangs that accentuate his bright blue eyes, an impetuous grin, a cocky swagger, and an enviable assurance. I have a tenacious attachment to him that I cannot conquer. When I'm not with him, I must see him. I must talk with him. I must know when I will see him again. Although he wants to see me, he doesn't match my intensity. I hate myself for allowing myself to be so subservient, and for having this frantic attachment to my phone, wondering every time it rings, *Is it him?* I've forfeited any and all control.

He says his standard poodle, Tony, is a better dog than our Shih Tzu Chin. That his family's Filipino housekeeper is better than our Filipino nanny. That it's better to live in Vancouver than it is to live in West Vancouver. And that he's a much better golfer than I am—but that doesn't make him such hot shit. It's not very difficult to be a better golfer than I am.

He wants to have children, and I want to provide him with whatever he wants, to the point that I'm actually contemplating having more children, despite my age. After all, more and more women are having children well into their forties. I could, too. I'll do anything to keep him. Despite my deep and pestering knowing that this is fantastical, I ignore my better judgment. I'm that desperate.

I hear Willow barge in through the side door. I stand up and go to the hall.

"Willow!" I exclaim, as she brushes past me and stomps upstairs to her bedroom. Once again, I'm at a loss for what to do. I pause and plead to God for direction, but nothing comes. I have ground to a halt in this no-man's-land. I'm stuck. The gears are broken.

The following Tuesday, January 14, I have a session with Lynn, my addictions counselor, as I do every Tuesday at one thirty. In the car on the way, I review my AA program in my head, remembering I will do anything not to have a drink again. "I now have 254 days of sobriety," I say out loud to myself.

Lynn's office is simple. There are two generic pictures on the wall—one of a bouquet of pink roses, the other of the imposing bow of a ship, as seen from the ocean in front of it. Lynn is sitting under this picture in a tan-colored, simple armchair, and I am in the matching love seat across from her—finding myself once again on the proverbial psychiatrist's couch.

After initial pleasantries, she asks what I want to cover today and I tell her about my issues with Willow and Dixie, and also my issues with Dave, which is where I begin.

"He tells me he loves me, and in the same breath he says he wants to be single and doesn't call when he says he will," I say, as her blue eyes look directly into mine.

Lynn is about thirty-five, with straight, shoulder-length blond hair and a pretty face masked somewhat by her eyeglasses, which lend her an air of intentness. With her methodical manner of delivery, she says plainly, "Concentrate on your own sobriety. Going out with someone this soon is like putting a microscope on your defects of character—those things you're looking for in step four. How's that going? How much sober time does he have?"

"I'm working on step four as we speak, and he has a year."

"That's not enough, Rosemary. You're like two babes in the woods."

I shift in my seat and fold my hands tightly, tap them on my lap, and take a deep breath. "But I'm just so sad and lonely and . . . well, horny, to be truthful. I don't want to be alone. I suppose the defect of character that the microscope is magnifying is my insurmountable insecurity. I'd rather have an unkind boyfriend than no boyfriend at all."

"It can only mean trouble," Lynn says with a sigh. "I guess you just want more pain, Rosemary. You're driving on a windy mountain highway, and there's a sign that says STEEP CLIFFS AHEAD, and you're stepping on the gas." She mimics stepping on the gas pedal with her right foot, holding an imaginary steering wheel.

"I'm so fucking tired of being sad and crying," I say, slumping. "Sadness seems to be my default position. I miss the love I had with Barry: pure and respectful. There was never any hurt or competition. We shone in each other's light. It's the kind of love I expect to get again, but I have a sense that I need to accept the reality that it may never happen."

I also tell Lynn about how Dave yells at the girls, like the time at Whistler when Dixie refused to get in the car when it was time to go home. It could well have been because she doesn't like him. Dave and Willow were already in the car, and I was going to lock up as soon as Dixie came, but she refused, plunking herself in the middle of the living room on the couch. Dave went into the house and yelled at her and said we'd leave without her if she didn't smarten up. And he meant it.

"Maybe she was afraid of him."

"Yes, maybe, with good reason, I suppose. He was already mad at her for her behavior at New Year's—also at Whistler," I continue. "I told her she could have some Mike's Hard Lemonade, and Dave got mad at her, not me. I figure if she was going to drink, it might as well be in the safety of our house, where I was there to supervise." I speak quickly as I download this information, now much more uncertain of the wisdom of my own actions than I've ever been.

Lynn looks concerned. "How old is she again, Rosemary?"

"Fourteen," I say, shifting in my seat. "I guess I didn't have the best role models for this. My mom provided wine for me and my boyfriend in high school, on the condition that we drink it at home."

It's only now, looking at Lynn, who's staring at me, apparently waiting for me to continue, that I realize most parents don't give their fourteen-year-olds booze. I feel sheepish, but Lynn's gaze holds no judgment, only an invitation for self-recognition.

I explain to Lynn how Dixie went outside and lay in the snow with no coat on. Dave came out and yelled at her and told her not to drink that Mike's Hard Lemonade. She yelled back that she wouldn't drink anymore because she didn't want to end up like her mother.

"I can still feel the daggers stabbing at the very marrow of my bones when I think of Dixie saying that," I confess. "Our lives are punctuated with screaming. We're still living in internecine chaos, just like before I got sober." I shake my head and put each hand out to the side, baring my chest and my heart in a gesture of surrender. "This is what I talked to Graham about at The Meadow. Am I thriving on this chaos, this calamitous energy? How do I stop this noxious cycle?"

Lynn reminds me of what I'm doing right, such as staying sober, and how much work that is in itself. "You need to continue to try to do 'the next right thing,' and things will improve," she says.

At the end of the session, I stand up and smile. "Well, I'm feeling a lot better," I say. "I guess you don't need to quit your day job!"

I've been sober almost one year. Somehow I thought that stopping drinking would solve all my problems, sort of like I once thought snorting a few lines of cocaine would solve all my problems. However, like the lines of cocaine, stopping drinking seems to have only given root to a different breed of tumult. I must keep reminding myself how bad it would be if I weren't sober.

Dave is insisting that the girls and I attend the one-week family therapy program at Desert Place Recovery Centre in California, where he got sober a year and a half ago. He and his family went to it, and it patched up some severe damage in their relationships. During the family therapy, he realized that he blamed his parents for his alcoholism. He believed that they had been demeaning toward and demanding of him when he was growing up, and that their behavior had driven him to drink. The program helped him realize that he was being arrogant, and that it was time for him to take control of his own life at thirty-six.

I admire Dave for being able to put a microscope on his own defects of character, but I don't often feel that he applies this same lens to our flawed relationship. He can be imperious and childish, but he also has tender moments. He says he worries about me when the children treat me badly. He kisses me softly on my neck and whispers, "You deserve to be treated better than that."

I melt when he does this. I'm so insecure that I suck up any positive attention he gives me and let it dominate my thoughts about him. I have difficulty standing up for myself, for fear of losing him. I know I crave the male attention, and while I'm not ready to do anything about these complicated feelings, at least I recognize my dysfunctional behavior.

This, I am told, is progress.

Before sobriety (or BS, as I like to call it) I would not even have recognized this as dysfunctional behavior. However, I'm not yet prepared to do anything about it, not prepared to do the next right thing, not even prepared to figure out what the hell that would be. I hang on to the slivers of tenderness Dave offers me, as they are what I need.

Dave is convinced that five days at Desert Place is what my dysfunctional family needs. I'm thinking it might be the only way to secure my relationship with him, as the girls are a big source of discord between us. There's a chance it would help us, too. I book a week for the three of us.

It's $2,000 for five days and includes group discussions, educational lectures, family therapy, personal goal setting, and, important for me, a promise that you will "walk away knowing what you can do to improve your family situation." I book us for Tuesday, April 29, to Saturday, May 3—my one-year sobriety date.

When I tell the girls about the plan, Dixie seems thrilled to have a week off from school. Willow, on the other hand, protests vehemently. She is concerned about her schoolwork and exam preparation.

"It's going to completely screw up my grade eleven, Mom. Besides, what do I say to all my teachers?"

I call the school and talk directly with the headmaster, Mr. Maxwell. He has been in this position for only a couple of years, and the jury is still out on his performance. I give him some context, explaining my previous behavior without going into too much detail—and I feel the shame surface, again.

To my shock, Maxwell says, "Congratulations, Rosemary. Getting sober is the best thing you can do for your children, and you." He speaks slowly, clearing his throat between pauses. "It takes courage to do what you're doing, and taking the family for therapy is a solid approach. You can all only benefit."

"Thank you, Mr. Maxwell," I say with relief, my shame replaced by pride that I'm able to face my bad behavior and am trying to turn it around.

We discuss the schoolwork the children will miss, and he assures me he'll make appropriate arrangements with the teachers. He even suggests he has a meeting with the girls to discuss the entire plan.

The next day, knowing that Mr. Maxwell is inviting Willow and Dixie into his office for this momentous conversation, a sense of impending doom paralyzes me. Near the end of the school day, I sit in my office, bracing myself for the onslaught I know is coming. They'll be home any minute.

I hear the garage door go up and, shortly after, car doors slamming. They come through the door from the garage, which is right down the hall from my office, and head right for me.

"Mom, Mom, Mom. What the hell? As if us talking to Mr. Maxwell will make a bit of difference. Do you know how embarrassing it was to be hauled into the headmaster's office?" Willow spews, as she pushes through my double brushed-glass doors.

I turn around in my office chair to face her, my desk at my back. She's standing about two feet away from me, and I can see she's flushed. She puts her backpack down, loosens her tie, and pulls it off. Again she says, "Mom, why are we going to California at all, this Desert Place, or whatever it is?"

Dixie pushes in behind her sister and sneers, "We're going to family rehab because Dave wants us to. Mom does everything Dave wants her to."

They're both looking down at me with ardent, penetrating eyes. I stand up, but I still can't find words to speak. My jaw is frozen. My mind is blank, numb, a defense mechanism; if I felt all the emotions that were going through me right now, I would likely implode. I pause, breathe, close my eyes, and pray.

Willow turns around, grabs her backpack, and stomps up the stairs and down the hall to her room. *Slam!* goes the door.

I'm standing face-to-face with Dixie. Her arms are folded, her mouth tight.

"We're staying in a hotel, right?" she says.

I know she's expecting the comfortable amenities that go with a hotel: rented movies, hot tubs, and room service. I dread having to tell her we'll be staying at Dave's parents' place.

"No, we're staying at Dave's family's condo." Dave and I were there earlier in the year. "It's cute and close to Desert Place. I think you'll like it."

As the words leave my mouth, I know what a feeble attempt I have made to dress up Dave's place. Truth is, although it's a great little spot, it ain't no hotel. Also, I would have booked us a hotel if Dave had not insisted I stay at his place and save the money. I don't care about the money, even though I should. I care more about doing what he thinks I should do. I'm afraid he won't like me if I don't.

"Dave's condo! See, I told you you'd do anything he says to do!

Why not a hotel?" With that, she turns around, slams the door, and goes upstairs.

I'm twisted into a state of demoralization and self-doubt, wondering if hauling them off to treatment is the right decision. Fuck. I take a deep breath and, putting my elbows on the desk, propping my chin on my fists, look out the window at the green bushes separating us from the neighbors. Their house is just visible through the foliage. Is there peace in their home?

19

"Cleanin' Out My Closet"
Eminem
Sunday, April 28, 2003

As we leave for Palm Springs I think, as dismal as the situation is, we are going on a trip together, and that's usually fun. I've created good little travelers. We love adventure, and Willow is now caught up in some of that, despite her vociferous protestations.

At the airport, we have Tim Horton bagels with cream cheese and check out the candy in the kiosk. We each pick out our favorite snacks: trail mix for me, Fuzzy Peaches for Willow, and Skittles for Dixie.

Willow tosses me the occasional hate stare to remind me that she really doesn't want to be here—Fuzzy Peaches or no Fuzzy Peaches. This I can handle, but it's a somber reminder of how tenuous the current peace is.

When we exit the airport at Palm Springs to look for our rental car, a welcoming surge of hot Southern California air and a cloudless indigo sky greet us. I stop briefly to appreciate that automatic and fleeting smile that always appears the very moment I walk from an airport into the warm, sunshiny weather of a vacation destination.

But this joy quickly dissipates when the current reality sets in. We ain't on no vacation.

We locate our rental, a Lincoln sedan, and now it's too hot out. I immediately try to figure out the air-conditioning, but when I turn it on, it blasts hot air. The girls are arguing about who's sitting in the front seat, and I snap, "Just get in the damn car. You can take turns in the front seat."

Dixie jumps in the front seat and looks for the CD player. Willow complains, "Dixiiiiiiiiiiie!" but settles in the backseat.

It's a thirty-minute drive to Dave's condo, and my brain is aflutter with all the things that can go wrong now. I know any sense of equilibrium we have is shaky. It's like driving on a gravel road, anticipating being struck by a rock. You know it could happen, but you don't know how hard the force of it will be.

I see Dixie pull out an Amanda Marshall CD. *Tuesday's Child* is a standard favorite of ours. She chooses "Best of Me," and as the first notes start, I feel my body shift. The beat of a familiar tune is enough to alter my negative state—enough to relax a little. I start to sing along, but not too exuberantly—lest the girls think I'm having fun.

Soon, we're making our way along the quiet, well-manicured street where Dave's family condo is. There are neat rows of townhomes and condominiums separated by graceful palm trees. I turn down the music; Willow immediately says, "No," and Dixie turns it back up.

I turn it off. "We're almost there," I say. "Can you guys please help me look for number 404?"

"I thought you've been here," Willow says. "Don't you remember?"

"Yes, I do, but they all look alike. Now, help me."

When we find the place, I pull into the driveway. "There's a pool, you know," I say, hoping this will be a positive distraction for them. As we open the doors, the warm outside air rushes into the car. "Why don't you guys go take a look?"

"All right," Willow says unenthusiastically, while Dixie hops out.

I watch them walk away, taking in the fragrant scent of the ubiquitous, lush gardens around me, grateful for a reprieve from their punishing treatment.

I haul the bags inside. The front door opens right into the living room, next to an open-design dining-kitchen area. There is a picture of Dave on the counter, taken about ten years ago—he must have been about twenty-six—looking tanned and dashing, with a big mop of messy hair. I would prefer for it not to be here. I think about him way too much as it is; I don't need any more reminders. Seeing the photo just makes me pine for him more.

There are three bedrooms. I put the girls' bags in the smaller ones and take the largest room for myself, the one Dave and I shared when we were here.

The two of them appear in the condo minutes later, somewhat breathless from their tour of the pool area.

"You've been running," I comment.

Ignoring me, Willow points to the photo on the counter and complains, "Why do we have to look at a picture of him?"

I go and pick it up, shove it into the closest drawer, and slam the drawer shut. "There. Happy?" I say, and then offer an olive branch: "Did you see the hot tub? Maybe we'll go in later?"

Willow rolls her eyes and shakes her head and turns away. "Whatever."

"Let's just get through this." I open the refrigerator, more out of habit than anything. Of course, there's nothing in there. "Do you want pizza for dinner? I saw a Pizza Hut on the way in. Dixie?"

Dixie is paying no attention, checking out the TV for movies to rent. She's already in her pj's.

"Want pizza, Dixie?"

She nods her head and says, "Hawaiian," without looking at me. I look at Willow, who nods, too. She sets herself up to study.

I tell them I'm going to get the pizza and to the 7-Eleven that we passed on the way in. "I'm picking up Coke and chocolate milk and regular milk and something for breakfast."

I get no response.

When I return, they're arguing about the volume of *Scary Movie*, which Dixie is watching.

"She's already seen it ten times," Willow complains.

"Oh, Dixie, Willow's trying to study. Turn the damn thing down."

Having basically given up any hope of peace in the kingdom, I decide that now is as good a time as any to let them know how early we have to get started in the morning. "We're leaving at seven thirty tomorrow morning for Desert Place," I say.

Neither of them acknowledges my comment. Dixie does turn down the volume of the television and moves so she is sitting ridiculously close to it, her nose almost touching the screen. Willow ignores me, folds up her math book, and opens her chemistry text. I guess they're still punishing me.

I put dinner out and let them know it's on the table. I eat two slices of pizza and leave the rest on the counter for them. I mumble, "I'm turning in. The pizza is here, and there are drinks in the fridge." There is no response, again. I retire to my room with a final "good night," which is also not acknowledged.

I go to my room and shut the door. I lie on my bed, which feels hard and uncomfortable, and stare at the white fan in the middle of the ceiling. I'm mesmerized by its constant turning. What was I doing when I was in grade eleven and grade nine, like the girls are now? I certainly know I was not at a treatment center for alcoholic parents. The summer before grade ten, I worked at a lodge in Georgian Bay, Ontario, serving meals and jugs of alcohol to conventions of truckers. I was underage but got away with it by lying about my age. The summer before grade twelve, I worked at a lodge as a waitress and dated the waterskiing instructor. I always brag today that I'm a good waterskier because "I dated a waterski instructor, you know!"

These are good memories. Am I creating only miserable memories for my children? Will they be completely screwed up? *Oh, Barry,* I think, *what am I doing? Please help me.*

Too bad there's no instruction manual for parenting. What kind of parents were mine? I remember Mom being more of a friend than a parent, and I try to remember whether I ever yelled at her. Yes, I think I did, but not very much. A memory floats up, of a time when I was about eighteen and told her to fuck off. All she did was turn to my sister and say, "She needed that." She never yelled at us.

In high school, my dad once heard me yelling at Mom and came to her defense—told me not to talk to my mother that way. But who is going to tell my children not to talk to me the way they do? Who is in my corner? I can't help but wonder if I would have become an alcoholic if Barry were alive.

I hear a knock on the door. "Mooom. Mooom! Open the door. Unlock the door," I hear Willow yell, as the door handle rattles. I ignore her. "Mom, come out of your room."

"No, go away. I need some peace." I shout back. As soon as the words spew out of my mouth, I'm guilt-ridden.

"Fine, be like that!" Willow retorts, shaking the door one more time. And then there is quiet—all but the self-reproach battering my psyche.

I bribe the girls out of bed in the morning with my adored version of McDonald's Egg McMuffin sandwiches: tons of cheese, and bacon on the side, smothered in syrup. "I'm very sorry for losing it last night. I shouldn't have yelled. I'll try to do better." The air is one of resentful acceptance.

On the drive to Desert Place, I grind my teeth in anticipation of an emotional eruption by either one of the girls after we enter the treatment center. We park, and when we get out of the car, hot air envelops us. An august mountain range looks upon us from a distance—dry, ochre-colored mountains that stand in stark contrast with the luminous blue sky gracing us from above. There is lush vegetation on the path up to the main entrance—on one side of the path, a green, leafy bush resplendent with red berries; on the other, a vast, manicured lawn that must have just been cut, as the scent of fresh cut grass lingers in the air.

"It's so pretty," I say inanely, as if that will make a bit of difference to the feeling that we are walking toward some sort of purgatory.

The building we are heading into is a modern structure, the outside walls made of a smooth, marble-type, cream brick, the big front door made of opaque glass bricks. I grab the wooden handle. It takes a bit of effort to open the door, it's so heavy.

The front lobby is large, with the main reception desk in the middle, like an island. There is a hint of eucalyptus in the air; I inhale greedily. A small pond with a fountain gurgles off to one side, and the generic paintings on the wall—geometric flowers in pastel colors, a sunset in the same muted colors and geometric style—are all nonoffending.

A young blond woman sits on the phone at a desk free of clutter. She sets the phone down and greets us with a perfunctory smile.

"Hi, I'm Rosemary Keevil," I say. "We're here for the family week."

She hands us each a name tag and asks us to fill them out with our first names.

"Have a seat," she says, gesturing to the tan-colored leather couches to our right. "Susan will be here shortly."

I'm too nervous to sit, but Willow and Dixie head over to the couches and each sit on one of them. I gravitate to the fountain and stare at the water, which is flowing over what appears to be a whale's tail. I take a deep breath and fold my arms under my breasts, my hands clasping either side of my rib cage. I presume the trickling water is meant to be calming to the likes of me—anyone coming through these doors to participate in any program here is in need of calming. But I'm going to need more than a bit of water trickling over a whale's tail to ameliorate my agitated state. I roll my shoulders and realize how tight my back is—maybe I can have a run later, or do some lengths in the pool. But even those options, I know, won't be enough to tame the tenacious knots in my shoulders.

A woman in a sensible business suit emerges through a set of closed doors that block off the reception from the main area of the treatment center. She's about my age, with well-coiffed brown hair and a warm smile.

"I'm Susan," she says.

"Rosemary," I say, and we shake hands. After I introduce Willow and Dixie, Susan leads us back toward the closed doors and slides a plastic card through a slot beside them to open them.

We pass a room labeled CHAPEL, and a nurses' station next to a sign that says MEDICATIONS DISTRIBUTED HERE, and then enter an area that looks like a large living room. Four large, olive-green leather couches sit in a circle around a large, square coffee table with books I recognize scattered about: *Alcoholics Anonymous*, *The Twelve Steps*. There are people occupying two of the couches already.

Susan introduces us to them, suggests we sit down, and says she'll be right back.

Left to make conversation, we learn that these are the other families we'll be spending most of our time with this week. What the hell are we supposed to talk about? What the hell is so wrong with us that we are here in this treatment center because our families are so fucked up? I have a sudden wave of fatigue and begin to entertain thoughts of giving up. What would happen if I just sat here and didn't make an effort to participate?

This, of course, is just a fantasy. I will muster the energy to do the next right thing and engage.

I can't get a read on how the girls are processing all this. Will they get angry, cause scenes, act out? Will they remain stone-faced (as they are now) the entire week and not engage at all?

I force myself to deal with the situation at hand. Here we are, sitting with a bunch of other families as torn apart as we are. I do what I do well: make conversation. Mom trained us in this department. She used to say that if we saw someone we knew on the bus on the way home from school, we should go and make conversation, even when it was the last thing we might feel like doing. My interior world may be a fucking fiasco, but I can still make people talk. And that's exactly what I do.

"Hi, my name is Rosemary, and these are my two daughters, Dixie and Willow." I motion to each of the girls, one on either side of me on the couch.

"Hi, I'm Frederick," says a handsome, well-groomed, sixtyish man. "And this is my wife, Sophia, and my son, Frank." Frank is about thirty, and his parents have the air of the well-to-do—poised and dressed immaculately. We make introductions all around the circle, and I turn to Frederick.

"Where are you from?"

"The Seattle area."

"We're from Vancouver, Canada, right next door," I say, as I look at the girls. "We love Seattle, don't we?"

They nod, and I continue, "What's your line of work there?"

"We're in the grocery store business," explains Frederick. We find out they are indeed a family that owns a large, well-known American grocery store chain.

There is a couple from Panama. He, Rodriguez, plays professional soccer and is dangerously good-looking, with an olive complexion, longish blond hair, and an infectious smile. I assume he's the guilty one. She, Carmella, is a voluptuous blonde, whose struggles with her English lend her an air of insecurity, although the strong accent is somewhat sexy.

Then there's us: a forty-eight-year-old, alcoholic mom with two daughters who, at fourteen and sixteen, are too old for the children's program. What will these families think of me? *"How could she behave so shamefully, the only parent of two teenage girls who lost their dad to cancer? Haven't they been through enough? What a mess she's making of their lives!"*

Meanwhile, Willow and Dixie, despite their seeming former resolve not to make any effort, have been drawn into conversations with these other folks, who, despite our differences, share brutally common family experiences. Willow and Dixie are gregarious. Similar to me, they genuinely like people, thank goodness.

"We went to Pike Place Market in Seattle. There sure were a lot of big, smelly fish," Willow says to Frederick.

"Great place, isn't it? We supply some foods to the market."

"The fish?" asks Rodriguez.

"Not the fish. They're from the local fishermen. You probably have great fishing in Panama."

"Yeah, I do some in my spare time," says Rodriguez.

"Yeah," Carmella rolls her eyes good-naturedly. "What spare time?"

"I fish in Seratami," Dixie chirps.

"What's a Seratami?" asks Sophia.

Before Dixie answers, Susan returns and takes a seat beside Rodriguez and Carmella.

"Welcome to Desert Place," she says, and hands out binders to each one of us with tabs such as: WELCOME, LECTURES, CHILDREN, FEELINGS, GOALS, RESOURCES, TWELVE STEPS, and NOTES. In a very friendly fashion, she explains the general rules, which include maintaining confidentiality, dressing conservatively (no clothing with alcohol/drug/sport logos), arriving to sessions on time, no private conversations with other people while another is sharing during group therapy, no eating in session (tea and coffee are okay), and no cell phones.

The rules established, Susan leads us to our first lecture. As we walk through the halls, I notice the framed art on the wall. These are clearly creations from children who've attended the Desert Place kids' program. I linger behind the group and study some of the art. One piece is so striking that it gives me pause. It's a picture of a large male—painted black, attached to a ball and chain, and under a dark cloud—with three people beside him. They look like a mother and two children dressed in bright colors, standing under a bright yellow sun. I can plainly see the inner turmoil this child is suffering—the rudimentary drawing crystallizes the life of a boy with an alcoholic parent who is a black cloud of despair, removed from the family cluster.

This is what I have been for my own children. Parents are meant to provide shelter for their children—not fear and worry. I hang my head in despondency. How can I ever reverse the damage I have done? I close my eyes and shake my head back and forth, dusting off the downheartedness and forcing myself to move forward.

I catch up with the others, who are already in the classroom-size lecture room, pulling the chairs out to sit down. The sound of metal legs scraping the tile floor fills my ears.

Once we're settled, the facilitator launches in.

"Hi, I'm Kyle. Welcome to Desert Place. I'll be giving you most of your lectures this week, but I prefer to call them talks. 'Lectures' seem so formal." He pushes his John Lennon glasses up on his nose and rubs his hand over his prematurely balding head. He must be about thirty-five. He writes on the sandwich board beside him:

Feelings are not right or wrong.

Feelings are comfortable or uncomfortable.

Coping with the feelings.

I take out my pen and start to write on the blank notepad provided for us, as Kyle explains, "We have to stop thinking about feelings as emotions we should or should not have. They just are. It's not our feelings that are the source of our difficulty with other people—it's how we deal with them or express them. The first step is identifying our feelings. This is work all of us need to do, not just the alcoholics among us."

This reminds me of something Graham said at the Meadow: "It's not the problem that's the problem; it's the *coping* with the problem."

Kyle continues talking while passing around a handout entitled "Core Feelings," which has pictures of faces on it, only one of which is happy. The other faces are expressing other emotions: anger, loneliness, fear, sad/hurt/pain, guilt, shame—all feelings I drank and drugged to numb. Feelings that I now know I need to recognize and acknowledge in order to decipher a functional reaction to them.

I glance at the children. Willow is yawning, and Dixie is doodling palm trees and whales. Are they absorbing anything? I feel sad and angry—angry they aren't engaged, which makes me sad.

Okay—now for the wisdom part. What is the functional reaction? *It's not the emotions that are the problem; it's the coping with them that's the problem*, I remind myself, but I'm stumped—stuck again in uncertainty, fear, and stress.

I check out the other families in the room. Most are listening intently, some are asking questions, some taking notes. Most are very present, except Willow and Dixie, and perhaps Frank, the son of Mr. and Mrs. Well-to-Do. He seems bored; maybe he's heard it all before.

"Emotional fluency requires us to have our feelings noticed, labeled, and affirmed," Kyle explains, and he goes on to say it's important to validate feelings, especially for children.

Those words echo in my head. *Validate? Validate?* When I was growing up, I was always told, "Chin up." We were expected to ignore our emotions and carry on as if we didn't have them. I have not validated my children's emotions as part of their upbringing.

I put up my hand and ask, "What about disappointment? How does a parent deal with that?"

"Good question," Kyle says. "It's hard for a parent to let a child be disappointed, but it's important that individuals learn to deal with not always getting what they want. In many circumstances, parents should give the emotional support the child needs while letting the child sort out their feelings on their own."

Oh my God, guilty again, I think, remembering all the times I've tried to placate Willow and Dixie when they've been unhappy or disappointed, by offering up a gift or some other distraction. I consider how hard I've made it on myself. I've tried always to make things perfect, but life is not fair, and it's been impossible to live up to my own standards. Like when I tucked the girls in at night: If I spent twenty minutes with one daughter and then only ten with the other, she would complain that I loved her sister better. So I would stay another ten minutes. It never occurred to me to say, "I do love you, very much, and that has nothing to do with how much time I take tucking you in."

The lecture lasts an hour, and although I notice the girls getting a little squirrelly, it is revelatory for me. Toward the end, I put my head down slightly, placing my left hand on my forehead, and stare at my notes. So many takeaways. What if I knew then what I know now? How is it I knew none of this while bringing up the girls? Here I am, in a treatment center for alcoholics and addicts, and I'm getting a crash course in parenting. Recovery, it turns out, is about far more than stopping drinking and drugging. It's an all-encompassing design for living.

At lunch, we sit with the family from Seattle—Frederick and Sophia and Frank—and chat between bites of burgers and salads. We learn Frank has been in Desert Place for six weeks and is going to secondary housing, where he'll live off campus with other recovering addicts (no family members allowed).

I'm sitting beside him at the end of the table, and while the others are involved in a conversation, I ask him whether it was drugs or drinking that brought him down.

"Crack," he says immediately, and not that quietly.

As I take a sip of my Diet Coke, I notice Frederick, Frank's dad, looking at us, and I'm concerned I spoke out of line. He finishes eating whatever is in his mouth, then leans over and says, "He was off it for two years and went back to it six months ago. Sophia and I made a decision to get him here as soon as possible."

Now Sophia is listening, too. "He was deeply into it for eight years before that. Oh my God." She closes her eyes, shakes her head, and then digs into her hamburger with a gusto that belies her sophisticated air, like she's letting go of pretenses. She looks at the girls, then at me, making a face that seems to ask me, *Is it okay to talk like this?*

I nod my head and give her a little smile.

We just met yesterday, and we're sharing deeply personal family aches. I see why this therapy is done in groups. We're creating a bond that allows for the unspeakable to be spoken, allows us to find a voice, surrender some power, and be noticed by others in similar circumstances, without being judged.

After lunch, we have the first session with our primary family counselor, Georgeanna. Her door is open, and she is sitting at her desk. When she sees us, she stands up, smiles, and introduces herself.

"I'm Georgeanna, and you must be Rosemary." She looks at me

and then toward my daughters, "And Willow and Dixie." She looks back and forth at them, as if asking who is who.

"This is Willow," I say, pointing.

Before I can introduce Dixie, she pipes up, "I'm Dixie."

"A real pleasure to meet you all. Such pretty names," she says. "Do take a seat."

Georgeanna gestures toward a love seat and a comfy-looking armchair. I head for the chair. It looks inviting, and my taking it will thwart any argument between the girls over who gets to sit in it.

Georgeanna, who is about fifty, is wearing a blue-beaded, caftan-type top. That, along with her flowing, wavy brown hair, soft voice, and eyes as blue as her top, makes her seem as mellow as a '60s flower child, which she could very well have been.

She explains that this is the first of three sessions the four of us will have together. We will also have group therapy with the other families.

"I'm sure you will find it all beneficial," she encourages us. "Here, we can go over specific situations and try to resolve them while learning healthy communication skills. Addictions can consume parents in ways youngsters simply cannot comprehend. When did you get sober, Rosemary?"

"One year ago, this week," I answer, and tell her about the death of the girls' father and my brother, my collapse into alcoholism and drug addiction when Willow and Dixie were six and nine, and the following six years of self-destruction. I also tell her about my father's alcoholism.

"Well, addictions become a family legacy that gets passed from generation to generation," she says. "Congratulations on stopping the cycle, Rosemary."

I have to pause and congratulate myself, too. I was raised in a household in which the emotional energy was unpredictable—in which my father's drunken rages sideswiped all of us too easily. But how can Georgeanna tell me the cycle is broken? My kids are surely already imprinted with the skewed emotional energy in our own household. I remind myself that I cannot undo the past—that what's important is what I'm going to do about it now.

Georgeanna wants us to discuss a particular issue that has been a bugaboo over the last year since I got sober. So far, the kids have said nothing, and I worry they won't cooperate at all. Anxiety is permeating my veins. I reach for my bottle of water and sip it, my mind racing over the past year. I try to zero in on one particular problem, but when I think of the previous year, it's as a blur of arguments and screaming: Dave angry at the girls, me mad at the girls, them mad at me, calls to the school telling them my girls will be late or absent.

"What about the time you and Dave went to California?" Willow pipes up, interrupting my thoughts. My fear of the topic at hand dwarfs my relief at the fact that she's talking and actually willing to participate.

"What about that?" I ask, realizing I should have said, *Guilty as charged.*

"You got that psychotic lady, Maree, to look after us. She had her three stupid little dogs there, and she kept saying weird, threatening things to us, like that we were devil children who were going to hell if we didn't behave. She called the school and talked to the teachers, and I told my counselor about her, and she suggested I stay with Robby, but I felt like I needed to stay to make sure Dixie and the house were okay."

Dixie butts in, "I was worried about the house, too, because she was just acting like a psychopath—"

"I was talking, Dixie," Willow says, and they start talking over each other. Suddenly, they are both enthusiastic about my misbehavior.

Georgeanna tells them gently to take turns and that Willow should continue, as she spoke first. But now I intercede and fill Georgeanna in on some facts.

"This last March, Dave and I went to his folks' place in Palm Springs—the one the girls and I are staying at now—for a week of golf." I pause to consider what to say next. "Hmm, well, I had an AA friend, Maree, take care of the children."

"She was crazy," says Dixie, bouncing a bit on the couch, as if to exaggerate her point.

At the same time, Willow repeats her earlier comment: "She was psychotic."

I glare at them to shut up.

"Now, girls," says Georgeanna, "It's your mother's turn to speak."

I go on. "I trusted Maree. I know her from AA. She happened to have three little dogs who came along. And she wasn't the only caregiver. Meredith, a former nanny and now a good family friend, stopped by to check in on the girls and help out as well."

I can see now that this was a textbook case of denial—a classic dysfunctional coping mechanism. I chose to believe the kids were lying just to get me to come home. I was absorbed by Dave—devouring up the dedicated attention I was getting because we were away on a vacation together.

"She took Meredith's baby into her bedroom with the dogs! Gus, the baby, was screaming!" says Willow.

Dixie adds, "Meredith was crying, and—"

Willow interrupts, "I called Mom and told her what was going on, and she ignored me."

I defend myself: "I thought they were just trying to get me to come home. They said they wanted to have the locks changed, and that seemed overly dramatic."

"She left and took all the house keys, and we went with Meredith to her house to get them, and she wouldn't answer the door," says Dixie.

Willow butts in, "We knew she was home because we could hear the dogs barking and Maree telling them to shut up."

The girls continue relentlessly about the dreadful details of that week. I'm a dart board, and they have very good aim. The darts dig in deep, and I'm bleeding inside.

I feel deeply embarrassed as Georgeanna takes this all in. Now I see how upset and scared they must have been. I can see I look like nothing short of a negligent mother, choosing myself over my daughters. Is that what I did?

I can't look at them or at Georgeanna. I hang my head low and weep. "I thought you were exaggerating, and that I should be able to have a holiday away with Dave, and you were just trying to get me to come home."

Mercifully, Georgeanna intervenes. She's gentle and even-handed. "I see two things happening here," she says, leaning forward in her chair, elbows on knees and hands folded. Looking at the girls, she says, "Safety is a basic human need, and it looks like you girls believe your safety was compromised during your mom's visit to California."

Hearing this throws me back to all the other times I compromised their safety, driving them drunk and high. What kind of mother am I?

"And it looks like you two," she says, looking at Willow and Dixie, "are ganging up on your mom." She turns to me. "You probably don't have much confidence in yourself as a mother right now."

"You can say that again," I whimper.

"You need to learn how to establish boundaries. Right now, for example, it's important to recognize you are being beaten up and take measures to stop it."

"Oh, really? Shall I try right now?" I ask.

She nods.

I think about it and am able to say, "I will not allow my children to gang up on me."

"Try again with a bit more conviction, Rosemary."

I breathe deeply, close my eyes, and repeat slowly, and with any degree of confidence I can muster, "I will not allow my children to gang up on me."

On our drive home that night, I vacillate between feeling totally unequipped as a mother and feeling validated by Georgeanna, who noticed that my children beat me up. But the berating continues in the car on the way back to the condo.

"Why did we have to come here?" Willow yells. "This is stupid, and right now I'm missing a really important exam! You're awful."

I reply in a measured tone, "We need to do this. It's the only way through it," although I have doubt in my own mind. Should we just leave now? No. I need to do the next right thing. But what is that, exactly?

Dixie says from the backseat, "And why do *we* have to be here? *You're* the alcoholic!"

This time, I'm the one who blasts the music loudly. As Amanda Marshall sings "Wishful Thinking," we all retreat to our emotional corners. Nobody says a word the rest of the ride home. As we walk up to the front door in silence, I decide to make an attempt at throwing my hat in the ring, even though I fear it will be received more like a matador's red cape and I'll be charged full-on.

"Look, Willow and Dixie," I start in, stopping at the entrance to the condo and blocking the door, "I'm really, really, really sorry about the Maree situation. That must have been dreadful for you. I'm sorry I forced you to come here. But I need to at least hope that it can help in the long run."

Willow tries shoving me aside to go into the house, but I stand my ground, putting my hand on her shoulder. "Please." I notice she's not resisting as much as she could. Dixie is trying to get by us on my right. I put my foot out to stop her. "Slow down there, buddy," I say, and nudge her back so she is beside Willow.

"Can we just try a momentary truce—a bit of dinner and maybe even a hot tub later? Or are we all too hot and bothered for a hot tub?"

Willow actually snickers at this, and Dixie perks up. "Can we have Japanese? Frank said there was a great Japanese restaurant near us."

"I don't feel like Japanese," Willow says, unwilling to pull out of her funk.

"Please, Willow," I plead again.

She nods slightly, puts her head down, and walks into the condo.

We seem to have stumbled upon some sort of delicate truce. We're all worn out from raw emotion. We manage to make it through dinner in a civilized fashion but nix the hot-tub idea when we get back to the condo—might be a little too much fun for a family in a straitjacket.

In the morning, I inform the girls that today is Family Group Therapy Day, and they both groan.

As I'm making my second cup of tea, I respond to their groans by saying, "I guess that sounds like a kind of a disgruntled acceptance. And I thank you for that." I take a sip of tea. "You never know—it could be interesting."

I'm seriously dreading the day ahead, too, but I can't let them know that.

"Sure," Willow says, all sarcasm. "I just want to get this whole thing over with."

When we get to the center, we're directed to the group-therapy room, where we meet up with the same people we had our sessions with yesterday. The room is painted gray and has a row of windows on one side. Ten black chairs are arranged in a large circle, facing each other. Another, small circle of three chairs is in the middle of the large circle, facing the center. We all seat ourselves.

"I notice nobody is grabbing the hot-spot chairs," I joke, but no one laughs or even acknowledges my comment.

Doddy, the facilitator—a plain-looking, fifty-something woman with gray hair pulled back in a ponytail—introduces herself in a deep voice. It's a voice that commands attention. I sit up a little straighter in my chair.

Detecting our confusion, or apprehension, about those three chairs in the middle of the circle, Doddy explains, "Each family will take turns in the middle circle. This is an opportunity for the client to make amends to his or her family." She pauses and looks around the circle at each of us and continues, "I know this sounds like an ominous task, but we have found it to be highly effective in healing the deep wounds that have formed. And there's a format. The client is to go over what it is that he or she wants to apologize for. It doesn't need to be everything, not an entire inventory, but it's a start. And the family members who are listening should remain silent."

"But . . ." I perk up and raise my hand to ask a question, then pause. "Can I ask a question?"

"Yes," replies Doddy.

"So, the family members are to give no feedback?"

"That's correct." She nods and folds her hands together. "We find this is the most effective way. The process sounds daunting, I know. It takes courage, but I know you can all do it."

I stare at the floor, avoiding any eye contact with Doddy, praying that I'm not the first to be asked to do this terrifying task. To my relief, Doddy says, "Why don't we start with Frank's family?"

Frank, Sophia, and Frederick all move to the three chairs in the middle of the circle. Then Frank rolls up the sleeves of his plaid shirt, takes his parents' hands, and launches into a frenzy of apologies to his parents. Finally, he looks at Doddy, as if to say, *Is that enough?*

Doddy nods gently. "You can go back to your places."

I'm envious of Frank's courage. After he's settled in his original chair, I catch his eye and give him a knowing nod, lifting my brows to commend him on a job well done. He nods back almost imperceptibly.

Then I hear Doddy say, "Rosemary, you and your family may go ahead."

It must be a defense mechanism, but I feel like I'm having an out-of-body experience. I'm looking down on my little family as we walk the few steps to the middle circle, the firing zone, in slow motion.

We take our seats, facing each other, so close together our knees are touching. I take longer than necessary settling into my seat. I take one of each of their hands in mine and look at them, my eyes moving slowly from Willow to Dixie and back again, while I speak.

"Um, I'm sorry . . . I'm sorry"—I look up to the ceiling, trying to fight the tears welling in my eyes—"for driving while drunk and high." I turn to Dixie. "I'm sorry for being high at Peter's bar mitzvah." I turn to Willow and say, slowly and quietly, almost like it's a secret, "I'm sorry I was often drunk at the dinner table when Robby was over. I'm sorry for the many times I drove him while I was drunk and high on pills." In saying this, I realize I'll have to make amends to Robby at some point, too.

As I continue to look deeply into my daughters' eyes, I see two innocent babes painted in adult miseries. *What, dear God, have I done to them? What damage have I done? Oh, Barry, I'm so sorry.*

"I'm sorry for making you come here, and that it upset you so." I continue to apologize for the plethora of times I have been a drunk and high mother. For all the broken promises, not being able to take them places when I said I would. For not showing up for that special dinner at the hotel in Hayman Island, in Australia, because I was drunk in the hotel room. For all the screaming I did when I was hungover.

Dixie keeps looking away. I'm saying all of this in front of seven other people. I look at Frank, who boosts my courage with a reassuring gaze. His mom looks sad, not judgmental. Carmella is crying; she puts her hand on Rodriguez's thigh. The others are looking intently at us, and I see them wearing my burden with me. I'm onstage, and the audience is absorbed in my emotions, understanding and relating, because we're all in this together; our stories are different but the same.

I consider whether now is the time to tell the girls about the cocaine. Is now the moment to purge it all, to tell them the worst of it? Fueled by the tacit backing I sense from the group, I continue, "And that time I drove on the wrong side of the road on the way to Whistler . . ." I stop and look at their hands in mine. I question myself, but we're here, aren't we? So I continue, "And I hit the rock beside the driveway and the police came to return my wallet . . . That time, I had actually had . . . I was, well . . . I had had some cocaine . . . which, um . . ." I pause again, take a deep breath, close my eyes, breathe out, and say, "I did cocaine often, and for that I apologize." I open my eyes and say, "I am so terribly sorry and sad and ashamed. I promise I will make this up to you. I'm sorry for being an unreliable mother who put drugs and alcohol ahead of my beautiful, brilliant, wonderful children, whom I'm so proud of."

Now Willow starts to cry, tears rolling down her face, though she remains motionless. But Dixie, in a somber state, stands up and walks, with great determination, right out of the room. I've gone too far. It was too much. What do I do now? I look at Doddy, who looks back and gives me a little nod, another near-imperceptible communication: *It's okay. Leave Dixie be for now. You can go back to your seats now. You did very well.*

Willow and I get up and take our seats back in the wider circle. She stops crying, but her face is flushed. Tears gush from my eyes, and Carmella gets up and hands me one of the Kleenex boxes. I blow my nose, wipe my face and eyes, and look at all the empathetic faces around the circle caring for me, figuratively holding me in their arms. I stop crying; their compassion and unadulterated acceptance has offered me a remission from my hell, however brief.

Rodriguez and Carmella go ahead with their own traumas, but I barely hear any of it. I'm too lost in my own bereavement.

I will never be able to undo what I have done. Never. I have destroyed the soul of our family, which already had a gaping hole in it from Barry's death. Maybe we're just fucked.

As we all get up to leave, Doddy walks over to Willow and me, stands between us, and puts one arm around each of us. I didn't take her for the demonstrative type, and she gives off a slight odor of sweat, but I appreciate her attentiveness.

"You don't realize it now," she says, "but this will have a healing effect. This afternoon, you can process this with Georgeanna. I know you'll find it helpful. And, Willow"—Doddy turns to her—"I know this is tough on you, but you need to know this took great courage on your mother's part."

Doddy has that authoritative way of speaking that makes you believe whatever she says unconditionally.

As we leave the room, I see Dixie in the center meeting area, sitting on one of the olive-colored couches.

"What about Dixie?" I ask.

"I'll go and talk with her," Doddy says.

"No, uh . . . I think . . ." I put my hand on Doddy's shoulder. "I'll go talk to her," I say.

Doddy nods her agreement.

Dixie is slouching and pouting, but at least she's here. I go to her and sit beside her on the couch, alert to any clues she may be emitting about her emotional state. She looks at me sheepishly as I brush the hair out of her eyes, and sniffs. "I . . . I'm . . . Mom . . . I . . ." Her eyes fill with tears. "I had to leave. I—"

"I know. I know. I understand why you had to leave," I say, and I put my arms around her shoulders and hug her. "I gave you too much information. I was afraid of that." Her arms are under mine, hugging hard as well. "This is a horrid thing for a fourteen-year-old to experience. It's horrid for anyone. I'm sorry I'm putting you through all this."

We're still hugging when I see Georgeanna outside the family-group room, talking with Willow and Carmella. Georgeanna notices me and approaches us. Willow follows.

"Hello, Georgeanna," I say.

"Hello. Can I sit down?"

"Please do. We're still reeling from the family-amends session." I breathe in and blow out.

"Yes, Willow was just telling me," Georgeanna says.

Willow sits beside me, so both of my daughters are flanking me. Georgeanna has pulled a chair over and is sitting facing us.

"You know, girls, this may seem chaotic now and worse than it ever was, but it's how family systems work," Georgeanna says. "You're all very intelligent, so I think today's afternoon lecture will appeal to you on an intellectual level."

She moves closer to us, clasps her hands, and leans in, like she's excited to be letting us in on an important secret.

"In the classical family systems theory, the family is a system composed of members in interaction with each other. The family has a rhythm that is greater than the sum of its parts. So even if one member of the family is an alcoholic, the family settles into a dysfunctional equilibrium, because systems yearn for balance."

"Wait, hold on," I say. "Equilibrium? We did not have equilibrium when I was drinking, and we certainly don't now. We couldn't be more off-kilter."

"Hear me out," Georgeanna says, hand up, palm out, a glint in her eye. "I'm not saying the dysfunctional equilibrium isn't chaotic—just that the reactions of the family members within the chaos are predictable. And this predictability is threatened when sobriety is introduced into the equation. That's why the entire family needs to readjust its mode of interacting when the alcoholic gets sober."

"Oh," I say. Then Dixie says, "Aha." And Willow, too, says, "Oh, aha." The three of us erupt in laughter, and it is a release of agony, a liberation of angst.

"You know, girls, the growth process for the family often requires a period of a different type of chaos in order to break down the former, dysfunctional equilibrium," Georgeanna continues. "This is what you're experiencing now—a complete and utter disintegration of your little family function—er, *dys*function. This has to occur in order to even start to build a functional foundation for your new family dynamic, your new functional balance."

So this is it. My family is experiencing the epitome of chaos—but it's a chaos we must go through before a new balance can work its way into place. We need to bottom out before we can start piecing ourselves back together, start the rebuilding process. That night I drove the kids drunk and high and blacked out, that was my rock bottom. And I was met with the gift of desperation. I was willing to do anything to get better. It's been a tough journey, but I'm doing it. And this is the next step. Now I have to repair my family. And the girls are on this journey with me.

I grab Willow's hand on my right and Dixie's hand on my left and stand up. I feel a sort of grainy gratitude.

"C'mon, girls. I know I have a lot of making up to do and we have lots of work to do and you're still mad and sore and hurt and it will take me a lifetime to make it up to you, but you came here and I want to thank you for that. Can we have a family hug?"

The three of us hug, and I squeeze the girls to me tightly. There's a seed of harmony here—in a most nascent stage, yes, but with room for growth.

"Mmm," I say, "someone smells like Herbal Essences shampoo."

"It's me," they say in unison.

"Hey," I say, "tomorrow is my one-year anniversary of sobriety."

We break the embrace, and Willow says, "Congratulations, Mom."

Dixie looks up at me. "Yeah, Mom, congratulations. You know, when you had no rules before, I thought you didn't care as much about us as Mandy's mom cares about her kids."

Georgeanna stands up slowly, looks into my teary eyes, and says, "You're living your amends to Willow and Dixie, Rosemary, by being sober and trying to do the next right thing. It may be a temperamental pilgrimage, but it's the very best gift you can give your children. Congratulations."

As she walks away, I nudge both girls back into a family hug—a gentle one this time—and savor it.

I look up and say out loud, "Barry—Daddy—please be here with us on this journey."

Epilogue

"Contacting My Angel"
Van Morrison

When we left Desert Place, we three were frenzied balls of raw emotions. Willow and Dixie and I had each been through open-heart surgery, and we hadn't been sewn back up.

The week's absence did not affect the girls' schoolwork. All through that time and the ensuing rough times, they remained bright students. I don't think I ever had to tell them to do their homework. They naturally wanted to excel.

As for Dave, I was invested in continuing our relationship, starved for male attention as I was. My sponsor didn't understand why I kept seeing him if I was hurting so much. Anyone could have predicted we were going to disintegrate. And we did, in August 2003, when Dave told me by phone that he was dating an Italian girl.

When Dave broke things off, I almost called Dimitri—my go-to sex-between-relationships Greek stud—to assuage the pain from this latest blow. But then it occurred to me this was likely an unhealthy coping mechanism—an old behavior that I had always used to alter my negative emotions—and Graham's words echoed in my head:

If nothing changes, nothing changes. Try to do the next right thing, Rosemary. I knew the right thing to do was *not* to call Dimitri. I didn't, and I was proud of myself.

This was one of many small steps. My consciousness had been alerted. I now had my radar primed to home in on potential dysfunctional behaviors. And I recognized a lot of them, though I sometimes chose to ignore them.

It continued to be difficult and painful with the girls. I had so much to learn. And I'm still learning, over eighteen years later. I still struggle with saying no to them, and they are adults with their own successful lives now. How each of them got there is their story to tell—or not.

These were often demanding and chaotic times, but I always tried to keep perspective—times could never be as atrocious as they were when I was drinking and drugging. I prayed. I imagined Barry touching Dixie's or Willow's heart, oozing healing energy. I closed my eyes tightly and willed him into their souls. I even invited Barry's deceased parents—Grandfather and Nana—and Uncle Rob along to help in the healing process.

Sometimes I felt as if Barry's death were a life sentence. Would any of this have happened if he had not died? When he was dying, I assumed, naively, that I would eventually settle into a "normal" life. But that never happened. Life just got more and more tough.

I also assumed everything would get back to normal after I got sober. But life continued to be challenging. Gradually, my daughters and I have all learned healthier coping mechanisms, but we are still works in progress. I occasionally see Sheena, the spiritual counselor who was responsible for getting me sober in 2002. I see both a therapist and a psychiatrist, who monitors my meds for depression. Other than that, everything is normal!

I know I cannot change the past. I know I will never lose my sadness over the death of my husband and the death of my brother.

I will also never lose the guilt I have over how I parented the girls in the absence of their dad, but I have acceptance. It's what I'm doing about it now that matters today.

Notes

1. Rick Atkinson and David S. Broder, "U.S., Allies Launch Massive Attack Against Targets in Iraq and Kuwait," *The Washington Post*, January 17, 1991

2. Rick Atkinson and David S. Broder, "U.S., Allies Launch Massive Attack Against Targets in Iraq and Kuwait," *The Washington Post*, January 17, 1991

3. Rick Atkinson and David S. Broder, "U.S., Allies Launch Massive Attack Against Targets in Iraq and Kuwait," *The Washington Post*, January 17, 1991

4. 4. Andrew Rosenthal, "War in the Gulf: The Overview—U.S. and Allies Open Air War on Iraq; Bomb Baghdad and Kuwaiti Targets; 'No Choice' But Force, Bush Declares; No Ground Fighting Yet; Call to Arms by Hussein," *The New York Times*, January 17, 1991

Acknowledgments

I would like to thank: my expert and invaluable publisher and editor, Brooke Warner; her excellent team at She Writes Press; Bill W. and friends; and the Starbucks at Caulfield Village Mall in West Vancouver, Canada, where most of *The Art of Losing It* was written.

About the Author

© Kent Kallberg

Rosemary Keevil has been a TV news reporter, a current affairs radio show host, and managing editor of a professional women's magazine. She has a master's degree in journalism and is currently a journalist covering addiction and recovery. Rosemary has two grown daughters with successful careers. She lives in Whistler, British Columbia, Canada, with her partner and her sheep-a-doodle. Rosemary has been clean and sober since 2002. This is her first book.

SELECTED TITLES FROM SHE WRITES PRESS

She Writes Press is an independent publishing company founded to serve women writers everywhere. Visit us at www.shewritespress.com.

Learning to Eat Along the Way by Margaret Bendet
$16.95, 978-1-63152-997-9
After interviewing an Indian holy man, newspaper reporter Margaret Bendet follows him in pursuit of enlightenment and ends up facing demons that were inside her all along.

Patchwork: A Memoir of Love and Loss by Mary Jo Doig
$16.95, 978-1-63152-449-3
Part mystery and part inspirational memoir, *Patchwork* chronicles the riveting healing journey of one woman who, following the death of a relative, has a flashback that opens a dark passageway back to her childhood and the horrific secrets that have long been buried deep inside her psyche.

A Different Kind of Same: A Memoir by Kelley Clink
$16.95, 978-1-63152-999-3
Several years before Kelley Clink's brother hanged himself, she attempted suicide by overdose. In the aftermath of his death, she traces the evolution of both their illnesses, and wonders: If he couldn't make it, what hope is there for her?

Insatiable: A Memoir of Love Addiction by Shary Hauer
$16.95, 978-1-63152-982-5
An intimate and illuminating account of corporate executive—and secret love addict—Shary Hauer's migration from destructive to healthy love.

Splitting the Difference: A Heart-Shaped Memoir by Tré Miller-Rodríguez
$19.95, 978-1-938314-20-9
When 34-year-old Tré Miller-Rodríguez's husband dies suddenly from a heart attack, her grief sends her on an unexpected journey that culminates in a reunion with the biological daughter she gave up at 18.

Raising the Bottom: Making Mindful Choices in a Drinking Culture by Lisa Boucher $16.95, 978-1-63152-214-7
Women share their drinking stories of hitting rock bottom—so you don't ever have to.